to TIMBUKTU

WORDS **CASEY SCIESZKA**
ART **STEVEN WEINBERG**

ROARING BROOK PRESS
New York

Roaring Brook Press is a division of
Holtzbrinck Publishing Holdings Limited Partnership
175 Fifth Avenue, New York, New York 10010
macteenbooks.com

Distributed in Canada by H. B. Fenn and Company Ltd.

Library of Congress Cataloging-in-Publication Data

Scieszka, Casey.
  To Timbuktu : nine countries, two people, one true story / Casey Scieszka;
illustrated by Steven Weinberg.
      p. cm.
  ISBN 978-1-59643-527-8
  1. Scieszka, Casey. 2. Weinberg, Steven, 1984– 3. Voyages around the world.
4. Travelers' writings, American. I. Weinberg, Steven, 1984– II. Title.

  G440.S355S35 2011
  910.4092'273—dc22

                                                        2010027627

Roaring Brook Press books are available
for special promotions and premiums.
For details contact: Director of Special Markets,
Holtzbrinck Publishers.

First Edition 2011
Printed in the United States of America

1 3 5 7 9 8 6 4 2

To our parents

FALL 2004

This is me, Casey. This is Steven. We're both from the United States, but absurdly enough we met here, in Morocco.

What makes everything a little less absurd is the fact that it's

the fall of our junior year in college
and like many of our friends, we're
studying abroad.

Steven made me a crossword during Arabic class today, which is what we're looking at right now. I'm excited (a new friend!) and flattered (he made it just for me!), but also seriously confused.

"But what do you mean 'The former king's nickname if he were a party guy'?" I ask.

"Exactly that," he says straight-faced.

"Okay, so something to do with Hassan the Second?"

"Right, right—but drop 'the Second' and what is a party guy?"

"A . . . what?"

"A Party Hassanimal!" he says triumphantly.

And for some reason, I laugh.

What I know about Steven so far: he was born in D.C., he goes to Colby College in Maine where he studies government, he is always drawing ridiculous cartoons, and he is fearless (maybe even shameless) about using the limited Arabic he has acquired in the past week, which seems to be making him lots of friends around town.

What he knows about me: I was born and raised in Brooklyn, I go to Pitzer College in southern California where I study sociology, I like to read, and . . . ? That I dress crazy dumpy? (I'm erring on the side of serious modesty to be culturally sensitive.) Oh the slow process of getting to know someone.

"So you get it? Hassanimal?" he asks.

"You know, traditionally you should be able to do a crossword on your own without say, the creator hovering over your shoulder giving you additional clues the whole time," I say and smile.

"Oh, but I never promised traditional," he says and smiles back.

I could sit here watching the sky change colors over the ocean for a whole lot longer, but I'm pretty sure I'm late for evening teatime with my host family. Then again, maybe not—really I have no idea. It's awfully hard to figure out what's going on when all I can say is: "My name is Casey;" "I am a student;" and "My father is a translation specialist for the United Nations,"which isn't even true, by the way, it's simply the vocabulary in Chapter One of our Arabic textbook. "I am truly lonely" also makes an appearance early on, which I suppose is a useful phrase to teach people when they are somewhere they've never been before without any friends.

Not that I don't have *any* friends, though. Because only a friend would make a crossword puzzle just for you.

A month or so later, it appears Steven and I are —*ahem*—a bit more than just friends. I would hardly say we're dating, though. Or maybe we are, but in that middle school kind of way where we are doing our best to hide it from our (host) parents and he mostly ignores me at school. And like any good middle school love, we know it cannot last forever since come the middle of December, when the semester ends, we will part ways and return to our separate lives at the opposite ends of the United States.

Is it naïve to hope that we can still be friends?

SUMMER 2005

Six months later, I am back in Morocco for the summer, sitting in an Internet café with Julia, my friend from college. Somehow I convinced her to come out here and learn some Arabic with me during the hottest months of the year.

"Ooooh," she sings. "Another e-mail from Steven?"

So it turns out we have stayed friends after all. A little more than just friends, actually, on the few occasions we saw each other before I came out here for the summer.

"What's it say?" Julia asks.

"Uh, something about a summer camp called Camp Chunder Camp. I think he and the friends he's living with at that cabin in Maine have created some kind of make-believe camp that—what? You're looking at me like I'm the one who made this up. It's Steven who's crazy. Not me."

"You're the one who likes him."

I can always count on Julia to tell it like it is.

"*Shnoo* 'chunder'?" asks our landlord/Internet café manager/ friend Mohammed who has been hovering around us this whole time.

"So Casey, is your Arabic advanced enough to explain that your boyfriend has a pretend summer camp with his friends named after the Australian word for puking?"

"You know, maybe it is, but I'm just going to pretend like it's not right now. And p.s. he's not my boyfriend."

"Right."

FALL 2005

Senior year begins. I am in southern California again, Steven is still in Maine and we are having *fun*. In between all the fun we are also taking classes, which can be fun too of course. I especially like my External Studies Colloquium where we eat food from around the world, prepare to visit local high schools to talk about the places we've studied abroad, and learn how to apply for post-graduation grants that will take us abroad again.

Over a spread of Turkish desserts our second week of class though, I am surprised to learn that the applications for most grants are due before Halloween. Which means we all need to decide where we want to be a year from now *right now*. I had hoped to put off the whole what-do-I-want-to-do-once-I'm-out-of-school question for a few more months, but it looks like that's not going to happen anymore.

We are told that when creating an application, the bottom line for most grants seems to be this: is what you are proposing to do going to increase mutual understanding between the U.S. and wherever your research takes you, while also teaching you skills you will use the rest of your life? Of course the details vary from grant to grant depending on where the money is coming from but essentially the message is the same: can we trust you to be a good ambassador out there?

plan Cc *plan* Dd . . .

My teachers make sure to point out that in order to be a good ambassador you're going to have to be happy. So don't apply to do something just because you know that's what the grant committee wants to hear. You've got to choose something that will get you out of bed on the other side of the world even when it's raining, you haven't made any friends yet, and you've got the travel shits like whoa.

For me I think that something is writing, talking to people about religion, and hanging out in schools. So I create proposals for a Watson Scholarship that would take me to Syria, Jordan, Senegal, Mali, Comoros, Malaysia, and France to write stories about the daily rituals of Islam in each of those places, and a Fulbright Grant with the U.S. government that would take me to Mali where I'd research the role of Islam in the education system there.

I won't hear back from either of them until the spring, so I'll just have to hold my breath and make Plans B, C, and D in the meanwhile. I keep wondering though, wouldn't each one of those places be that much more fun to see with Steven? So I send him my applications and the next day he leaves me a message. "Hey Casey, I read your essays and they're, uh . . . amazing and—not that there was supposed to be—it's just—there's just no place for me in all this."

But if we really wanted to, couldn't we make one?

WINTER 2006

It's January now, a full year since Steven and I parted ways after our semester in Morocco, and we are in New York giving it a go. We figured a few weeks together during winter break would be a good way to decide if we should be trying to make any promises to each other.

So here we are now, in Central Park.

"I just don't get it," I say.

"I know—is it a group wedding or something?"

"I guess so."

"Maybe it's a Korean tradition."

"Why Korean?"

"I thought you said they were Korean."

"No, you just did."

It's worth mentioning that last night we reached a new "relationship milestone." "I think we are in love," he said.

"Oh, do you?" I asked. "I mean—sorry, you just said it so funny—I love you too."

And now we're surrounded by weddings.

Yeah, it's not in the least bit awkward.

Now that we've dropped the L Bomb, it's time to have the talk about Our Future Together. So, on a snowy night, tucked into the warmth of a neighborhood bar, we go neck-deep into all the uncertainty.

What comes up first are the two grants I've applied for and won't hear back from until the spring.

"Well, we'd make sure you had your own project too. It wouldn't be like you were just following me," I say.

"Yeah, but what could I possibly do that would take me to Comoros and Syria and all those other— You know, I don't think I can even go to Syria since I've been to Israel. "

Hmm.

"Well, what about with the Fulbright? We would be in Mali the whole time. I'm sure you would be able find your own job with an NGO or maybe with a newspaper?"

"Even though I don't speak French?"

Hmm, again.

"I don't think I want to do any newspaper stuff anyway. The only reason I joined freshman year was so I could make the cartoons, and now I'm writing all these articles and copyediting. I'm only doing it because I like working with all my friends."

"And because now you can make your cartoons as big as you want and put them anywhere."

"Yes, that too." He smiles and I kiss him.

"Okay, so not a newspaper."

"Not a newspaper."

We drain our drinks in studious silence.

"Another round?" I ask, standing up.

"Yes, please."

When I come back with round two, Steven looks like a classic portrait of someone deep in thought.

"I think I want to spend more time painting," he says, his eyes still focused on something that no one else can see.

"Yeah?"

"Yeah. I should really be taking advantage of having an art studio at school and the time to do it."

"Definitely!" I say and think of the work of his I've seen. It's damn good.

"That Chinese art class I had got me really excited about painting again. Hey, what about China?"

I like China. I went for a summer when I was sixteen with a small program led by three rockin' graduate students who took twelve of us on an epic linguistic-cultural-culinary adventure. I've taken several Chinese anthropology/history classes in college and—

"I like China," I say.

"Yeah, that could be really cool. I could talk to my brother about it since—"

"Oh yeah! He's living in Beijing with his girlfriend, and teaching English, right?"

"Yeah, from what I've heard so far, he likes it. I could ask him about the different schools and—"

"Now we're getting somewhere!" I say. "Cheers!" We each take hearty gulps. "Unless I get one of those grants."

Hmm.

We look a little grim again.

We start to talk in circles.

Circles, circles, and tangents—Should we be deckhands in Croatia? Herd reindeer in Lapland? Finally we have a stroke of mutual genius and decide that before we get into any specifics we need to pull back and look at the big picture and ask ourselves: What are our goals for the first few years after college?

And guess what? They match.

1 Get out of the country.

2 Pursue our creative interests
(visual art for him, writing for me).

3 Be together.

So doesn't that mean we could go anywhere?

Well, so much for narrowing things down. At least we know that almost anything we come up with should fit our criteria.

Having made the promise to be together after graduation, we head back to our separate schools to finish senior year. We still don't know where we'll go or what we'll do after graduation, but we know we'll do whatever that is together. Maybe we'll go all around the world with the Watson, maybe we'll wind up in Mali thanks to the Fulbright, maybe we'll go to Mali regardless, hopefully we'll go to China first. . . . At this point it's up to the Powers That Be.

Spending the spring of your senior year three thousand miles away from your new love sounds pretty shitty. And sure we clock a fair share of hours on the phone together, but honestly (*honestly!*) it's not such a drag to do the long-distance thing right now. There's something kind of liberating about it actually. It's like we've been given these last few months to just shamelessly focus on ourselves—on our schoolwork, on our friends who will soon be scattered all over the place, on *whatever* we want—all

the while knowing that we've got something good waiting for us on the other end.

Now just to be perfectly clear— I am NOT recommending long-distance dating as a lifestyle. It's certainly a whole lot more fun to have a certain someone in your bed instead of on the phone. *But*, for a finite amount of time, during which both parties are feeling per-sonally fulfilled in other ways, it can be done.

SPRING 2006

We manage to sneak in a visit each during the spring. Steven comes to Pitzer for the formal my roommates and I are throwing in the morning since our landlord said we couldn't have parties at night anymore. (Hah.) And when I fly out to Colby I am treated with a trip to the L. C. Bates Museum so we can feed our mutual love of bizarre museums and übercreepy stuffed wildlife.

We make up for lost time together by driving cross-country after graduation in the obviously mini Mini Cooper I've been leasing, packed with all my college crap. We have two weeks to make the trip back to Brooklyn before I get on a plane to India for the summer (a friend's wedding, who knows what else?). A few days after that Steven will fly to China to visit his brother Michael and his girlfriend Jessica who are winding up their year in Beijing. Hopefully Steven will like it because we've officially decided that China is the first stop of our ADVENTURE.

Our plan has turned out as follows:

- Teach English in Beijing from August to January.

- Make our way through Southeast Asia until March.

- Somehow get to Mali so we can be there from March until December. (Hooray for being awarded the Fulbright!)

Getting out of the country? Check. Working on our art? That check will be up to us once we get there. Being together? Big fat check.

Here we go.

PART

I

CHINA

INNER MONGOLIA

Beijing

Suddenly summer is over, our diplomas are tucked away in our parents' houses, and we're on a plane to China. We've been hired to teach English in Beijing for six months by the same company Steven's older brother, Michael, worked for. All we really know about the setup is that they'll ship us out to a few different schools around the city and that they have an apartment waiting for us. The same apartment where Michael and Jessica lived last year. (Switch one Weinberg for another.)

After thirteen hours in the air we stumble off our plane and pray that our bags will have arrived with us and that someone named Vivian from the school will actually be waiting to take us to our new home.

And behold—already, dreams do come true! We have our bags, and there *is* a nice young lady named Vivian holding a sign with our names on it. We should have wished for more though, because as it turns out we're going to have to wait four *more* hours for another teacher to arrive.

That's how we wind up having the first meal of our International Adventure at the airport KFC.

"Michael! Michael!" Vivian yells to Steven. "What do you want to eat?"

"For me? Oh, just a Coke I guess. Uh . . . Casey, do you want anything?"

"Sleep."

After four hours spent watching other people arrive and head off to their various adventures outside the airport, the other teacher finally arrives ("Hey," is about all we can eek out by now) and we're off to Mr. Sun's (the school driver's) van with Vivian.

It is immediately obvious that Mr. Sun loves Steven's brother. Apparently, during the year Michael lived here, the two of them spent a lot of time talking NBA each morning on the way to school. So Mr. Sun automatically likes us, which is excellent, except for the fact that he therefore wants to talk NBA with us right now. We drop the couple of team names we know, and in the expanding silence we all realize we're going to have to find a new common ground.

I'm having a particularly hard time socializing since I can't help but notice we seem to be driving through especially dark and spooky neighborhoods while Vivian keeps insisting we're close. As much as I can't wait to get to our new place, I hope we're not close at all.

We pull into an unlit alley, the big block buildings closing in all around us. Mr. Sun is slowing down. Vivian is telling him something I don't understand and pointing at an enormous shadow up ahead.

And then we stop.

"This is your home!" she says, and throws open the van's doors.

"My mom can never come visit," I whisper to Steven. Up five flights of winding, barely lit stairs — open the door —

Creek . . .

We flick on the fluorescent lights, then quickly turn them off again. As scary as all the shadows and cobwebs are in the dark, they're even scarier in the harsh light.

"Let's just go to sleep," Steven says. "We'll deal with this in the morning, right?"

You'd think that after such a long trip we'd sleep until noon. Instead we're wide awake by five. In the soft morning sun, the apartment looks a whole lot more welcoming than it did last night. We roll over to get out of bed.

Squeeeeeeak.

"Oh that'll be just great," says Steven. Laughing, I push him out of bed.

We pad around our new place barefoot, opening cupboards, going through the books left on the shelves. The place is roomy, but kind of has the feel of a slapped-together dorm since about ten different people have lived here, all in very temporary ways, and each has left behind random things they no longer wanted.

"I think we should rearrange some stuff," I say. "We can turn it into a place that feels more like ours."

"I like where you're going with this," says Steven.

"I can't believe we *live* here!"

"In China!"

"I know! Okay," I clap excitedly. "How about we start with the bedroom. We could move the bed to the back wall so it's not so close to the window and—"

"Yeah, yeah, sounds good!" We go back into the bedroom and each take a side.

Squeeeeeak screeeeeeeeech!

"Um, maybe we should wait until after nine to drag all this stuff around?" suggests Steven.

"Probably a good idea. We don't need the neighbors hating us already." We push the bed back quickly then stand there, looking around.

"What do we do now?" I whisper.

"I don't know," he whispers back.

"My god. I don't think I've been up this early since I was four years old. It must be terrible to never sleep in once you've got kids."

"Yeah, unless you stick them in front of the TV or something."

And that's how we wind up spending our first morning in China watching *Dumbo* on the couch in our pajamas. (Hooray for all the bootleg DVDs we inherited!)

"We're grown-ups now," I say, cuddling up on the couch as Steven puts the movie in.

"Watching *Dumbo* in our pajamas," he points out.

"Hey—we can do whatever we want. That seems pretty grown up to me."

After the movie, after moving things around, we're hungry.

"How about Chinese?" I suggest.

"Sounds good to me," Steven says.

We put on our shoes and step out into our new neighborhood.

We have six days to settle in before we start our weeklong teacher training, so we take that time to wander, hit up some classic tourist spots, and eat our way through the city.

One of our first trips beyond our walking radius is to the Dirt Market, the famous outdoor antique fair that once upon a time had (duh) dirt floors. Supposedly you can find some great bargains. That is, if you bargain. And I mean *bargain*.

The first time I came to China with that summer program six years ago, it exhausted and unnerved me to have to haggle for everything. Couldn't there be a little price tag on things that I could check out discreetly and decide privately if I found that fair? My negotiating skills improved when I went to Morocco. Those medina merchants will make or break the haggler within you. It turns out, I just had to dig a little deeper to find that poker-faced/ ain't budging/will do the walk-away bargainer I had somewhere in me.

So at this point, despite my limited Chinese being extremely rusty, I feel ready to whip out my toughest haggling game.

Then I see Steven bargain.

Never mind that he only learned his numbers yesterday, or that his grasp of tones is about as good as his musical rhythm (endearingly earnest, yet terrible)—this guy gets his point across: there is NO WAY he's paying whatever you just said he should pay and you are INSANE and STUPID to think he might ever even consider it.

And just like that, without ever consulting, we've got a Good Cop/Bad Cop routine.

It's already more fun to have a partner in crime.

Living with someone can feel like a perma-slumber party. *Hooray!* You're still here! We can stay up as late as we want and play all the time!

There comes a point though, (maybe five days in?) when you realize there are some things you prefer to do alone. And that's when you have to devise ways of having "together but alone time."

For Steven, it turns out to be simple enough. Give him a flat surface and something with which to draw or paint, maybe some Bob Dylan or Beck, and it's like he's not even there anymore. He's *out* there, on that other mental plane where time passes without us knowing and daily stresses disappear.

I can get to that place too. Just not with Steven in the room.

 So I write a story at the desk in the living room,

play guitar in the kitchen,

write in my journal in bed.

When Steven's paint is drying, he wants to play again. When my hand starts cramping up, I want to play again.

Good thing we live together now and can play all the time.

It's our first day of teacher training. After a hearty dumpling breakfast from the vendor on our corner, we walk the three minutes from our place to the big office building where Shane English School's headquarters are. Up to a high floor, skipping numbers four and thirteen, which the Chinese find inauspicious, the elevator doors open and here is our new life: the administrative offices and cubicles, the classrooms, the drawers of flash cards, the smell of dry-erase markers and, of course, our new coworkers.

There are twelve other teachers. Some of them sound American or Canadian, some sound British, some are not talking so it's hard to tell.

We're shuffled into a room by Leonard, the English-born principal/coordinator/trainer. Leonard's energy and friendly conversation fill the awkward gaps in between our sporadic introductions. And then there's the Chinese staff: Diana, the boss at the top, and a handful of shy young ladies who will help us with a little bit of everything. We see

Mr. Sun and wave heartily. Surprisingly enough, he seems just as excited to see some "familiar" faces in the crowd.

Steven and I sit apart. We don't want to be that couple that's always together and therefore never makes any other friends. But as we sit down on opposite sides of the room we realize that there are three other couples and they're all sitting together. Now we look like that couple that's already fighting. Oops.

Our training is the usual round of humiliating ice-breakers with even more embarrassment to come: in order to learn the games we'll play in our future classes we have to play them now.

Duck Duck Goose anyone?

We crawl around like elementary school kids and sit through PowerPoint presentations like unlucky high-schoolers. But this is not to say that we don't learn a ton. Among many other things, Leonard teaches us how to smoothly transition between activities, what exactly a diphthong is, and perhaps most important, to not take it personally when the really little kids cry upon first seeing us.

After a week of training that leaves us feeling somewhat prepared (Leonard promises we'll learn some things best by just doing them), we're finally going to be given our schedules.

The moment of truth has arrived!

Leonard reiterates that he tried to keep couples together, that some of us will spend all of our time at one school, others will split their time among as many as four, some will teach preschool, some will teach professional nurses, some will have days off that aren't on weekends and on and on. Come on, give them to us already!

He calls our names one by one and we come to the front . . .

Yes! Or, wait, *what*? Our schedules are an indecipherable spreadsheet of acronyms and times.

We run up to Mr. Sun to see if he can help. He looks at it. "Shangdi?" he says.

"Uh, yes, this is our schedule, do you—"

"No—Shangdi school?" he asks. "I drive Michael to Shangdi school every day." We look at our papers. We don't seem to have Shangdi anywhere.

It looks like Mr. Sun is going to have to find a new basketball buddy.

After much consultation with the rest of the staff, we can come up with a basic profile for each place where we'll be teaching:

1. San Fan Junior High: An elite public school where we will be spending most of our time as conversation teachers (nitty-gritty grammar will be left to the Chinese teachers).
2. Zhong Guan Cun Elementary: A public school where we'll each teach one first-grade class.
3. Shane (the company that hired us): Private classes on Friday night and Saturday, including preschool, kindergarten, first, and second grades, as well as one-on-one tutoring.

4. Beijing Normal University: A private afternoon
   class every Friday for elementary school kids.

   Some of us will be driven to our schools by Mr. Sun, some of
us are on our own but will be reimbursed for any subway/bus/
taxi rides. All of us are a little perplexed but hoping for the best.
I'm especially hoping that Steven and I will get used to a Sunday/
Wednesday weekend.

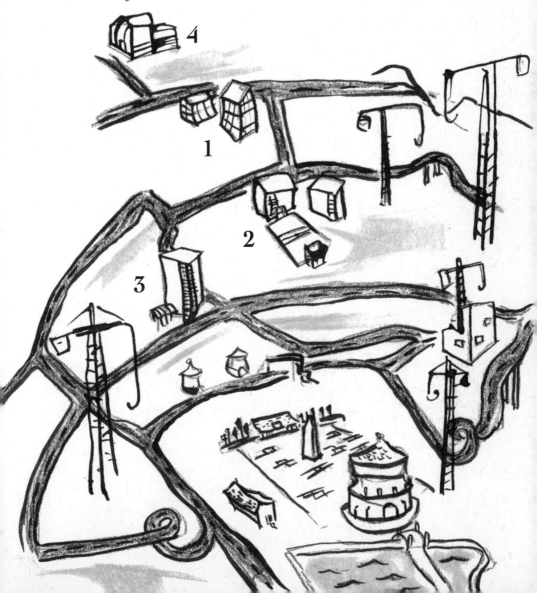

Now that we have our schedules, everything feels a bit more real. We have our very own apartment! We have jobs! We have salaries!

About that last one: it's time we figure out exactly how we're going to deal with money as a couple. Over a lunch of cold sesame noodles, we decide to simply pool our salaries together since they're exactly the same. We have our own Chinese bank accounts set up by the company, so we'll each take out our own money; but as far as paying for things goes, it'll be like "You paid for lunch so I'll pay for dinner." And by the time we're done with teaching come January and traveling around Southeast Asia, we'll put together whatever we have left. Which is looking like it might be a lot. You can live

so cheaply in Beijing. Two bedroom apartment? Three hundred dollars a month. Three-course feast at the restaurant down the block? Dollar fifty each. Twenty-two ounce beer? Twenty cents. (Yes, *twenty cents*. I think I found the carrot to lure my younger brother out here to visit.)

Is it a bold move as a new couple to share money like this? It certainly rests on the hope that neither of us is secretly looking to fleece the other for all their worth and then leave after a month. And I know some of my friends think it's a little nuts—but then again, so was moving across the world together, right?

But as my mom told me before I left: "If you can share bodily fluids, you can share money."

Thanks, Mom.

As our fellow teachers head off to their first days at new schools, Steven and I have another week until our classes start. (Our schools just happen to have different schedules.) So we take the opportunity to check out Tianjin, a city nearby.

On the train ride back to Beijing, we realize we're feeling anxious. "I just want to start teaching already," I say.

"I know. Me too," Steven agrees.

And suddenly our new phones beep as we receive simultaneous text messages:

COME TO ZGC ELEMENTARY. CLASS 3:15

COME TO ZGC ELEMENTARY. CLASS 3:15

As much I as appreciate the lightning-quick response from the work gods, I wish they would have taken a moment before granting my wishes to realize that I am on a train right now, coming back from a long weekend, dirty, tired, and bedraggled — aka in no shape to teach my first class.

"What time is it?" I ask Steven.

"Two forty-five."

"So we have half an hour to get back to our place, shower and change into teacherly clothes, find that school we've never been to, and prepare a lesson for a class we've never met." Words like *impossible* and *failure* flash through my brain. "No way."

"I think we have to do it," says Steven.

"But your brother said we should be firm about stuff like this!" I try. "If we let them yank us around in the beginning they'll always be pulling crap like this—giving us ten minutes' notice, sending us somewhere new, unprepared. We should say no."

"Or we could say okay and show them that we're hardworking and cooperative from the get-go, which will give us leverage later on."

Of course I agree with him. However, I am the kind of girl who has her outfit for the first day of school picked out by August 1, the kind of girl who gets happy heart palpitations when the supplies list is handed out in class, the kind of girl who does NOT come to school with dirty hair and no pencil. And that's as a student! As a teacher—well, I don't know what my standards are yet, but I'm pretty sure they don't include being late and disheveled and winging it.

"But—" I say, without much force.

"It'll be fine," he says, and starts to smooth down his I-look-kind-of-insane hair. "It's just the first day. The first day is always a little crazy anyway."

And a little crazy it is, but in the best of ways. It turns out you don't need clean hair or much of a lesson plan to wow a bunch of first graders. If you know a variety of dance-intensive songs to get them going (like "The Hokey Pokey") and lullabies to bring them back down (like "Twinkle Twinkle"), you're set for a good thirty minutes. The rest of the time can be spent learning names and simply making silly faces while saying "Hello." What's surprising, though, is how sweaty you can get doing those few simple things. By the end of the forty-five minutes, I am dripping like I've just performed an entire acrobatic opera by myself under heated stage lights.

Sweat aside, the post-workout high is *amazing*. All of us new teachers are absolutely beaming, talking over each other and dancing around excitedly, each giving accounts of the most precious/hilarious/delightful things that happened in our classes. As we leave the building like a gang of giggling students, Steven and I find each other.

"Wasn't that insane? How much do you love teaching?" I squeal.

"I can't believe they were actually doing what I was saying!" Steven says.

"I know! And that they were having so much fun!"

"Yeah, my class was laughing almost the whole time!"

"Mine too!"

"Especially every time I turned around to write something on the board."

"Really?"

"Why are you saying it like that?"

"Like what?"

"Like that! You sound suspicious."

"No way! I'm just really happy this is all working out."

To celebrate the success of our first day, a whole gang of us walks over to the International Beer Garden a block away from school.

It's no "garden," but at least it's outside. And there's certainly a lot of international folks and, of course, beer. The crowd is friendly, and gets progressively friendlier as the night goes on. We meet tutors, bankers, travelers, business people, students, and other teachers from all over the world. If you were ever going to run into someone from another part of your life in China, it would be here.

This is also a good place to get to know the non-teacherly side of our coworkers. Steven and I originally thought most people would

be fresh out of college like us, but instead they're nurses, translators, German literature PhD candidates, budding political scientists, and photographers. For nearly everyone, being an English teacher is not a part of their professional goals, but rather, a means to an end—the end being an extended trip to China. When people ask us what we "really do," or at least what we "really want to do one day," we're not sure what to say. Are we a painter and a writer? Teachers? Can we even call ourselves teachers yet?

At the end of the night we realize the best part about going to the Beer Garden just might be that Shane comps the taxi ride home. Because, even though it's well past midnight, technically we're coming back from school.

(AB)USING MANDARIN CHINESE

Learning Chinese is hard. But there are some aspects that make it easy too. This is how it all balances out for a beginner:

This is a four-tone language. (Flat, rising, falling, and falling then rising.) So the same word can mean totally different things depending on how you sing it. And you *have* to sing it. Because, for example, *ba* can mean *eight*, *father*, or *target* depending on the tone. We're often demanding that taxi drivers "listen," when we're trying to get them to "stop." (Flat tone vs. rising tone.) Of course, we could do worse. Rumor has it "mother-in-law" and "water buffalo" are only a few tones apart.

BUT

You don't have to conjugate! Just plop any old verb after a pronoun and you're done. (*Wo chu* = I go, *ni chu* = you go, *ta chu* = he or she goes.) Good-bye tedious verb charts of Romance languages.

Written Chinese is character based, meaning there's no alphabet that you can use to sound out words. Just thousands and thousands of little pictures that for the most part don't look anything like what they mean. Despite all those years in school, you are illiterate again.

BUT

At least you don't have to think about spelling! And besides, you'd be surprised how far just a few characters can go. Dining with a vegetarian? Avoid all items on the menu with the character for "meat:" 肉. Trying to catch a train home? Scan all the characters for "Beijing" and point to that one: 北京. And you can always feel good about "one, two, three:" 一二三.

Chinese is a difficult language to master. Especially if your native language has no tones or characters.

BUT

Almost no one expects you to speak it! And when you do, many people are pleasantly surprised and excited to help you through whatever transaction you are attempting to make.

For us, the best part about having only basic Chinese skills is that it brings us closer to our youngest students. We can easily trick them into believing that we're fluent because we know *their* kind of Chinese: colors, numbers, basic emotions, simple commands. And on top of it all, we sound just like them. Because apparently, when you mess up your tones, you sound exactly like a little kid. It's no wonder the guy on the corner loves it when we ask for, "Dumpwings pwease!"

We have a meeting today with the head of the foreign-language department at the junior high, San Fan, to acquaint us with what we'll be doing there three days a week. She sits us down in the teachers' lounge, hands us a book, and says: "You will teach this to every class in the school."

"How many classes are there?" I ask hesitantly, trying to look professional and capable, not sweaty and scared. (There were a *lot* of kids playing Ping-Pong in the yard when we came in.)

"Thirty-six," she says, straight-faced. "I have split the school in two. Eighteen classes for you, Steven, and eighteen classes for you, Casey."

I laugh nervously and try to play it off as teacherly joy. She opens the book and continues. "You will teach one unit during each forty-minute lesson."

"Wait, hang on—" starts Steven, clearly remembering that we technically signed a part-time teaching contract and that eighteen forty-minute classes per day is above and beyond what we'd even call overtime. "How often do we see each class?"

"Once every two weeks. Actually, it will be quite easy. You will only have to prepare one lesson every two weeks!"

"So we will teach the same lesson eighteen times in a row for two weeks?" I venture.

"Exactly!"

"Every two weeks, eighteen times in a row?" clarifies Steven.

"Exactly!"

"Oh."

Back at our apartment, Steven and I go through The Book.

Unit One: Lions.

"Lions?" he groans.

Unit Two: Harry Potter.

"Harry Potter?" I whine.

The rest of the chapters we will cover in the coming five months include Bubble Gum, the Leaning Tower of Pisa, Valentine's Day . . .

We slump into our couch and try to think of how on earth we are going to make lions sound cool to one thousand six hundred pubescent kids eighteen times in a row.

We're thinking that the best way to make even the most insane/ mundane unit seem interesting is to teach it in a way that none of the students' other classes are taught. That is to say, with games, with jumping and screaming, with skits, with music and art. So much of school here is focused on memorization and rote learning—essentially sitting quietly and watching the teacher talk for forty minutes straight, something Steven and I have zero interest in doing.

So the first time we meet each of our thirty-six classes at junior high, all of our students seem a little confused—okay, maybe even horrified—by just how far we have thrown the usual lesson plan out the window. But by the end of those first classes, it's easy to see that soon enough our problem is not going to be how to engage them, but how to reign them back in and quiet them down. These kids are ready to *rock out*. So I guess it's not a huge surprise that when they give themselves English names, a class list includes: Chapter, Zero, Super-Teeth, Dad, Michael Jordan, Gin, Boss, Nestea, Sniper, Elvis, Mummy Vista, Everybody, Satan, Name, Old Ben, and Henry VIII.

It is *really* hard to not laugh when you call on Dad.

To wrap up the lion lesson, we hand out some homemade cartoons and tell everyone that their first homework assignment is to write a caption for the one they're given.

Two weeks later (since we only see each class once every other week), we're back and ask everyone to hand them in. Plenty of kids have forgotten or misunderstood and colored them in. Of the ones who got the assignment, some have written rather straightforward captions.

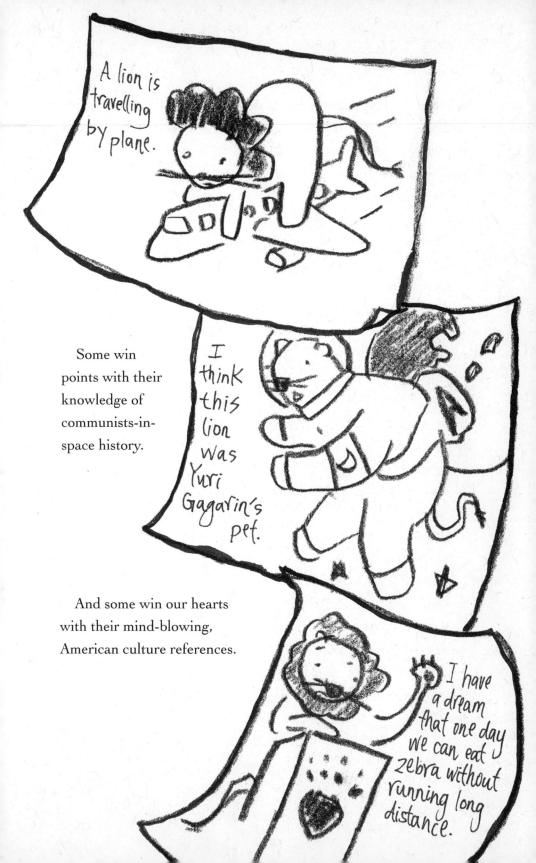

A lion is travelling by plane.

Some win points with their knowledge of communists-in-space history.

I think this lion was Yuri Gagarin's pet.

And some win our hearts with their mind-blowing, American culture references.

I have a dream that one day we can eat zebra without running long distance.

So our student roster is as follows: we've got the junior high kids at San Fan, the adorable first-graders at Zhong Guan Cun (where we taught our first lessons), a Friday afternoon class at the University elementary school (where for all intents and purposes we are babysitting), and then there's the company headquarters, Shane.

At all the day schools we are mostly left to our own devices, given the vaguest of guidelines, and set free. Shane, though, is a private supplementary school where the possibility to have overworked students and overinvolved parents is, well, quite possible. So the pressure's on.

There are "performances" for parents, "tests" for the children, "performance tests" for us teachers, and on top of it all, the fish-bowl. I mean, the break-room, where we all try to relax/prepare in between classes while being observed like captive animals.

The teachers all cope differently with break-room time—some throw themselves into making detailed flash cards and abuse the laminating machine (ahem, Steven), others take turns acting as a bouncer to keep out the throngs of children, some check NHL stats online . . . we all try our best is to simply ignore the madness until the bell rings. At which point the real madness begins.

The classes we have at Shane can be rowdy to say the least. (Think flying flash cards.) But in the eye of the storm, Steven and I each have a one-on-one student who always saves the day. For me it's Linda, for Steven it's Rudi.

Eleven-year-old Linda and I become BFF halfway through our first tutoring session when we realize we both adore writing stories and playing piano. There's a brief moment of disillusion when she confesses her love of all things Harry Potter and I'm perhaps not as enthusiastic . . . but it's overshadowed by our shared love of hanging out together.

With her mom in tow—did I mention that?—scribbling away notes on pronunciation and idioms on the sidelines, I'm initially nervous and skeptical. But Linda's mom turns out to be 101 percent positive and supportive. When I can't remember exactly how much I covered last week, there she has it in her handy little notebook and on top of it all—gasp!—Linda remembers every little bit because they've reviewed it together.

Steven is jealous. Not just of my budding relationship with Linda ("Baby, she gives me things you can't!") but of his lack of

a one-on-one connection with a Chinese kid. Then he's assigned to Rudi.

Rudi's dad is an all-star comedian who's on TV nearly every night, he plays ice hockey, and at the tender of age of nine mousses his hair. (Whatever. Linda rocks too.)

Initially Steven is floored by just how fluent Rudi is. Then he's floored by the meaning of what he's been saying: "I scored ten goals in the game last night, I can play most of the *Moonlight Concerto* by now, and did I mention that I'm going to Canada next week for a tournament?"

But the real key to Steven's heart is an entirely different skill. One that Steven himself worked so hard to cultivate as a child.

"Can I show you something? That's where my team practices. See that building over there? The really, really tall one? And—"

"*Holy shit*, thinks Steven. *He's doing the same thing I did to my teachers! Delay! Distract! Digress! I LOVE this kid.*"

The only downside of our one-on-one tutoring sessions is that sometimes, much to our dismay, Linda and Rudi are too busy to come.

It just makes the next week that much better.

MINORITY TRADING CARDS: COLLECT THEM ALL!

Searching for bargains at the Dirt Market one Sunday, Steven comes across a pack of what might be called "Chinese Ethnic Minority Trading Cards" circa 1984. They are *easily* the best find of the day. And although we can't really read the Chinese, Mongolian, Korean, Arabic, or Tibetan on the back of the cards, the pictures on the front of each are certainly worth their thousand words. We have the feeling they're not exactly P.C., but we just *have* to have the whole set of smiling women in traditional dress doing chores.

About minorities in China: when people in other countries say "Chinese," they're usually talking about *Han* Chinese since they make up about ninety percent of the population. But there's the other ten percent, which is made up of a whole bunch of other ethnic minorities. (The Chinese government officially recognizes fifty-five.)

Some biggies are Zhuang, Manchu, Hui, Miao, Uyghur, Tujia, Yi, Mongol, and Tibetan. And when I say "biggies" I mean BIGGIES. We're talking sixteen million Zhuang Chinese. That's about twice the number of people living in New York. (These populations are growing, too, since minorities are not required to abide by the One Child policy. And neither, for that matter, are rich parents it seems, since plenty of our students have siblings. Hmm.)

Where do the many groups of ethnicities live? All over China. If you *had* to vaguely map it out, you could say that the farther west you go, the more prominent the minority populations are. Although here in Beijing, like any international metropolis, there's a mix of people—in our neighborhood there are Tibetans selling jewelry on the sidewalk and Uyghur Muslims running noodle shops. But for the most part, it's a Han city.

We'd like to learn more about the country's diversity, but honestly, we're kind of scared to ask too much. There are so many varying degrees of taboo here, and from what we have gathered, Han-minority relations can be a touchy subject. (Think Tibet.) Both of us were lucky enough to have traveled to western and southern regions of China on trips before we came to live in Beijing, so we've been somewhat exposed to the cultural vastness and variety of this country. But we know there's a whole lot more. Maybe these tacky cards, at the very least, can remind us of that.

外国人
FOREIGNER

Since we have a minuscule kitchen and it's so damn cheap to eat out, we wind up dining out down the block nearly every night. Big brother Michael and his fluent-in-Chinese girlfriend say they all but lived here as well. So the first time we go, we make sure to bring a picture of them.

The waitresses go from confused (Who are you? Who are these people?) to ecstatic (It's you again! But my how you've changed!) to even more giggly and pleased (Our dear friends left but they sent us replacements!).

Initially we order whatever the other diners are enjoying. Pointing at food is a lot easier than saying the Chinese word for it. But you can't point your way through everything, so after a few weeks, we decide it's time to move beyond this killer combo of charades/scattered Chinese I learned in high school, and into the world of more sophisticated communication.

We hire a kind and soft-spoken Chinese woman about our age named Jessica to tutor us at our place once a week. She's the girlfriend of Glen, one of my teaching assistants, and he promises that she is so good we will be fluent in no time.

Jessica prefers to go by her English name with us, maybe because we keep butchering the way we are supposed to sing the syllables, thereby accidentally calling her something terrible. She says she'll teach us any vocabulary we request and even how to read and write if we're interested. (Interested? Yes. Have enough time to study? No.) So Steven and I cut right to the chase.

"Teach us how to order food."

So she does. And soon enough the ladies who run the restaurant down the block are impressed with our culinary knowledge and we are immensely and enjoyably full from dishes we order without any pointing involved.

For our second lesson, we learn colors and food-related adjectives so that when the name of a specific dish escapes us we can at least ask for, "Green, salty, not fried, cold" and get that chopped cucumber salad that's so refreshing.

This all translates as: we eat *a lot* in Beijing.

LIFE AS A GROWN-UP

Adults are always warning that there are a lot of boring, tedious, and necessary responsibilities that come with living on your own.

It turns out, as long as you live on your own somewhere foreign, all of those dreaded responsibilities can be fun!

"Check out this crazy ATM I can hardly use. Good thing you're here to help me, overly friendly man in uniform!"

"Ooh, grocery shopping. I've never felt this alive picking out seafood!"

"You mean we need to fill out five *more* forms to send this one letter? Yay!"

And even if you slip up and, say, forget to pay that electricity bill on time, living on your own is still a blast because now you can have a black-out party all night long.

Steven has decided it is time for a haircut. And even though I can do a mean job with kiddy scissors right here at home, he wants to get a "real" haircut.

Hah.

As he leaves, I remind him what we've been told about hair salons here: "The ones with the red swirly barbershop poles and dark rooms in the back are for more than just haircuts, if you know what I mean."

"Yeah, I know."

Does he?

When he comes back half an hour later, I am somewhat surprised to see him with shorter hair.

"So you got a real haircut."

"What's a *jiao zi* again?" he asks immediately.

"Dumplings, why?"

"I think they were laughing at me because my head is shaped like a *jiao zi*."

And then I am laughing at him because his head *is* shaped like a *jiao zi*.

"So you didn't get a massage or anything?" I ask when I can finally manage to breathe again.

"Well, no. But everyone who came out from the back rooms all tarted up definitely looked disappointed when I kept insisting that all I wanted was a haircut."

"And that's why they called you a *jiao zi* head? Because they were mad?"

"Yes."

"It had nothing to do with the dumpling-like ridge on the top of your skull?"

"What?"

"Nothing." I hold it in this time. "What do you want for lunch?"

"I hate to say it, but—" he rubs a hand over his head. "*Jiao zi*."

If we're not lesson planning, teaching, or eating out, we're probably at the small park near our apartment where we snack on banana chips, play backgammon, and hang with

our neighbors. We're often the only folks over six and under sixty.

Knowing the sunny days aren't going to last much longer, we clock a lot of hours out here in the first few weeks.

WHERE DO ENGLISH TEACHERS COME FROM? WHERE DO THEY GO WHEN THEY'RE DONE?

By now we've figured out that it goes roughly like this:

You have a certification/degree in teaching English as a second language (like ESL or TOEFL).

You have a college degree or more. The higher your degree, the higher your salary.

You know someone in the school/ You're fluent in the local language/ You have a knack for talking your way into things for which you are underqualified.

You go back home.

You renew your contract with your current school.

You create your own schedule with a different school, or pick up some private tutoring to cut out the middle man.

You teach at an organization/school like Shane.

You go teach English in another country. Maybe somewhere nearby with a similar system, like Korea.

I want a world map to put up in the bedroom. The idea is that as I'm lounging around in bed, I will inadvertently learn all the geography that I never quite retained in middle school. Because frankly, I'm sick of feeling stupid next to Steven, who can tell you the location and capital of every damn country in the world.

So one evening, while picking up some banana chips from the corner vendor, we see that right next to the guy who sells pirated DVDs is a guy who sells maps. Excellent!

"Check it out! A map—just like you were talking about!" says Steven.

"Except it's labeled in Chinese," I point out.

"Quiz me! Quiz me! I bet I know them all!"

So I quiz him. And guess what? He knows them all. Or does he? Because *how would I know*?! The whole reason I want a map is that if I were given one in Chinese, I would *not* be able to re-label it in English. I try to express this point, but Steven is so excited, his love of maps and geography bursting all over the place, that I don't push it.

We bring the map home, hang it up on the wall, and instead of learning while hanging out in bed, I brood and wind up having angry internal monologues that go something like this: "Memorizing capitals is stupid . . . political history is boring because it's all male politicians and memorizing dates . . . everyone has different kinds of intelligences and so what if mine don't include regurgitating names!"

I'm about as good at feeling stupid as I am at keeping a poker face when I'm annoyed.

"Casey, what's wrong?"

"Nothing." I keep my glare steady and focused on the map. I last about six seconds before I explode. "This map is in Chinese!"

"You knew that when we got it."

"*You* got it."

"Fine, let's take it down."

"No, don't take it down. You like it, right?"

"But you don't like it. And you'll just get mad every time you look at it."

"That's not true." That is *so* true. So luckily, before we lock ourselves into a cold war, Steven comes up with a peace plan to please all parties: we will have fun with it.

We spend the rest of the evening listening to classical music and drinking gin and tonics (to enhance the air of colonialism, haha) as we redraw all country lines with a fat black marker. We chop up Africa in a grid since historically that has worked so well, we give Mexico back most of the South West and finally unite the entire Caribbean as one. So now, when I'm laying around in bed, I'm not learning geography through osmosis or mentally ranting against all politics, but rather, thinking about how damn sweet Steven is.

Steven decides to play with the first-graders during a break between classes.

Steven is taken DOWN.

Steven sets new
teacher-student
boundaries.

So here we are, doing what we do quite a bit these days: lesson planning.

Students think teachers are getting off the hook with no homework. That's because lots of students have never had to lesson plan. Lesson planning *is* homework. And instead of getting a grade, you get a salary, and instead of "fail," *F* stands for "fired."

So, Steven and I work hard at being prepared.

Lesson planning for me means laying out a detailed outline for class, putting together any extra materials I might need like flash cards or a worksheet, and coming up with a few backup plans in case an activity doesn't seem to be working out.

Lesson planning for Steven includes similar elements, but most of that outline exists in his head and nearly all of his planning time is devoted to making flash cards. Detailed, bizarre, beautiful flash cards. And rather than holding on to each set, he makes new ones nearly every time. (Steven is to the laminating machine as a Hummer is to gas.)

I'm sure none of our former teachers would be too surprised by our different approaches.

Some of our best lesson planning, though, happens for our junior high classes at San Fan because we do those together. A little bit of planning here, some spontaneity there, an art-heavy assignment here, a writing game there . . .

And slowly but surely we've been influencing each others' styles: Steven's got a teacher's planner now and I'm *really* getting into drawing coloring spreads for my preschoolers.

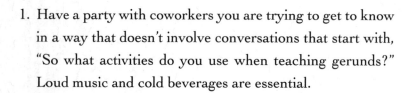

PANTS-OFF CASUAL

Follow these five easy steps
to befriend your Beijing
neighbors:

1. Have a party with coworkers you are trying to get to know
   in a way that doesn't involve conversations that start with,
   "So what activities do you use when teaching gerunds?"
   Loud music and cold beverages are essential.

2. Wake up the next morning craving pancakes, then remember that you bought
   some mix at a grocery store in order to
   make the aforementioned food for your
   neighbors as a way to introduce yourself
   and your American ways. Decide that
   making pancakes to make amends for a
   loud party is a good idea. Especially if
   you get to save some for yourself.

3. Make the pancakes. Use a wok since that is the only pot
   you can find in the apartment. Realize that the curved
   edges make flipping surprisingly easier than in a flat pan.

4. Look up the Chinese character for "gift," then copy it on a piece of paper you put on the pancake plate. Ring the bell across the hall.

5. Meet your neighbors who hang out pant-less. Try not to look at their exposed underwear as you sit down with them. Eat pancakes. Make friends with the couple who insist you call them Mama and Baba, and believe them when they say they couldn't hear the party and they love the pancakes.

Date Number One

Steven and I never really "dated" before we got here. We'd ridden camels together and flown across the country to see each other, but had never gone on a "date" per se.

So when he asks if he can take me out on a first date I gladly accept. He's secretive and suave about it. "Dress nicely, as you always do, and I'll pick you up at seven," he says. When I ask how he plans to pick me up at a place where he also lives, he says there are some other "preparations" to take care of so he'll already be out. Plus, he can change at the gym. (We recently joined the Hong Kong Boss VIP Fitness Club just down the road. Primarily we did it for our health, but I'd be lying if I didn't say we were very taken by the name.)

So romance is in the air! At exactly seven, I'm downstairs, all primped and made up with, I kid you not, butterflies in my stomach. I get progressively more nervous as time ticks on and still no sign of Steven. Just as I start wondering if he's having second thoughts, up pulls a taxi and out steps Steven, shaved and looking sharp with a rose.

It turns out he's made reservations at one of Beijing's finest restaurants, a Brazilian place with tablecloths, heavy silverware, candles, English menus, and a full bar. Our mojitos are divine, the pork chops delicious, the conversation playful—what a perfect first date!

Then we make the ultimate First Date Mistake. We talk politics.

There's something about him growing up in D.C. and studying government in the Northeast, and me growing up in Brooklyn and studying sociology in California that gets us in this terrible gridlock. He winds up playing the cynical realist, and I the dreaming optimist. And even though on paper we agree about the Big Stuff, talking about it seems to be a sure-fire way to get us both pink-in-the-face mad.

And so, our first date sadly ends without a good-night kiss, and a second date doesn't look like it's in the cards. Lucky for us, we've already skipped that whole part, and the next morning we can get back to living together.

Teaching is chugging along nicely now. We're not so nervous anymore, we're finding that balance between following our lesson plans and going with the vibe of the class, and we're not wearing ourselves out so much.

Most of the time.

Yeah, that other part of the time we've got these kindergarten classes at Shane. Mine consists of ten boys who are fond of chucking flash cards and one girl whose survival tactic is mostly the cold shoulder. (I refer to her as Princess Judy because she often wears a tiara.) Luckily I have a great T.A. named Silen who can lay down the law in that piercing Chinese that makes even me stop and shiver.

Steven, on the other hand, seems to be having the opposite problem. "I can't get them to do *anything*," he laments one afternoon in the park.

"Because they're just running around like mad?"

"No, no, I wish. They just sit there."

"How many of them are there?"

"Well that's the other part," he says. "It's different every time. Last week I had

eight so yesterday I planned this number game but then only two showed up. I don't know what to do with them! They just stare at me."

"Like little zombies. I know. Sometimes that would happen at the preschool I used to work at. But there are ways to engage them. First off—are you standing at the board?"

"Yes."

"Get down on the ground so you're as small as they are."

"I tried that but they all backed away—I think they're scared of my big nose!"

I laugh. "Well you were probably too close to their faces, that's all. Just sit down and start slowly, start low key, and then gently bring them to a higher level of energy with a song that speeds up or something. It's like a party you know? It might be a little awkward when everyone first arrives—"

"Right."

"And smile, smile, smile. They're probably looking at you all worried and scared because that's the same look you're giving them. You're doing it right now actually."

He laughs. "See? It makes me nervous. It feels like I'm faking it sometimes."

"Faking it?"

"Faking being a teacher."

"Fake it til you make it."

The next week, Steven fakes it pretty well. "We began the class really quietly just like you said, and I let them all touch my nose, then I touched their noses then we ran around the room pretending we were animals—I think it went really well."

"Did you get any English in there?"

"Hey. One step at a time here."

OUR SHORT GUIDE TO BEIJING STREET FOOD

Beijing street food is:

    a) delicious

    b) cheap

    c) lovingly called "the commoner food" (*jia bian xiao chi*)

    d) ALL OF THE ABOVE

1. *Baozi* are succulent steamed dough balls packed with spiced pork and biting ginger bits. Keep an eye out for stacks of circular bamboo baskets. And move quickly! Because these hot treats are often gone before lunch.

2. *Kao hong shi* are coal-roasted sweet potatoes that can turn any cynic's heart warm. Look for a large oil drum on wheels near a subway stop. Eventually you'll be able to follow your nose to them. They greatly improve a long walk home after work.

3. *Yuan ro chuan* are grilled skewers of spiced lamb meat with the occasional sinfully good pocket of fat that bursts like pure joy in your mouth. Stumble into one of these stands outside most bars and nightclubs. Mind the pointy ends. There are more glamorous ways to go blind.

4. *Jie bing guo zi* are almost more fun to watch being made than to eat. (Almost.) There's batter spread over a hot plate in a swift circular motion, an egg cracked on top, scallions and hot pepper bits thrown into the party like delicious confetti, a giant crispy egg noodle and a mysterious (to us at least) brown sauce dribbled over it all right before it's folded into a crepe/burrito roll that you can hold with both hands greedily. A most excellent brunch choice after a long night out.

And by the way, *hao chi* means *delicious*, literally *good food*. Throwing that one around with the vendors almost always gets a smile.

Upon moving into our apartment we inherited a collection of perhaps two hundred DVDs. Yet even with this substantial library, we are occasionally tempted to check out what that guy has lined up on the sidewalk outside Subway. (Yes, the sandwiches.)

"Oh he's got *Cars*?" Steven says, crouching down to look. "I've been wanting to see that! It's supposed to have incredible animation."

"Look he's got *The Break Up*. Vince Vaughn is always funny."

A dollar later, we settle into our couch to enjoy a private screening of *Cars*. The animation is superb, but the English subtitles are . . . first off, unnecessary since the audio is in the original English, and second, written for an extremely violent gangster film, definitely not for *Cars*. ("Just kill him now. Do it now, I said!")

It looks like buying a DVD for ten percent of the usual cost might mean getting ten percent of the quality, too. *Damn*. We blindly attack our remote control and magically manage to turn off the subtitles. Success! We spend the evening enjoying *Cars*.

The next night proves to be a bit more difficult. As Steven puts in *The Break Up* he asks, "Are you sure he said this is in English? The title on the cover is in Russian."

"Yeah, he definitely said it's in English. And if not we can always turn the subtitles back on."

Of course it's not in English, so as Vince Vaughn bellows away in Russian we press all the buttons on the remote until we get the subtitles back on. What we get is snippets of this flashing on the screen at the lightning pace of their comedic banter:

-Good of! Good of! Hence lemons twelve on kitchen!

-Lessen velvet lemons kitchen!

-Of twelve thirteen crooked pile inside?

-No.

-No. Guest door father simple lemon! You!

At first it's hilarious. Did they directly translate the Russian subtitles into English? Did someone get paid to just put random English words onto the screen to vaguely pass as subtitles? Maybe two minutes go by before we each have a headache.

"Can we turn it off?" Steven asks.

"Yes please," I say. The screen goes black. "Well I guess we knew they were going to break up anyway."

"Maybe it was over lemons."

"Good of! Good of! Catch nothing hamburger tree!" I shout.

"What?!"

"I said, let's check out what other DVDs we have."

One of my friends from college studied abroad in Beijing. She's still in touch with her host family (a mom, a dad, and a daughter our age) and so we've been invited over to their house this afternoon to make dumplings. Honestly, we're a little nervous. "What are we going to talk about?" Steven asks in the cab ride over.

"Well, worse comes to worse, nothing," I say, trying to make us feel better. "You can blame a lot of socially awkward things on a language barrier."

As it turns out though, our tutor Jessica has prepared us perfectly for such an encounter. We exchange greetings (How are you?), we talk about the weather (It's so chilly now!), we make jokes about animals (Steven is like a monkey, yes?), we compliment each other (You are so clever!)—all while making *jiao zi*, which we can discuss as well (These are pork dumplings, yes? We also like egg and spinach ones but these are the best!).

After stuffing and folding the *jiao zi* they are put into bamboo baskets to be steamed. We look at photo albums, watch some volleyball on TV, and laugh about how small the slippers that they've lent to us are on Steven (size thirteen, he'll never find any shoes that fit in China). There are times when it's quiet, but not uncomfortably so. Steven and I keep exchanging looks of, "There was *so* nothing to worry about. This is fun!"

Soon enough the *jiao zi* are ready and, of course, delicious. We eat them until we have round toddler bellies and talk some more while digesting. There is a dictionary on hand, which is helpful.

Especially when Steven starts telling anecdotes from the past few days that are a little too complicated to express and not quite interesting enough to slave over translating. (It's part of his charm!) They are patient and generous and fun—we can totally see why my friend has stayed in touch with them through the years.

"That was fun," I say in the cab on our way home.

"And delicious," Steven adds.

"It felt so nice to be in someone's home." It's frigid outside and the cabbie has the window down since he's smoking, but our bellies are still warm. I put my head on Steven's shoulder.

"*Wo ai ni,*" I whisper.

"I love you too," he says and laces his chilly fingers into mine.

We've been here just over a month and already it's vacation time. Golden Week comes in the beginning of October and for nine days, it's like Thanksgiving but with 750 million people going to see their grandparents.

We could easily spend the week avoiding the travel chaos by exploring still-new-to-us Beijing, but then we read about the Inner Mongolian grasslands while flipping through our guidebook. Now we can't stop dreaming about the life that's only a two-hour flight away where we can gallop across rolling hills on horseback to our cozy yurt under a sea of stars.

Even though we normally avoid travel agencies like the plague, big brother Michael swears we're going to need the help. And of all weeks in the year, now is not the time to just wing it. After a phone call, we get an initial itinerary from the agent via e-mail.

"What's a luxury yurt?" I ask.

"Oh no," says Steven. "Traditional racing? Traditional wrestling? Traditional dance?"

We call them back and explain that all we'd like to do is ride horses, wander the grasslands, and sleep in a yurt. "Okay, no problem," the lady says. "I will send you a new itinerary tomorrow."

The next day we get our new schedule and it's exactly what we asked for. Not a "traditional" activity on the list. Now just to be clear, we would love to experience traditional Mongolian culture. It's just that we can't help thinking the average Mongolian doesn't race, wrestle, and dance all in one day, every single day.

After a quick flight and a car ride we pull up to our camp that's looking a little . . . uh . . . not so yurt-in-the-grasslands-y?

"Are they seriously going to make us take welcome shots of rice liquor at ten in the morning?" I whisper to Steven as a man in traditional costume hands us small cups.

"It would seem so. Wait—are those yurts made of concrete?"

"Steven, I'm experiencing an overwhelming sensation that our travel agent simply deleted the racing and wrestling and whatnot without actually changing a thing."

The first day we stagger around our little "luxury yurt village," trying to avoid the Disneyland-esque shows of traditional activities and singing with synthesizers. Once we escape from the fenced-in compound, though, it's beautiful. Stark and not so green this time of year, but *beautiful*.

"This is nothing like Beijing," says Steven as we lay down on the side of a hill, not another person in sight.

I settle down next to him and look up at the sky. "*This* is what we asked for."

The next day we wake up early to have that ride through the grasslands we've been dreaming of. Our guide for the morning is the Mongolian cousin of Captain Jack Sparrow (of the *Pirates of the Caribbean*). He is staggering, swaggering, bejeweled, and possibly drunk, but oh so charming in his eyeliner and sunglasses with one lens. He takes a liking to Steven right away. Maybe it's because at six foot two Steven looks so silly — I mean *stately* — on his small horse. "He is very good-looking," Captain Sparrow tells me more than once.

We spend the morning trotting and galloping around the hills, our butts getting progressively sorer with each second, while Captain Sparrow talks a lot. Since we demonstrated a basic level of Chinese during our introductions he has decided we are fluent. I'm sure whatever it is he's been pointing out to us is fascinating. Then again he could be venting the details of his recent divorce and we'd never know the difference. Either way.

We dismount near a small, real yurt where he insists we each smoke a cigarette. (Hell, yesterday we took a shot at ten in the morning and three more before the sun even set.) Then we hear a buzzing in the distance. Captain Sparrow squints into the horizon, then starts nodding slowly as a smile spreads across his face. It's a woman on a moped with what turns out to be a bag of "traditional" outfits. We can pay a dollar each to put them on and take pictures if we want. It takes maybe two seconds to go from,

"I don't know, is that kind of weird?" to "Oh, hell yeah! Get me standing by my horse like this!" Captain Sparrow acts as our art director and photographer, ushering us into the deeper grass to hide our inauthentic shoes.

After reluctantly giving back the costumes, we gallop home to our concrete yurt village and spend the evening alternately massaging our sore butts and laughing hysterically at the pictures we took. We can't wait to get back to Beijing and send them to our families.

Back in Beijing we feel refreshed and ready to take on a new unit at the junior high. Two weeks of lions was tough, two weeks of Harry Potter was surprisingly tougher (it's *really* hard to cater to a room divided by diehard fans and those who couldn't care less). Next up: Bubble gum.

Bubble gum? You know at this point, we'll take anything.

Steven and I get down to lesson planning. We've found that our classes are most interesting when we include some kind of creative group work. Who wants to hear the teacher talk for forty straight minutes anyway? Not us. So for this unit on bubble gum we decide we'll read the passage about its invention by so-and-so in 18-whatever aloud, play some games with the new vocabulary that'll get them out of their seats and moving, then split them into groups where they'll create their own inventions and end the class with presentations of said creations.

Monday comes and we're so ready to get into this unit and see what these guys invent. It's going to be hilarious! I get to my first class, hand out the copies that are on the teacher's desk thanks to the student in charge of that (there is a designated teacher's helper in each class—I wonder if it's the really cool or the really nerdy thing to do?). We read the paragraph about bubble gum's invention, play the vocab game, and then get straight to the inventing. There are a few not-so-surprising inventions, like money trees and glasses to see through people's clothes. And then there are the ones that absolutely need to be made, like, *today*: knowledge milk (drink it with a question in mind and during digestion you will find out the answer), mechanical fish that help grandparents swim, flying houseboats and, the remote control that can take back whatever you just said.

Steven gets to his classroom, psyched for his day of inventions and—uh-oh. The teacher's helper forgot to make the photocopies. One hundred eyes are upon him as he realizes he's going to have to wing this first lesson.

Okay, he thinks, *I'll just tell them about the invention of bubble gum instead of having them read about it. No problem!* Except he doesn't remember what the passage says. Had this been the tenth lesson it wouldn't be a big deal, by then he could recite the passage in his sleep. But this is the first lesson. So he begins like this:

"Today we're going to talk about bubble gum, which was invented by . . . uh . . . Johann . . . Bubble! Yes! In, uh . . . eighteen . . . seventy . . . nine? Right. Now repeat after me kids!"

And they do. So if you ever come across a Beijinger who believes that bubble gum was invented by a man named Johann Bubble, well—at the very least you know where they went to junior high.

Despite really enjoying my life here, and despite being able to stay in touch with everyone back home via e-mail or phone, I am seriously missing my people.

Steven seems to be taking it a little a better, which is not to say that he doesn't love his family and friends as much as I love mine. We're apparently just dealing with it differently. When I started tearing up last night over how much I miss everyone and asked him how he copes with it he said, quite simply, "I guess I just expected it. I knew I wouldn't be seeing anyone for a while." Maybe I didn't expect, in the face of all these stimulating and new experiences, to still miss everyone so much and morbidly worry that not all of them will be around when I return.

So I'm alone in a sense. My new teacher friends aren't yet true friends (why are we just not clicking?) and my best friend who's here with me doesn't feel the same way I do (how dare he!)—and yet I can't even really *be* alone since we're in this small apartment together. The closest I can get to isolation is to go into the extra bedroom that houses our fridge and scribble miserably about the sad reality of international adventures containing more loneliness and boredom than anyone remembers once they return home.

Steven comes to check on me—do I want any dinner? A back rub? To watch *Arrested Development*?

Not really.

I can hear him listening to Bob Dylan, drawing, drinking a beer. And it bothers me that he can be so content when I'm feeling so miserable.

Around midnight, he knocks. "I'm going to sleep." He pauses.

"Good night," I say and start wondering just how alone I want to be. I hear him walk away and get into our squeaky bed. In the dark of my room I feel like crying and yelling at myself. Ten minutes later I hear him get up again.

"Can I come in?"

"Yes," I say and wipe my eyes.

"I want to sleep in here if that's okay."

"Okay," I say and he folds his limbs into the bed with me and falls instantly asleep. I hate him for being able to do that. And I hate him for coming in this room. No, I love him for coming in this room.

Once my hand starts cramping from writing and I feel like I've exhausted myself enough to sleep, I turn out the light and close my eyes. Settling in wakes up Steven. "Are you okay?" he asks as he gets up. I nod, part yes, part no. I hear him walk to the bathroom, flush. Then nothing. I let five minutes go by before I check on him.

He's in the other bed. Why is he in the other bed?

Now I'm back to hating him. And myself.

What am I doing here?

I'm somewhere in between sleeping and thinking. The blue light of morning is starting to brighten the sky. I've spent all night worrying that it was a mistake to come to China, to be so far from my family and friends, to be teaching English to rich kids in a country that could use so much more help than that, to move in with a guy I don't fully understand. My eyelids are puffy but finally they're heavy and I know I'm close to sleeping.

The door squeaks open.

"Casey? What are you doing in here?"

"I'm trying to sleep."

"What happened last night?"

"Were you drunk or something?

"No I only had two beers! I just—I thought I came in here to be with you and—"

"You did, but then you just left."

"I what?"

"You went to the bathroom and never came back."

He steps into the room all the way.

"I—I must have been sleepwalking or something. I'm so sorry."

"It's okay."

It is okay. The sun is rising and everything is going to be okay.

"No, really. I'm sorry. That must have been so confusing. I hope you didn't think I was mad at you."

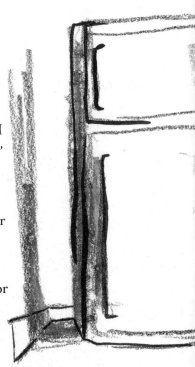

"Get in here."

We hold each other and listen to the quiet morning noises of our neighborhood.

"I'm sorry you miss everyone so much."

"That's not your fault."

"Did you sleep at all?"

"Not really."

"And you never ate dinner. Want to go get those egg sandwich pancake things and watch the old people dance in the park?"

"Yes I do."

And so we do.

WE HEART HAND-PULLED NOODLES

Not only are they great fun to watch being made and damn delicious to eat, hand-pulled noodles provide us with some necessary comfort at two key times in the day: during lunch while teaching at junior high and late at night.

We come across the lunchtime noodle joint by simply stumbling out of the school gates and falling into the nearest restaurant. Here, the bowls are big and greasy and hot and, similar to "our restaurant" (the one back by our apartment where we have dinner every night), we're the only foreign folks around so the waitresses get a kick out of our Chinese.

Then there comes a point when we know we're not just oddities, but valued regulars. We know this because they start letting us fend for ourselves as we try to find a seat, they stop staring at us as we slurp just like them, and they start saying, "See you tomorrow" in the same way they tell that old guy who's always in here too.

Initially this transition is welcome; it can get kind of annoying to have people staring at you when you're just trying to eat. But then, as much as we hate to admit it, we start to feel not so special anymore. Oh, the constant paradox of trying to "go native." How much do you want to live locally? How much do you want to be that foreigner who—look!—does such a good job of living locally?

And now it's Ramadan—the Muslim month of fasting. This is relevant to hand-pulled noodles in that this delectable dish comes from the one to two percent of the population that's Muslim living mostly in the northwest. And so, as the family that runs this joint pulls the noodles and keeps the beefy broth simmering all day, they're STARVING. (We know, because we've done it before. Back in Morocco we tried the first couple of days of fasting with our host families and found it rather terrible.) But you know what? They don't get cranky, they get *friendlier*. The last day of Ramadan comes and after downing our usual bowls of noodles we are presented not with the check, but an enormous plate of cookies. What for? For celebrating Ramadan with friends. We look around and see that we are the only customers with cookies.

Guess who feels special again?

One of Steven's friends back home, Noah, is also a teacher. The two of them decide, after sharing stories of the hilarities of being at the blackboard, to create a pen-pal link between their elementary school classes.

Noah's class writes first. Mail! From America! How exciting! Steven tosses his original lesson plan for the day and puts an example response on the board. He gives his kids two sessions to write their responses because while there are only seven of them, there are twenty-five kids back in America each expecting their own letter.

It's a good thing that Frank is one of Steven's students.

Frank is what you might kindly call "high-energy." He's funny, he's uncooperative, he's entertaining—he's difficult in a classroom. But you know what else he is? A one-man letter factory. While everyone else slaves away on a single letter, going through drafts and drafts and carefully choosing exactly what they want to communicate, Frank pumps out at least ten letters.

"Letters" meaning crayon drawings of muscle men engaged in various activities.

"Frank," Steven tells him as he hands in yet another. "These are great, but don't forget to write something in English on them, okay?"

Soon there will be a handful of children in Massachusetts who believe most second-graders in China are named Frank and have biceps like cantaloupes.

It seems as though some of our junior high kids are catching on to a few things: mainly, that we don't know all sixteen hundred of their names, and that we won't be giving them grades. (That's left to the grammar classes run by the Chinese English teachers.) For the most part, these are the students who play with their cell phones in the back, or do their homework for other classes when we are going over new vocabulary. At first, Steven and I let it slide, or we give gentle warnings. We want to be the fun teachers! We want to have a good time! But after a while it starts to snowball and soon we have to start confiscating chemistry worksheets and giving lectures we'd only heard from the other side. I find myself saying things like, "You must know all of this already—that's why you're talking when I'm talking, right?" (That only happened once. I swear.)

It's surprisingly hard to not take it personally. Steven—who wasn't the most dedicated student when younger—has an "I'm-growing-up moment" as he realizes that he had often been that kid spacing out in the back that drives him so mad now. (At this time, he wishes to apologize to all his former teachers.)

"But your experience helps me, you know?" I say during an afternoon coffee break at a McDonalds. "I always loved school—well, almost always, and I sat in the front row, and never went a class without participating."

"Oh you were *that* kid," Steven says and rolls his eyes playfully.

"Yes that kid." I laugh. "So I just don't understand these kids who are so disinterested and, frankly, disrespectful. It just makes me so mad. But now I try and picture them as you."

"As thirteen-year-old Chinese me?"

"You know what I mean! It really helps. It gives me more patience. More faith."

We sip our coffees quietly until Steven breaks the silence.

"Frank is going to be one of these kids once he's in junior high, isn't he? I just know it."

"Like he'll go from being 'energetic' to just a 'bad student'?"

"Exactly. Did I tell you that I saw his mom outside school the other day and she told me 'Frank is bad,' and I wanted to be like, 'Nooooo! Frank is great!' "

"Just keep telling her that, and keep telling him that too."

"It's going to be so sad when Frank starts hating school."

"Well, maybe he'll always love English class because of you?"

"Nice try."

Now that it's getting chillier, it's easy to spend our days off all cozy in our place. But we're trying to keep up our adventure-seeking spirit, and that's why today we're going to Da Shang Ze, the industrial neighborhood that's been converted into artist studios and galleries. It's the kind of place that was probably excruciatingly cool a couple years ago and now, with plenty of good press and a restaurant or two with English menus, has become a bit of a scene.

We stroll quietly through the galleries and drool over the wide open spaces, the arching windows, the bizarre old factory gadgets that have survived this transformation. The art too, of course.

"It's just so wild to think that none of this could have been shown here fifteen years ago," Steven says, his voice quiet with awe. We pass photographs, abstract paintings, prints, sculptures, video pieces. . . .

"How weird is it that people are converging on this idea that art is something that's to be appreciated in quiet spaces with white walls?" says the sociologist within me. Steven is formulating a different thought in his head.

"What if we lived here?"

"We do."

"No, I mean—in this exact kind of space."

"Well, that would be incredibly cool."

"I know! What if this was our crazy loft and we had our bed up there and some kind of living room set up over here and then all this space to just make stuff? You could have a writing corner with a million different typewriters—"

"And a grand piano in that corner—"

"Yes! And you could play when I was painting over here and—"

And we go on for a while.

"We'll have a studio someday," I say.

"I know, I just—I kind of want to get to that right now. It's not that I don't like teaching, it's just—"

"It's okay," I say. "It's okay that it's not your calling."

"I mean it's totally fine for now. I just—"

"You just want to live here and paint all the time."

"While you play piano and type away."

"Really. One day we'll have a studio," I say.

Because I want it too.

Meandering through more cobblestoned alleys on our way back out to the main road to find a taxi, we stop in a hallway near a photography gallery to look at the enormous photos hanging on the wall. They are giant—four-foot-by-six-foot giant—color prints of thousands upon thousands of Red Guards in Tiananmen Square in the sixties. Red Guards were the young people who made up Mao's strong youth base during the communist Cultural Revolution. They wore red armbands, and plenty of them carried around "The Little Red Book," Mao's book of sayings. I've read a good deal about the Red Guards—how this generation was robbed of its youth and education, sent to the fields to do "real" work that wouldn't breed "subversive" and "backward" tendencies like school or religion could, how fear tactics scared them and other citizens into submission or at least silence. But I've never seen a color photograph of Red Guards, let alone one so huge and full of detail.

"My god," I say, openmouthed. "It's just so much more real to see it in color." We step closer. "Look at these people! They look just like everyone walking around nowadays—I mean, not the arm bands and whatnot, but their faces.

Check it out, she looks just like that teacher from Zhong Guan Cun!"

"Oh, weird! She really does," says Steven, peering closer.

"This is tripping me out, I . . ." I trail off and look at all the faces, the wrinkled jackets, the arm bands that were hastily pinned on. Where are these people now? How do they feel now about what they supported? Do they think it was the only way to survive that era? Do they have any idea that their photos have been blown up to be part of an art installation forty years later in a place that has an Andy Warhol-esque portrait of Mao down the hall? I try to calculate how old these people are now. Sixty something? How fucking crazy is it for them to have children who, at the age that they were Red Guards, might be going into business—capitalist business—that deals with companies in Europe or Japan.

"This is so weird, Steven. "

"We don't have to go yet," he says.

So we stay. And look. And wonder. And then head back home, giving everyone over fifty an extra look up and down.

So here we are, *adults*. We are no longer required to do anything. It's liberating! It's . . . *full of pressure*. Because now that we can do whatever we want, we're constantly asking ourselves: *Is* this what we want to be doing?

Yes and no.

For Steven it's *yes* because he's in China and he's using his free time to draw and paint and make strange little books, and *no* because in the end, he doesn't really want to be a teacher. Overall he's happy to be knocking potential professions off his list—like journalism, which he once considered, or teaching—and is slowly but surely dipping himself into the chilly pool of being an "artist."

And me? Am I doing what I really want to be doing? *Yes*, because I've often considered teaching, maybe even starting my own school and *no*, because I also want to be a writer and a sociologist among a zillion other things that maybe I haven't even thought of yet. Where Steven's process of

elimination gives him a sense of freedom, mine sometimes brings me a sense of gloom. I find it depressing the more my potential paths narrow. Not that I ever wanted to be a concert pianist or an Olympic gymnast, but those possibilities are nearly *im*possible now.

I think what's stickiest about all this is that while I'm exploring teaching as a possible long-term path, Steven isn't. So when he occasionally blows off lesson planning to keep drawing, I feel like he's somehow disrespecting my potential profession.

And, of course, it doesn't help that this situation also taps into our whole he-was-a-back-row-doodler-who-then-got-his-act-together-in-college and I-was-always-a-good-student-who-now-as-a-grown-woman-will-still-make-only-seventy-cents-to-every-dollar-he-does-no-matter-if-I-did-better-in-school thing.

Sigh.

We'll just have to keep moving forward and see.

Good morning! Chinese students don't have gym class in the way Americans do. Instead of playing chaotic (and traumatic) games of dodgeball or tag, they participate in synchronized aerobics that occasionally verge on dance. It's quite entertaining, even soothing, to watch so many kids all dressed alike, moving like one giant entity.

Except for the whole counting into the loudspeaker thing.

The school we live within earshot of has a sound system that includes some megaphone-into-microphone-then-out-to-long-range-speakers action.

At least we know our numbers up to eight *really* well now.

Somewhere along the line, Steven and I decide to give dating a second try. "How about you take me out this time?" he suggests.

Since the whole traditional pick you up/bring a flower/out to a fancy dinner thing didn't work out too well, I come up with something different. Here's a blow-by-blow of how it goes:

6 p.m.:   Kick out Steven so dinner can be made.

7 p.m.:   Invite him back for a Mexican feast. Enjoy some non-stir-fried vegetables and the exotic taste of taco seasoning.

8 p.m.:   Take him out to the main road and pretend to hail a cab downtown then pull his hood over his head and abduct him into the karaoke joint right behind him that he's been dying to go to.

8:15 p.m.:   Book a private room and buy a six pack.

8:20 p.m.:   Have a small hernia laughing at how bizarre it is to have a private room in which you will serenade each other.

8:21 p.m.:   Let Steven pick the first song.

8:22 p.m.:   Watch him belt "Genie in a Bottle" with just as much soul as Christina.

8:25 – 9:15 p.m.:   Sing! Sing! Drink! Sing!

9:16 p.m.:   Marvel when a uniformed lady comes in to inform you that your time is up. My, how time flies! Book another hour.

9:17 p.m.:   Buy another six pack.

9:18 – 10:15 p.m.:   Sing! Sing! Drink! Sing! Now you understand all the rage about karaoke!

10:15 p.m.:   Reluctantly leave your booth and echo-y microphone behind.

10:16 p.m.:   Discover that the food buffet downstairs is free with your booth purchase. Why not have some dessert? And some dinner again?

10:30 p.m.:   Take Steven back outside and get in a cab for real this time.

10:45 p.m.:   Pull up to the dance club Propaganda.

10:46 p.m.:   Get stamped, hit the bar.

10:50 – ??:?? a.m.:   Hit the dance floor. Hard.

??:?? a.m.:   Keep on dancing!

??:?? a.m.:   Find your way to twenty-four-hour hand-pulled noodles.

??:?? a.m.:   Get home, pass out still sweaty.

My family is coming to China for Thanksgiving.

I know that when we first pulled up to our apartment I said my mom could never visit, but really that was the jet lag and the dark and scary shadows talking. After clocking many enjoyable and sunshine-filled hours in this darling apartment in this fantastic city I feel sure Jeri will love it.

Or at least not hate it.

At the very least I know my dad, Jon, is going to be in culinary heaven with noodles aplenty and I'm banking on my two-years-younger brother, Jake, being impressed by the vast quantities of large, cheap beer. So I'm not too worried about them.

To prepare for their arrival, Steven and I spend a serious amount of time scrubbing and sweeping and fluffing. (Did I mention my mom is an interior designer?) We arrange for them to stay in a modest hotel only two blocks from our place, we go on teaching and eating dumplings, and then all of sudden, they're here.

After shedding a few tears of joy upon our reunion, Jeri gives her first review: "It's just like Chinatown."

And in some ways I suppose it is, which excites me now as I think about how one day, when we're living in the States again we'll be able to go to Chinatown and feel at home.

We show them our apartment ("Oh, I love what you've done! How darling!"= Success!) and whisk them down to our kitchen, aka the restaurant.

We're so excited, as are our waitress friends, to show them this place and feed them all the delicious dishes we've come to love. We've been planning what kind of feast we'll order them for days.

Then I look at them as they try to get comfy on the squeaky seats with their coats still on and I realize: they're not seeing this the way we do. The fluorescent lights, the disposable plastic cups, the old guys smoking cigarettes giving commentary about whatever's on the tiny but loud TV.

"Are they cooking the chicken with a blowtorch back there?" Jake asks.

I'm sure it's just the jet lag and the dark and scary shadows talking.

Steven and I do our best at being Beijing guides, taking the gang to the city's classic must-sees (like the Forbidden City and the Great Wall) as well as our personal must-sees (like the park and the twenty-four-hour noodle joint). But we are the most excited to show them our regular, everyday life by taking them to school. (Unfortunately we can't convince Jake to come. "Lady, I go to school. I know what it's like," he says. And that's why I love him.) We settle on our first grade classes at Zhong Guan Cun since they are the most action-packed and adorable.

The Chinese T.A.s are abuzz in the teachers' room. Most are perplexed by how young my parents look compared to Chinese people their age, and all are absolutely wowed by Jeri's bright red, curly hair. She's been wowing folks left and right with that actually, getting plenty of stares and pointing fingers. She even made a kid cry this morning.

The bell rings and we hurry down the hall as children run past screaming happily. My dad follows Steven to his classroom—boy, that's going to confuse everyone—and my mom files in after me. "You can sit in the back," I tell her. Everyone watches as she settles into a tiny chair.

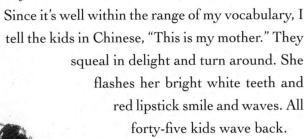

Since it's well within the range of my vocabulary, I tell the kids in Chinese, "This is my mother." They squeal in delight and turn around. She flashes her bright white teeth and red lipstick smile and waves. All forty-five kids wave back.

It's quite hard to get them to turn around and face the blackboard again. But this is one of my best classes, so I can get about two-thirds of the kids to watch me at a time. The rest are taking turns pretending to sharpen their pencils in the back so they can get a closer look. A few bold souls are brave enough to touch a curl. Jeri is a real sport about it, pretending she doesn't see the shy kids who creep by slowly, sticking her tongue out at the silly ones. She even sings along for "Twinkle Twinkle" as I wind down the class.

When the bell rings again, the kids are all over her, talking talking talking, maybe hoping she'll speak better Chinese than her daughter. She's excited, too, as is my dad who I can see down the hall, struggling to make his way through the swarms of curious kids. "Watch out, they'll take you down," warns Steven.

My parents are riding that same high Steven and I had after our first class. They're bursting with all the darling things the kids did. Jeri is telling Jon about our class, Jon is telling Jeri about his. I ask Steven how he introduced my dad and he says, "I didn't. But I totally made him participate in the games."

"They all seem like smart kids, they probably figured it out," says my mom.

"Maybe a little *too* smart," my dad says. Jon swears that during a round of "Head Shoulders Knees and Toes," the kid sitting next to him leaned over and whispered: "Small head, big ass."

School was such a hit that Jon wants to come see one of the junior high classes the next day. "Just to warn you, it's a unit on talking birds," I tell him.

"That sounds better than—what was that other unit?—bubble gum?"

I sit my dad down in the back, introduce him to the class, and then get straight to it. The older kids play it a bit cooler than the little ones. Instead of turning around to face him the entire time, they do sly things like drop their pencils and sneak a peak when they're bent down.

The reading passage is about Puck, an African gray parrot that, before dying in the mid nineties, learned how to say 1,728 English words. We have a little discussion about whether or not we think Puck actually knew what he was saying, play some Hangman with the new vocabulary, and then move on to our trusty "creative" work.

For this unit, the students imagine that they have a talking bird of their own and come up with a list of twenty words or phrases they would teach it to say in English.

I am so happy that my dad has decided to visit one of these classes. It's my eighteenth (and therefore last) one, so I've got the

rhythm down pat and, surprisingly, I'm still not sick of teaching this unit because there's something about talking birds that, I don't know, sets these kids free from their cages? (Aharharhar . . .)

So far I've gotten a most excellent mix of vocabulary lists for our imaginary birds. There are the kids who have a selection of basic, polite greetings like "Hello," "How are you?" "Good Morning," etc., the kids who list the last twenty vocabulary words I gave them (oh, how clever), the kids who spend a lot of time studying American pop culture ("I love Leonardo DiCaprio," "Just Do It," "I'm Lovin' It"), and the ones who think I'm somehow going to count "very good" and "very very good" as two separate phrases. And then there are the geniuses who have lists that look like this:

No Parking

I am the God

Can I smoke here?

I don't have a sense of humor

Donkey-ASS-mule

Where is Alfonso?

I feel very nervous

Seriously. That's my student Henry VIII's list. It's not twenty phrases but I plan on giving him full credit.

The biggest laugh of all, though, happens when my dad and I return home and Steven tells us the best phrase he got today:

Puck is a loser.

The family visit is coming to an end. We've crammed in a few last-minute activities like seeing the Forbidden City (which unfortunately turns out to be entirely under construction), Peking duck for Thanksgiving dinner, and perhaps most important, introducing my brother Jake to fellow hockey player Rudi (Steven's hockey-playing one-on-one student). Once Rudi gets over his initial astonishment that Steven has brought in a real live, American hockey guy, they play Battle Royale and discuss who would win in a fight on an oil tanker, Roy or Gretzky. (Gretzky may be crafty, but Roy would most likely simply outpower him and toss him off the tanker. What a waste of talent, eh?)

And now that it's everyone's last night in town, we're going to make it memorable. We have another delicious duck feast in our neighborhood and do some bar hopping in the swanky part of town where the ex-pats hang. There are a few standard foreign guy/Chinese "escort" couples around, which prompts me to (against my better judgment) repeat an anecdote another teacher told us about how someone came up to him asked him if he wanted a "goalie," which totally confused him until he realized the guy was asking if he was interested in a Mongolian prostitute.

Jeri is dutifully horrified, Jon's gasping "No! *Goalie?*" and Jake is all but rolling on the floor laughing. For the entire cab ride back

he's cracking variations of goalie jokes. (He loves to push our politically correct buttons.)

Someone suggests we have a nightcap at the hotel bar so we all go in. It's quiet at the main floor bar, but there's music coming from the basement. "Let's check it out, cruise some goalies!" says Jake, running for the stairs. We all shake our heads and laugh, but follow him anyway. Downstairs it's significantly darker and appears to be a karaoke bar.

"Oh, sweet! Let's get a room!" says Steven.

A woman comes up to my dad and starts to negotiate. He's doing his best with gestures—big nod yes, all of us would like a room; yes, just one room; yes, all *together*. Steven and I get in there with bits of Chinese but the woman is still looking perplexed. Disturbed even.

And then a door opens and out file six women adjusting their red silk dresses and one man tucking in his shirt. A wave of realization pulses through the group. "Goalies!" says Jake.

Back upstairs it takes two or three nightcaps for all of us to stop laughing. Jake is definitely the most disturbed of the bunch by the idea of our family plus prostitutes in one private room. "Serves you right for making goalie jokes all night," I say.

"Get me back to America," he says.

And the next day, that's exactly where they go.

Now that we're done hosting, we get back into our groove of teaching, eating at our restaurant, working out (and taking advantage of the hot showers) at the gym, Chinese lessons with Jessica, going out dancing or staying in to watch a DVD or read a book. Speaking of books: all I want to read right now is a fat elephant fact book. Sometimes I just get fixated on things like this. Before elephants it was classical composers. Normally I'd be able to satisfy at least part of this must-learn-about-elephants urge at a library or bookstore, but alas. I just pine and whine.

Until one day, "An Elephant Fact Book" magically appears on our table:

Yes! I know SO MUCH about elephants now.

I have the sneaking suspicion Steven had something to do with it. Especially since fact number eight is one of his spare passport photos with the description, "This is not an elephant." So when Steven leaves for "boys night out" with the other gentlemen teachers the next night, I spend that evening in creating "Elephant Haikus: Haikus About Elephants."

Have you seen my hat?
It makes me look like a pro.
(At life, not tennis.)

The next morning, Steven describes what it was like to go to Korean Hooters with the boys, be deemed the one with the best Chinese, and thus have to be the one to ask, "*Yo mai yo titties?*" (You might not speak Chinese, but you know what he's saying.) Then he finds the haiku book.

"I think a little poetry is just what I needed to get my sophistication back."

I've babysat a bunch before, and for the most part I've really liked it. But you know what? I'm not supposed to be babysitting right now. I'm supposed to be teaching English. So this Friday afternoon setup we have going on at the University really isn't working out for me. Or anyone else, for that matter.

The only part of the class I like is hanging out with Glen, my assistant. He's Jessica's (our Chinese tutor) boyfriend. During the break, it's fun for me and Steven to use our new vocabulary with him and make him proud of his girlfriend. Everything else about this class however, is NOT fun. Like when the kids scream like zoo animals, or when they stand on their chairs, and definitely not when they throw milk at me like one miniature punk did today. Steven says he's always confiscating Ping-Pong paddles. "That's better than ducking them," I remind him.

This experience, at the very least, creates a feeling of camaraderie among the teachers. Each bus ride home we commiserate and pray for these student mutinies to come to full fruition so we can just walk the plank in peace and be over with it all.

Today I feel especially defeated because after the milk incident, something even worse happens. There's this girl in my class and I can never remember if I gave her the English name Ella or Emily. Then, when I sit them all in a circle to discuss the inappropriate dairy-launching, I realize why I can never get it straight: I named one Ella and her *identical twin* Emily.

It's at times like this that we wonder what, if any, good we're doing here.

BRRRRRRRRRR

As the temperature changes, so does life in Beijing.

Brisk: Outdoor International Beer Garden closes shop for the season.

Chilly: Thermoses for hot tea are never out of reach.

Cold: Long underwear is the new black. It's sad (and unsexy) but true.

Very Cold: The dreaded Winter Cold makes the rounds. Nothing like interacting with hundreds of sniffling kids a day to test the immune system.

Bone-Chilling Cold: Our hot water heater becomes a lukewarm water heater and thus we become those kind of people who shower "every other day or so."

I-Can't-Remember-What-Warm-Weather-Was-Like Cold: Restaurants (like classrooms) still insist on keeping their doors open but hang thick plastic flaps. The beer is now literally ice cold, but we prefer dumpling steam facials and hot tea.

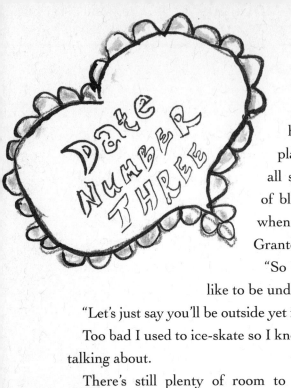

Date Number Three

It's Steven's turn since I took him out last time. He's been planning for a while, being all slick and secretive. He kind of blew it the other day though, when he started giving me clues. Granted, I manipulated him into it:
"So what should I wear? I don't like to be underdressed you know."

"Let's just say you'll be outside yet inside."

Too bad I used to ice-skate so I knew exactly what he was talking about.

There's still plenty of room to be pleasantly surprised though. We begin with breakfast for dinner, which I greatly appreciate since I've been having these relentless dreams about bacon. (The Chinese do really good pork, just not enough bacon.)

During the cab ride over to the ice-skating rink we both pretend like I don't already know where we're going. That is, until we get lost. And then we both have to start explaining in our Chinese/charades where we're trying to go. ("Cold cold go, in a house. Dance in cold. Near hotel." "How could he not know what we're trying to say?!")

It turns out Steven asked his one-on-one student Rudi for directions to where his hockey team practices. And believe it or not, the nine-year-old boy was wrong when he pointed to the biggest building in the skyline.

Eventually we make it. And it's well worth the wait. My bacon has settled and I'm fulfilling all of my early-middle-school-figure-skating fantasies.

And as if this weren't enough, he ends the evening by taking me to BED. Which is 1) perhaps bold for the third date but maybe not so unreasonable three months into living together 2) as he knows, my favorite place to spend my free time, and 3) the name of a hip bar in the old part of town.

We're nearing the end of our teaching contract. All the other teachers have signed up for a full year and, maybe it's the Beijing winter, but a few have simply had enough. One left just a few weeks ago without a word to the bosses. And two more are on a plane right now, having left a laundry list of their complaints behind. Last night, these two invited us out to an early Christmas dinner at T.G.I. Friday's so they could tell us in person all the reasons why they're quitting. That dinner made us realize how much we randomly lucked out—how great most of our students are, how cool it is to have such a varied schedule, and just how lucky we are to be given autonomy in planning our classes.

So I can't say we're exactly thrilled when our boss Leonard calls us in, after finding the aforementioned list from the leaving teachers, to tell us that he's going to have to change our schedules. "We need you to take over all their classes," he says, looking sad and serious.

"But—but what about *our* classes?" asks Steven.

"We can't just leave them," I say. "Why are their classes more important than ours?"

"Because that contract is bigger."

And just like that, there's no more bubble gum at San Fan, no more screaming first-graders at Zhong Guan Cun, no more Friday afternoon classes at the University (ok, so that change feels

pretty good — I could do without the milk launching). We're to finish out the workweek and after Christmas weekend, start at a new elementary/middle school called Shangdi. It's all business, contracts, and money.

Fueled by the desire to leave more than a faint legacy of laughs behind, we hurl ourselves into our last few days with our classes. The first-graders cry when we tell them we won't be coming back, the junior high kids are a bit baffled, some even look betrayed. It's not a good feeling to say good-bye like this, so quickly and not on our own accord. We don't feel like we're being responsible, even if we're doing what our boss is telling us to do.

In the end, I'm just happy that I get to teach the Valentine's unit to my best and last class at San Fan before we go. The creative assignment is for the kids to write a Valentine to anything in the world they love. And had I not been around for this last day, I would have missed this gem:

Dear Fly,

I love you. If you are a mouse I am cheese. If you are a cat I am a mouse. You are a fly, so I want to be shit.

The teacher in me tells my student: "Normally that's not such a nice word to say, but I understand why you're using it here." The student in me adds: "Great job, though. Seriously."

Steven and I both like to read in bed before going to sleep. Me novels, Steven nonfiction. I like to read about a place where I'm not. It's an escape. Steven likes to overdose on the history of his surroundings. I kind of get the best of both worlds because while I'm reading my book, Steven likes to tell me the highlights from his.

Lately he's been reading a recent (and controversial) biography of Mao by Jung Chang and John Halliday called *Mao: The Unknown Story*. Steven's mom, a librarian, mailed it to him and we were quite surprised to see that it made it past the censors since it's banned here. (Ooops.) He's been enjoying it thoroughly, but not sleeping entirely well thanks to the detailed accounts of the atrocities committed under Mao's leadership. And although I've read a good deal about recent Chinese history, I am happy to be learning even more through Steven.

"Did you know that when people here were starving after the Great Leap Forward Mao was sending aid in the form of food to Eastern Europe?"

"Oh my god. Really?"

"As a kind of 'fuck you' to the Soviets and a way to make it look like everything was going just fine back home."

"Yikes."

Toward the end of the book, Steven starts reevaluating certain things. "You know, I kind of get it," he says to me tonight as we're tucking in after spending our day off in Tienanmen Square. "From about 1920 until 1980 or so, everything was such a mess here. Of *course* people aren't banging down the Party's doors in the name of democracy right now. Things are finally calm."

"Not ideal," I say. "But for the most part calm. You're right."

"I can't imagine it will last forever like this, but—"

"But it's not nearly as bad as it once was." I tuck myself under his arm. "It'll be interesting to see what kids like our students will grow up and think about Mao and Communism. Everything is just so global now, I wonder if they'll have less tolerance for censorship etcetera because of exposure to other ways of life."

"I don't know. I wonder."

"It looks like we'll just have to come back to China one day and find out."

It's mid-December and it's a winter wonderland out there, but we're cozy and warm by the roaring fire as we prepare for the holidays and all our family traditions that bring us joy this time of year.

I mean—it's freezing and gray outside and we're just as frigid in here as we wait for the kettle to boil and whine about who should take all those empty Tsingtao bottles downstairs to be recycled.

"You do it."

"No, you do it."

"Wait. Neither of us will have to do it. I have an idea."

And that is how the beer bottle menorah is born and our holiday season begins.

Neither Steven's nor my immediate family are particularly religious. As for heritage, his is Jewish-ish; mine is a Catholic/Protestant mishmash. So when the other teachers bemoan the fact that they are missing out on all their religious and familial traditions going on back home, we just kind of sit there and shrug.

Tonight, though, we are hopping on board this whole winter holiday thing. We line up nine twenty-two-ounce bottles on the windowsill and stick in our leftover didn't-pay-the-electric-bill-on-time candles. Steven says a Hebrew prayer (or what he remembers of it), lights the necessary wicks, then tells me the first installment of the eight-chapter story of Hanukkah.

"Once upon a time, the Syrian Greeks decided to invade Israel."

"Aren't you supposed to start with the Maccabees?"

"Hey—who's the Jewish one here? I don't care how many bar or bat mitzvahs you went to. I'm saying it starts with the Syrian Greeks."

"You are *such* a government major. Politics, politics, politics."

I cuddle up next to him on the couch under our mountain of blankets.

The next night we exchange gifts as well. Because what fun would this holiday be for us young folk without presents? Erasers shaped like penguins, sugar cubes, a pair of sleeve protectors, "rock 'n' roll!" picture frames.

When Jessica comes over for this week's Chinese lesson, she sees our makeshift menorah and asks, "Is this a countdown to Christmas?"

"Well, not exactly—"

She looks at us kind of sadly, almost as if we had just told her there's no such thing as Santa.

"Actually. Yes. Yes, it is. We're counting down to Christmas now."

The countdown is over. Christmas is here! *Here* being the Hong Kong Boss VIP Fitness Club holiday party. The event is kind of like a flashy talent show. There seems to be some karaoke action, some performance yoga, and what might be best described as "fitness dance fantasy." Nothing says "Merry Chrismas" like their misspelled banner and a mostly naked, absolutely glistening body.

We drink our fair share of free Chinese wine (the CEO of a vineyard also pumps iron here) and enjoy the show until they finally kick us out.

The next morning, we greet Christmas with the enthusiasm of children. Children who each drank a gallon of iffy wine the night before.

But after some black coffee from the ever trusty McDonald's (I have never patronized this chain so much in my entire life—it's all for the coffee and the soft serve) we're ready for this holiday morning. Not that we have a tree, or presents to open, or extended family coming by for ham. Still, the holiday cheer is in the air. Especially once I remember that actually I *do* have a present to open! It's from Thomas, a junior high kid from my best class at San Fan. He's talked to me a lot about his love of model planes, so I have a sneaking suspicion about what my present is. . . .

I open it up and what could be better than a model plane? A model Swiss house!

"Yay! It's like a mini dollhouse!" I squeal. "You want to make it with me?"

Steven holds his head. "I think I'm just going to paint a little in the other room. Maybe lay down again."

Hours pass, time swirls as I glue all the little pieces together—the frame, the roof, the windowpanes, the shutters, the chimneys, the doors. . . .

"This is so great!" I announce to myself.

I keep gluing and gluing—

And gluing, gluing, gluing!

When I'm finished I run into the other room to show Steven. "Casey?" he asks, "Are you high on shitty glue?"

"Look at my house! Look at my crazy little Merry Christmas-house!"

MAKING A TRAVEL PLAN

We've got a little less than a month left in China now, so we're starting to plan our upcoming Southeast Asia trip. (Remember, the original itinerary was China through January, Southeast Asia for February and some of March, then Mali until the next December.)

There's a lot to be said for planning ahead when traveling. Perhaps an equal amount could be said for the joys of finding your way on the fly. Many a bowl of noodles have witnessed us trying to determine our desired balance between these two traveling approaches for this trip.

Some aspects are out of our hands. Like visas. For example, Vietnam requires you to say exactly when you're

coming and going. Other itinerary items we need to work around include precisely when we can visit my dear friends Alexandra and Kate, who are each teaching in different towns in northern Thailand. We also need to make sure we catch a flight from Bangkok to Paris that we booked. (Believe it or not, it's awfully hard to find a direct flight from Thailand to Mali. Paris is a good airline hub and great neutral place for our parents to visit us and meet each other for the first time. Did I mention that's now in the works?)

So we have a few established posts along the road, and a fat guidebook to bring along. But it's looking like no matter what we say, our scale always tips toward finding our way on the fly.

We've reached the point where our life in Beijing doesn't feel so foreign anymore. It's exactly what we hoped for that night we first arrived—that we could come back to our apartment after a long day of teaching and sigh, "I'm so happy to be *home*."

At the same time, we know that we won't be in Beijing much longer so we should therefore get out and see as much of it as we can in the weeks we have left. And besides, we have a few more days of vacation until school starts up again. So that's how we wind up at the Beijing Natural History Museum. You might say our paths have long pointed there since Steven's and my motto for museums is, "The more bizarre the better."

After a final photo shoot with the dinosaur statues outside, we take a long look at the museum building before leaving.

"Man that's ugly," I say.

"I know," says Steven. "What a Stalinist block of cement."

"It's really a shame so much beautiful architecture was lost to the Cultural Revolution."

"I know. Kind of amazing that you can just knock down history with a bulldozer."

We turn the corner and enter a rubble-ridden war zone.

"Holy shit, what happened here?!" I say. But I know the answer before I've even finished asking.

The Olympics.

It's more than a year and a half away, but the city is already ringing with the jackhammer echoes of "preparation." As the hotels and stadiums and CCTV tower go up, the *hutong* come down. These courtyard houses and cobblestone alleyways that have long survived cycles of revolution and change are, for the most part, doomed. We hear bits and pieces about unethical evictions, about the folks who try to fight it, but overall, not much at all since the Chinese media inevitably spins those stories into narratives of "progress."

We walk small paths through the piles of demolished brick. The wintry tree skeletons do nothing to ease the mood. After a while we find a restaurant where we can warm our bellies with a big plate of stir-fried eggplant.

We wonder aloud if the parts of town where the *hutong* have been recobbled and the courtyard houses converted into funky restaurants are any better. Is that bringing good businesses while maintaining some of the local history? Or is turning an old man's tailor shop into a trendy T-shirt store just as bad as demolishing it?

"Fucking gentrification," says the girl who grew up in ever-changing Brooklyn. "There's never a straight answer."

"Fucking Olympics," says Steven. "Who goes to those anyway?"

We start our new gig at Shangdi today. Instead of walking or taking taxis to get to school, we now get the Mr. Sun/subway combo. He picks us up at the crack of dawn and Steven and I do our best to impersonate "morning people." A couple of steamy dumplings and subway stops later, we're at our new school, ready to go.

It doesn't matter that we show up not knowing what classes we have and with what books, because we know how to wing it now. We are prepared to be unprepared.

And it's fun to have a whole new gang of curious faces who think our old tricks are new tricks. And it makes us happy to know that we can connect with kids all across this city; it makes us think we can do this anywhere.

That cynical voice in the back of our heads keeps wondering, though, if this is in fact a "connection," or if any foreign face would do. No amount of positive parent/boss/T.A. reviews can entirely clobber that fear.

At least we don't have the time or energy to dwell on that in the classroom.

The teachers' room is another matter. All we have is time to dwell. Cold, freezing, frigid time to dwell on all those things we don't really want to think about. Like is it even possible to teach these kids anything in just three weeks? Is it too late to become better friends with the teachers we now share all our break time with? Did we cherish the time at our other schools enough? Does this model of native-speaker-teacher education work? Is this the reality of the international adventure our friends and family think we're having?

To keep our minds away from the self-defeating questions and our icy hands warm, we take to rewriting Chinese Doraemon comics.

As Steven explains it to me, Doraemon is a Japanese cartoon robot cat from the future that comes back to the past (which is actually the present) to hang out with this kid who is the grandpa of the kid who made the cat. (Think about it for a second . . .). A whole bunch of Wite-Out later, we have a new book with updated text that thoroughly entertains us, slightly befuddles the other teachers, and definitely impresses the kids who catch a glimpse of it in Steven's bag.

But still, there is so much time spent waiting in between each class. And it's so. Damn. Cold. Seriously—what's with the open windows in winter?

The last few weeks are one cold blur of pitch-black mornings and jumping children whose names we'll never have the time to learn. Poor Steven spends all his time giving the same oral test to the entire sixth grade. Just a cog in the wheel, he feels terrible failing kids he never even had the time to teach.

We can't tell if we're so ready to leave because we've timed this just right, or if the mind gives up only once it knows it can. Either way, we don't talk much with the other teachers about our plans for Thai beaches where we'll wear sarongs instead of scarves. We can't imagine that's something they want to hear about as

they face another six months of this same thing. (So glad we signed up for shorter contracts than they did.)

"I think my nose hairs are frozen," says Steven.

"We'll get *jiao zi* for dinner. You can defrost over the steaming plate."

"I'm going to miss *jiao zi*."

"Me, too. But I can't wait to taste real pad thai."

"I can't wait to just draw all day."

"Soon enough, Steven. Soon enough."

Even though we had to leave our other schools so we could take over the classes at Shangdi, we insisted on keeping our one-on-one tutoring with Linda and Rudi, as well as my prized preschool and first grade classes, and Steven's second grade one.

Now, inspired by the fact that we'll be leaving so soon, we are going full throttle in these classrooms. Singing, dancing, jumping, working up huge sweats like we did in the beginning before we knew how to preserve our energy. The fun factor kind of takes a nosedive, though, when we have to tell the parents we're leaving.

"But *why*? Why go to Africa? It's not as nice as China. And very dangerous," one parent says to me.

"Uh . . . well, this has always been the plan?"

The staff at Shane knew upon hiring us that we would be leaving at the end of January.

That was in our contract. But it looks like the parents weren't quite as aware. Some are disappointed because their kids are having genuine fun while learning with us, some are mad because their children have gone through too many teachers and the inconsistency is academically and emotionally detrimental, some probably couldn't care less as long as there's another white face lined up behind us. I say *white* because I had a junior high kid ask me if I wanted to replace his current English tutor and when I asked why that wasn't working out he whispered, "He's *Jamaican*." Even Leonard admitted that the school's unofficial policy is to grant the parents' wishes for white teachers.

All in all, part of me is really going to miss this whole scene. Like how one of my first-graders, Mary, always makes her parents wait for me to pack up after our evening class so we can take the elevator down together while holding hands.

The other part of me is packing for the beach.

With only a few days left in Beijing, I've finally fallen prey to those little sniffly noses and have been in bed all day. So Steven lets me be and goes to the gym alone. When he gets home two hours later, his fingers are cold and he smells like coffee. He sits down on the bed and it squeaks.

"Remember that guy from the gym who speaks English?" he says. "After working out, I took the elevator down with him and we kind of struck up a conversation and he was so friendly. And it turned out we were both going to the Starbucks downstairs so we sat together and he told me all kinds of crazy shit!"

"Like what?" I ask sitting up a little.

"Well, it kind of started when we saw a million people getting on this one bus and he was like, 'Don't you wonder why it's so crowded on that bus?' and I was thinking 'Well, no, because lots of Beijing is really crowded' and then he went into this whole thing about the Olympics and how everyone is getting pissed about how they're taking over and so the government is trying to do things like make buses cheaper to appease people. And then he started

telling me about how people like him, who aren't *really* rich but have some money, have immigrants working for them as housekeepers or nurses and how that's all getting totally messed up because the government made that law about everyone who isn't registered as a Beijinger has to leave Beijing for the Olympics, remember? And so his mom has a nurse, a lady who comes from some other town and she's going to have to leave and she's not going to have any more work and how he doesn't know who's going to take care of his mom—"

"His English must be really good."

"It is. He said he worked in Canada for a while and was telling me about how he doesn't get to practice and how living abroad gave him a different perspective on media and he's convinced he's watched online—"

"Wow! He really opened up."

"I know! It was *so* cool. It just made me think about how much more interesting our time here could have been if we spoke fluent Chinese or if we knew when we could push certain topics—"

"Oh I know."

"I mean, this was the first in-depth conversation I had with a Chinese person about all this stuff. Otherwise it's just barely mentioned, if that."

"If that," I repeat. We are silent for a moment.

"Man," Steven says, shaking his head. "I wonder what else everyone is thinking but not saying."

It's January 22nd. We're leaving Beijing tomorrow. So we're absolutely gorging ourselves on fish-flavored pork, steamed eggplant, diced chicken with peanuts, lotus root dumplings, and cold beers in tiny plastic cups.

Taking a brief intermission between courses, we set down our chopsticks to stop shoveling and call over Big Mama (as we call the lady who runs the show here).

"Mai dan? Xian zai?" she asks, surprised that we'd want the check already.

"No, no, no," we say in Chinese. "We have something we give you because we leave tomorrow." I hand over the model house I

made Christmas Day. Maybe it's regifting, but really, there's no way it could survive in my backpack through Southeast Asia. Plus, we've added a personalized element: our passport photos are taped inside so you can see our giant heads through the miniature windows. Maybe it's creepy, maybe it's sweet. We'll see.

Big Mama howls in laughter and calls over all the other waitresses and cooks. Ha! They love it.

Now a part of us will continue to spend each night in this restaurant, on the shelf behind the cash register nestled in between bottles of terrible rice liquor, watching the dumplings come out from the kitchen and the empty plates go back in.

We have to get back to our apartment now, because the other teachers are coming over for a little going-away/giving-away party. Big Mama makes us promise that we'll come back tomorrow for lunch before we go. We promise, and run upstairs just in time to greet our guests.

We make a low-key night of doling out the books we can't carry, the DVD player we certainly won't be using, the flash cards we won't be needing anymore. There are echoes of the first party all around, but now there's no more wondering if these people will

become our new best friends. It's already over. So we're all being friendly in the way that you can be only when you're no longer required to be together.

Once everyone leaves with parts of our apartment tucked under their arms, Steven and I are left in a sterile place that looks eerily like it did when we first arrived. But now we know what all the shadows are. And we'll sleep one last night here in this place that we have surprisingly, comfortably, called home.

We return to the restaurant for lunch as promised, only to be told by Big Mama that we have to come back *again* once we have our bags and are really leaving. So we pack our toothbrushes and other last-minute items, close our apartment door for the last time, and head back down. "*Zai jian, zai jian, zai jian*," she says to us over and over. Good-bye, good-bye, good-bye. She wraps us both into her bosom and I can't help but get teary-eyed.

"We'll come back," I say to Steven as we're walking away. "Right?"

"Oh yeah, definitely." He says. "Right?"

"Someday."

We stop by Shane one last time to hand over our keys and say good-bye to the staff. We realize we're the first teachers of this group to leave announced. It turns out to be not that momentous. Some hugs, some good wishes for our travels to Africa. Sometimes the Chinese are big on ceremony, other times not so much.

The bell rings and swarms of children exit from the hives of each classroom. Teachers drag their feet behind them clutching flash cards and dry-erase markers. I see my old kindergartners running down the hall to their parents.

"Excuse me," I hear someone say behind me. It's the mother of Tom, a former student. He's holding her hand, looking mad. "Tom wants to know why you're not his teacher anymore." I tell Tom, who gave me constant hell (his favorite English word was "no"), that I'm going to Africa. He says something to his mom in Chinese. "He says he likes you and wants you to stay."

No shit. Really? Who'da thunk? I give him a hug and when I pull away he's smiling. At this moment something bowls into me and since I'm crouching, I nearly topple over. "Casey! Casey!" I hear a small voice squeak around me as I regain my bearings. It's Princess Judy, the only girl in my kindergarten class, the one who wore her smug disgust of the boys as often as she wore that plastic crown. Her mom rushes over and says Judy wants to take pictures with me before I leave. The next thing I know I'm smiling, flashing the peace sign with kindergarten royalty. She's beaming, and I've got a shit-eating grin too. "Steven!" I call out. "Will you take some for me?"

As the paparazzi circus winds down and Princess Judy squeezes me one last time, Steven escorts me to the elevator where I can get teary-eyed discreetly.

"I love those kids," I sniffle.

"I know," he says. "And see? They love you too."

"Your kids love you too, you know. They just didn't have class tonight."

"Damn straight they love me! They requested a photo shoot long before I left."

"Casey, do you think they have hand-pulled noodles in the south too?"

"Are you hungry already?"

"Maybe."

"Good night."

"Casey?"

"Yes?"

"I'm so excited to start a cartoon-a-day journal."

"I bet you are. You know, you're not Teacher Steven anymore.
Now you're Painter Steven, or Artist Steven."

"And you? Researcher Casey? Writer Casey?"

"I don't know yet. I'm thinking Wild Traveler Casey for now."

"I like that."

"Me too."

FRANCE

Dubai, UAE

MOROCCO

MALI

PART II

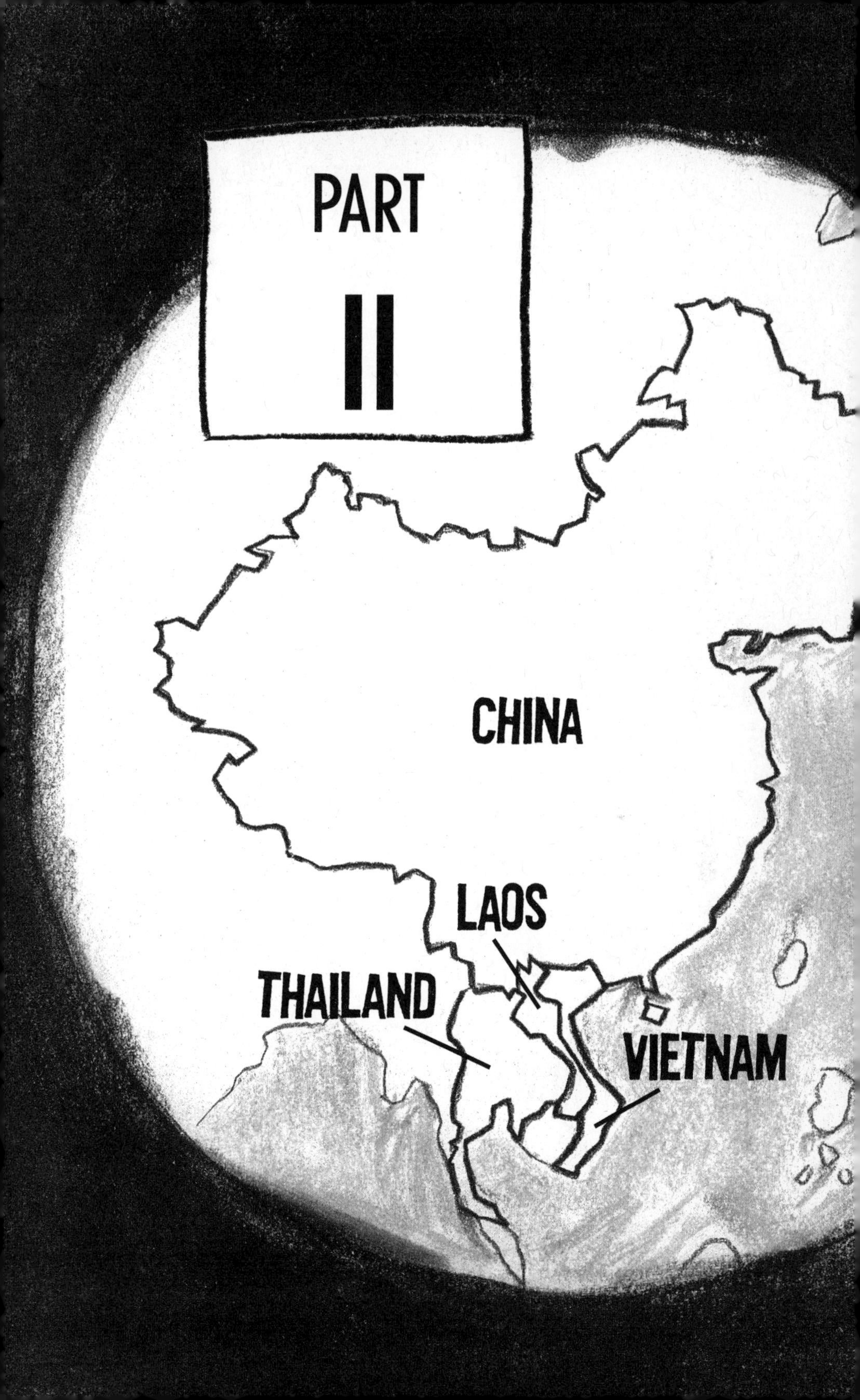

The first stop on our two-month tour is Shanghai. The night train ride passes quickly as we sleep, tuckered out from all of our good-byes, and all of a sudden we're here.

"It doesn't even look like China," I say as we take in the view of the city from the south side of the river.

Steven points to something passing by. "Check out the giant floating TV."

Shanghai was but a fishing town a hundred and fifty years ago. Then the Treaty of Nanking ripped it open for foreign trade and everyone swooped in. Now the city is an odd mix of cobblestoned alleyways, stately colonial-style banks, and modern highrises. It's not at all like the blocky uniformity of Beijing.

"I'm still cold," I chatter and put up my hood.

"But at least we didn't have to get up at six to teach!" We do a little victory dance that warms us up in every way.

Free to do whatever we please, we wander and catch sight of a sign with a dinosaur. Steven the dinosaur fiend is hot on the trail and eventually we find ourselves at a Natural History Museum with many a stuffed animal. Excellent! And then a noodle joint. Also excellent. (We love being on vacation!) We sit huddled together on small stools in the alley restaurant and laugh at the dozens of photos we took. When lunch is served we warm our faces in the rising steam and slurp it down with delight. We're on the move, we're doing whatever in the world we want to do, we're free!

We're tourists.

Even when we ask in Chinese, "Ten each? Really?" the old man doesn't back down from his inflated price. Even when someone else comes up and pays only four for the same thing right there in front of us, he holds firm. If he let us pay less now it would be admitting that he was trying to rip us off, and that would be "losing face," as the Chinese say. So instead we lose money and hand over twenty and give him menacing glares that he doesn't see because he won't look us in the eye.

And just like that we are thrust out of the cozy womb of residency and into the world of anonymous travel.

Getting ripped off is an inevitability of traveling. Of course, there are ways to decrease your chances of getting fleeced: speak as much of the local language as possible; don't buy things around major tourist sites; look to see what other people are paying for something before handing any money over; and don't display wads of cash. Our time in Morocco showed us that speaking the local language seems to help the most—not only with getting local prices, but with every part of being abroad. It shows you care enough to try; it surprises and delights most people; it makes you friends.

But what are we going to do in the rest of Southeast Asia? We'll learn some basic greetings and numbers from our guidebook. But surely that won't be enough.

Since we're still in China, it feels like we're not *entirely* tourists yet. This may not be Beijing, but we kind of get what's going on here. But we're only going to keep descending deeper into the realm of tourism the farther away we get. In just two weeks, once we're out of China, we might not even realize when someone takes advantage of us—because how are we supposed to know what a plate of pad thai should cost? How will we ever know if they're laughing with us or at us?

Hmm.

Back at our hostel, we flip through the communal guidebooks to put together a Vietnamese cheat sheet. An older woman in a blue, bejeweled beret sits down next to us and, as it happens when you're traveling, we get to talking.

A former Montessori schoolteacher originally from the States, she's been living in Shanghai for nearly twenty years. We tell her we're teachers too (or were) and she tells us about the changes she's seen sweep through here, and how she's spent most of her grown life taking care of her elderly mother. It feels good to listen to someone other than us speak English. She continues to tells us more about caring for her mom and—wait a minute—did she just say something about "all of that sexual energy that has been bottled up for years"?

Yes, she did.

We are trying so hard to hold in our laughter that we almost miss it when she asks us where else we're planning to travel. We get it together and tell her our plan: Vietnam, Laos, Thailand. She shudders. "I could never go to Vietnam. My youngest brother fought there. He came back okay, but no—no matter what it's like now, I could never, ever go there."

And now we're not thinking about this lady's bottled up sex drive, or the dollar forty we just lost, but about war and change and the passing of time. Will our generation's children go backpacking through Iraq? I kind of think so. I hope so. Maybe you have to be in a city like Shanghai to believe that change can come so quickly.

WHAT TO EXPECT WHEN YOU'RE EXPECTING

"Steven, you're showing!"

"Am I?"

"What about me? Do I look pregnant or just fat?"

"Uh—neither?"

When on the road, there's nowhere safer to keep your valuables than on your body. Hence those unsightly but unavoidable personal travel pouches that are supposed to discreetly clip around your waist. Steven and I can't stop calling them our "foopahs," F.U.P.A. being a rather crass acronym for that "fat upper p#@$! area" that some women have right below their belts. (It's terrible, I know, but like any bad nickname, it has stuck.) We're going to be wearing them for the next two months as we make our way through Southeast Asia.

Here is what we keep in these oh-so-important pouches.

Passport, obviously.
Some American dollars.
Yellow fever vaccination card.
Traveler's checks.
Emergency credit card.
Emergency Pepto-Bismol.
Extra passport photos.
Giant wad of *quai*. (Why is there not a Chinese bill that's bigger
than $10?)

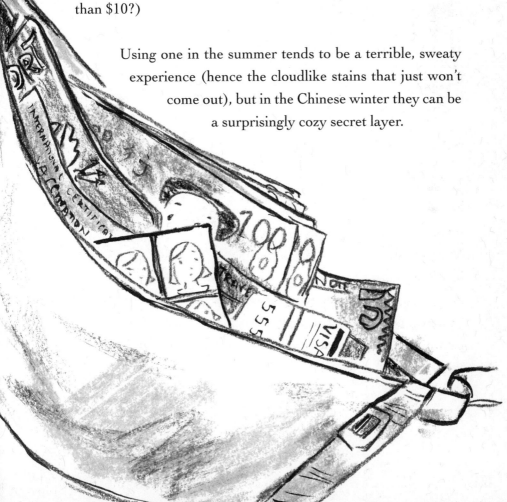

Using one in the summer tends to be a terrible, sweaty
experience (hence the cloudlike stains that just won't
come out), but in the Chinese winter they can be
a surprisingly cozy secret layer.

After barely three days in Shanghai, we hop an hour and a half train farther south to the city of Hangzhou. Here we will wander the shores of idyllic West Lake, and more important, meet up with Jessica. Although she usually lives in Beijing for school, by happy coincidence she's home for a winter break right now. The prospect of sharing a meal with her family at their house sounds even more inviting than it did two weeks ago when she proposed it back in Beijing. Already we're craving a dose of real, local life.

She meets us at an intersection and walks us to her apartment building. Her neighborhood looks much like the one we lived in back in Beijing—that is to say, lots of big block structures that are hard to tell apart. Which I guess explains why initially she rings the wrong doorbell. "They all look the same!" she laughs at herself. "And now that I live in Beijing it's hard for me to remember!"

We all laugh together as we climb the stairs, and I realize, so happily, that Jessica is our friend. Our real friend who wants to introduce us to her family. We keep thinking about how difficult it was to make Chinese friends. Jessica is our one big exception. Maybe because we saw her in our home. Maybe because we saw her so frequently. Maybe because she's just so damn nice and thinks we're funny. What if we had seen even more of her? Six months once felt like a lifetime, and now feels more like a quick tease.

By the end of dinner, we're counting her mom and dad as our friends too. Mom cooks a feast fit for ten and provides enough beer for a college party. (Apparently Jessica told her about all those Tsingtao bottles laying around our apartment.) Dad wears his quilted house pajamas and is awfully shy until the conversation turns to American politics at which point he reveals himself to be Hillary Clinton's Number One Fan. "She's my senator back home!" I tell him proudly.

We do our best to show off the Chinese that Jessica has taught us, especially all the slang. Jokes about being crazy and who's got a "broken brain" ("*Ni de naozi haule,*" I tell Steven when he drops his chopsticks) get us a lot of laughs and get Jessica some serious kudos. We also make sure to *tell* her parents what a great teacher she's been. Jessica plays down the praise and turns it around, telling us that we were instrumental in her getting a job with a company based in Hong Kong. "Before I was so nervous

to speak English, but because I went to your house every week and we spoke so much, I was not as nervous for the interview. Thank you."

It might just be all those hot peppers in the beef, but either way, I'm tearing up.

Eventually it's time to bring our bulging bellies back to the hostel. Our new parents dole out bits of last-minute travel advice — warning us to never let our bags out of site, to keep our passports on our bodies at all times. "Yes, yes — we have these," I say and lift my sweater to reveal my oh-so-chic "foopah." Mom looks at me, then at Steven and bursts out laughing. It turns out she'd been wondering how someone so tall and skinny could have such a fat belly. (Apparently mine just blended in? Oh well.)

After many good-byes, it's just us again, out in the chilly evening air.

"I wish we'd spent more time with Jessica in Beijing," I say and loop my arm into Steven's.

"Me too. It just went so fast and —"

"How about we promise right now to make it an absolute priority when we're in Mali to make Malian friends?" I say and put my hand out.

"Done," Steven says and we shake on it.

Thirty-six hours is a long time to spend on a train. But that's how long it's going to take to get from Hangzhou to Guilin. I've done a ride in China this long before, and really it's not as heinous as it sounds. Okay, sometimes it is. Like when the train screeches to a stop when you're in the "toilet" (aka hole that leads straight to the tracks).

Other times, it's achingly lovely to watch the greenery of the countryside roll past. Steven and I spend many of these hours simply looking out the windows. Moving on the ground really gives us a sense of just how immense this country is, and makes us think about how what we saw in Beijing is such a tiny sliver of all that is China.

Riding this train is also making me think a lot about the last time I was here, nearly seven years ago now. The Beijing I remember from then was full of bicycles, with some roads not even fully paved. The Beijing I'm leaving now is a crowded web of highways gridlocked with cars and cranes that bring destruction and growth simultaneously. Back then, would I have laughed at the idea of the Olympics coming? Or at the idea of me returning to live and teach with my boyfriend? Maybe. But at this point, I can take comfort in the fact that I have no idea what my life will be like seven years from now. Even seven months from now is mostly a mystery.

When we're not dreamily gazing out the windows, we're reading, or eating instant noodles, or getting to know our cabin mates.

For the first night it's just us and the Snorer. But in the morning we get some disheveled-looking newcomers who pull out a half-drunk bottle of *bi jiou*—an absolutely terrible rice liquor—and set it on the communal table. And, oh, it's ten in the morning.

At the next stop they get off and buy some spicy noodles and chicken on the platform and return to eat. They offer some to me and Steven. I politely refuse, but Steven's empty stomach gets the best of him and he accepts. They offer us some swigs of *bi jiou* as well and, much to my surprise, Steven again accepts. One of us should probably stay sober to keep an eye on our bags and what-not, so I just watch as the three of them get rip-roaring drunk.

Through a mixture of our Chinese, our phrasebook, and lots of charades, we get into some interesting "discussions." We talk for a while about how these guys are truck drivers and how it upsets them that drugs like speed are such a big part of their profession's scene, how China is getting way too crowded despite the one-child policy. At one point we get stuck as they're miming what looks to us to be peering with a microscope into someone's midsection, and then making a splash. Then suddenly it dawns on us that they're talking about sex-selective abortions and female infanticide. It just might be the most in-depth conversation we've had with a Chinese citizen yet.

Ten hours later we pull on our backpacks and quietly leave the train while our cabin mates are snoring. "I love those guys," Steven whispers. His belly audibly grumbles. "But man I hate *bi jiuo*."

We get our land legs back in the city of Guilin. Steep and dramatic limestone mountains called karsts jut out of the middle of the city just like the ones in ancient scroll paintings that we've seen in museums. The sun is out and shining and the food here is a whole new spicy challenge. We spend the day wandering around in a happy fog, stuffing our faces. We buy tickets for the next day to take a boat down the Li River to a delightful town I've been to before called Yangshou, and then fall deeply asleep in a hostel bed that doesn't rock.

The next morning I have to face the fact that although all that street food was cheap and delicious, I'm paying the price now, cowering in the bathroom. Despite the odds, I make it to the boat without incident. (Okay, there was a very close call on the bus ride to the boat.) We push off shore and almost instantly realize that we must not have learned our lesson after Inner Mongolia. We have just signed up for Chinese Tourism Hell and there's no escape. (Although at least there's a bathroom.)

When synthesizer and flute duets aren't blasting through the crackling speakers, someone's yelling into the microphone monologues we can't understand. Guides point to a picture of the

mountains that are passing outside our windows. And people are *taking pictures of the picture*. Naturally we take pictures of them taking pictures of the picture, and for a brief moment we're laughing hard enough for me to forget that my insides are about to explode.

The river looks peaceful and untouched—as long as you ignore the boys with nets on long sticks begging and the Chinese tourists who throw money at them. The mountains, though, are magnificent and truly pristine. But after a few hours we just kind of want to be there already. Steven goes to the top deck to see if he can spot Yangshou up ahead.

And that's when we turn around.

It turns out the river is too low for our boat. So we ever so slowly return to where we first embarked and get back on a minibus—a minibus that stops at two different giant jade stores where other groups of tourists wander around looking lost and confused. When our group guide asks us specifically for more money since she's going to take everyone to see another town along the way, we decide to bolt. We would walk the rest of the way there just to not have to listen to another synthesizer song, but luckily a motorized tricycle with a back hatch filled with people comes along. We squeeze in with all our crap and breathe huge sighs of relief.

As we putter along, I start getting nervous that the town we're entering isn't actually Yangshuo. I don't remember these big roads, or the photo shops and karaoke bars, the traffic. Where is the little quaint town tucked in the valleys of the karsts lining the river? The one with only a few small hotels

and cobblestone streets and fishermen on floating bamboo platforms with cormorant bird companions? Was that a different town? Has it been built over?

It takes a full day for me to even partially believe that this
is the place I once went to. Then we rent bicycles and head
out of town to the rice
paddies.

"Oh yes," I say as we pedal around a corner. "This is it. This is the Yangshuo I remember."

We spend a week here, biking through the rice paddies and floating on bamboo rafts down the calm rivers, eating fried beer fish at plastic table shacks or eggs and toast on the tourist strip we both love and hate. We celebrate my twenty-third birthday on the river and Steven gives me a hot pink parasol with white trim that he somehow convinced a local seamstress to add, all in an effort to re-create the one I had when I was little that I once described to him. (He listens *so* closely sometimes. I have to wonder what other arcane shit he remembers.)

The fixed entry date on our visas for Vietnam is creeping closer and closer. We realize that we have not yet learned how to prepare our favorite Chinese dishes so that we can one day cook them for ourselves back in the States. Tourism comes to the rescue when we spot a poster advertising a cooking class. It's the perfect activity for our last day here, especially since I've been feeling ill in mysterious ways and biking around hasn't been as pleasurable as it first was. (Is it a stomach bug? Is it a bladder infection? Will it just go away already?)

We meet our teacher at the specified time and place and realize we're the only ones signed up since it's off-season. Fine with us, we say, and follow her to the market where we will pick up our ingredients. Actually, she does all the buying, since we are too busy staring at the roasted dog carcasses hanging from hooks around us to think about eggplant prices. (Contrary to popular belief—or bad humor—dog is not a very common ingredient in China, so we are a little surprised to see it here.)

The classroom kitchen is in a beautifully refurbished farmhouse fifteen minutes outside of town. At our individual wok stations we steam dumplings, stir-fry eggplant and simmer beer fish, absolutely delighted to learn the secrets to Chinese food: oyster sauce and a smoking hot wok. Outside in the garden we enjoy our creations in the middle of the jagged mountains and flat fields. Sure we'll be able to cook this at home. We're just not convinced it could ever taste the same without this view.

Back in town, we tuck our recipes into our packed bags and head over to the White Lion Hotel. A few days ago, while strolling around, we caught site of their sign listing how much it costs to sponsor a kid's education for a year. We'd just been talking about how the Robin Hoods in us wish we could take our money from the rich parents of Beijing and give it to the needier students in the countryside. *Et voila*.

Anna, the Chinese woman running this charity, is spunky and friendly and so happy to see that we have returned like we said we would with envelopes of cash. She tells us about all the different things our money can go toward: jackets for farmers, school supplies for children, dental work for those in need of it. She even calls over a girl to show us her missing teeth. We're a bit mortified, but neither of them are, so we get over it, share some tea, and laugh about how missing teeth makes you whistle.

Usually we can only offer our time not money, but now it's quite the opposite; we're about to leave, and we've got stacks of Chinese *quai* we won't be able to legally exchange for any other currency. (We exchanged most of our *quai* for dollars with a new teacher, but apparently overbudgeted for our time in China.) It may be the government's overpossessive way of controlling money, or it may be that this money really does need to stay in China, not with us.

We tell Anna we'd like our donation to go toward any education projects she sees fit. Beaming, she promises to keep us updated via e-mail on exactly how she uses it, and even to send pictures. We shed our winter jackets and hand them over, asking her to give them to whoever needs them since we certainly won't be using them in Southeast Asia. The girl with the missing teeth puts on mine and smiles. We wave good-bye and head off to one last meal of eggplant, shredded pork with carrots, lotus root dumplings, and spicy tofu.

"To China." We cheers and down the last of our last big bottles of Tsingtao.

MEET VIETNAM

Casey: Welcome to the show, Vietnam!

Vietnam: Thank you. Or as my people say, *cam on*.

C: Ah yes. *Cam on*. That's easy enough. What about the rest of the language? Will Steven and I be able to pick up much of it as we go along?

V: I don't think so. You thought Chinese was hard. We've got all these other nasal sounds going on and an alphabet that will rock your world.

C: Oh. I see. Well, can you tell us some more encouraging things about yourself?

V: People tell me I'm very beautiful. I have lush jungles, pristine rice fields, bustling yet quaint cities, and a stunningly long coastline on the South China Sea.

C: Sounds delightful!

V: And I have delicious food. Crispy springs rolls, steamy noodle soups, dried squid with unripened mango, and house vodka.

C: Dried squid with—

V: Just trust me. You'll love it.

C: Let's talk about your neighbors China, Laos, and Cambodia. Do you get along?

V: At the moment, yes. Although we've had our differences in the past.

BREAKING NEWS

MEET VIETNAM

finally... great coffee in Asia · Watch out for mope

C: Speaking of tumultuous relationships of the past—tell me about your current relationship with the United States.

V: It's excellent. You'd never know we were once sworn enemies. Why, you know the dreaded P.O.W. prison dubbed the "Hanoi Hilton"?

C: Of course. I hear it was a terrible place.

V: Well, it's no longer around. Instead we have a real Hilton in Hanoi. Imagine that!

C: So it's not awkward at all to have Americans come and—

V: Not at all. Truly. Lots of my people even accept American dollars as currency.

C: That seems a bit bizarre.

V: Maybe. But it's better than trying to calculate how many Vietnamese *dong* there are to the dollar. You have to multiply by fifteen and divide by seven then subtract your age and— it's very complicated and difficult to do while bargaining on the spot.

C: I see, I see. Is there anything else you'd like to tell us about yourself at this point?

V: I'm part Buddhist, part Communist, and my capital city is Hanoi.

C: Thank you for your time, Vietnam. I mean—*cam on*.

V: *Cam on* to you too.

C: One last note to our viewers: please, tune in next week when we meet Laos!

1:05pm   78°

ey're not watching out for you! · Hanoi Museum is not t

Five hours, one bus, and one motorized rickshaw later, and we're at the Chinese-Vietnamese border. There's a fence, a small building, a few guards with guns—mostly it looks like a lot of people hanging out with bags. After asking around, we figure out that for some reason people are only let in once every half an hour—so rather than deal with the steady trickle of folks as they come through, the border patrol purposefully creates a big bottleneck. In China lines are deeply underappreciated (so much so that the government is making people practice forming them before the Olympics), and it's looking like it's going to be the same in Vietnam. Once given the green light, we all bum-rush the building, throwing our passports at the different border staff who then slowly and tediously do mysterious things to them behind the bulletproof glass. By the time we emerge, the sky is significantly darker and everyone seems to have disappeared. For a moment we stand, dumbstruck, with all our bags and no local currency. We'd kind of been counting on the Vietnamese side being more than a country road and a few parked cars.

"Taxi?" a man says from behind us. We flip to the back of our guidebook and attempt to ask him to take us to a town not too far away. Apparently he understands. Then again, what else would we be saying? "Please sir, leave us here where there is nothing"? Once we're in his cab we tell him we don't have any money.

"He took that awfully well," I whisper to Steven as we pull away.

"Yeah. Probably because he's going to kill us and take our stuff." Instead, he drives us to the

nearest town and helps us to navigate Vietnam's black market money exchange run by middle-aged ladies with big bags of cash and worn-down calculators. It's all remarkably easy. We change money at the market rate (which we'd looked up online before leaving—see, we weren't *totally* unprepared), pay our driver, find a clean and cheap hotel right across the street, feed ourselves at a menuless restaurant, and watch, of all things, MTV before happily passing out.

Getting to Hanoi the next day seems to be a bit harder. At first, anyone we ask denies that a bus station even exists in this little town. Then once we finally find someone who can help direct us there, we can't find a taxi. So, naturally, we hop on two strangers' mopeds with all of our stuff in tow, and squeeze into a minibus heading to the capital. Or at least that's where we thought it was going—now the driver is telling us they're actually driving *through* Hanoi, not stopping there, so we should get ready to jump out when he gives us the cue.

"He's not slowing down!" I panic.

Once on the ground Steven says, "See? Who needs bus stops?"

I do.

Flinging ourselves into Hanoi traffic is actually a rather apt introduction to this city, where every spare inch not occupied by people is filled with mopeds. Roaring, squealing, spurting mopeds with families stacked five deep on the seat and groceries for a month piled on the handlebars. Our guidebook recommends you move slowly and make eye contact with drivers to humanize yourself so they'll be less likely to mow you over. Yikes.

Once we are comfortable enough to multitask avoiding mopeds *and* looking around, we realize that Hanoi is darling. Especially the old quarter where buildings are no more than eight feet wide by regulation. The weather is pleasant— perfect for a stroll around the city's lake, or an exploratory spring-roll crawl down the rows of food stalls, or an afternoon coffee at a café (Steven is happily running back into the arms of his caffeine addiction). This city feels like a *real* city, with an urban heartbeat and blood pumping with residents, not just tourists.

I take advantage of Big City life and head to the doctor to see what it is exactly that's been making my unhappy body disagree with my happy mind. "All your good bacteria have gone," the doctor tells me. Uh . . . ? She gives me some pills and promises I'll be better in a week. I believe her because I really want to.

While I'm at the doctor, Steven takes the afternoon to catch up on his cartoon-a-day journal at a café by the lake in the middle of town. Even without reasons like doctor's appointments we're trying to make an effort to take some time for ourselves. (Funny how easy it can be to forget to.)

We celebrate Steven's twenty-third birthday together (we're only nine days apart) with plenty of spring rolls and mugs of ten-cent beer. I give him three rubber stamps: a monkey, the Laughing Cow (of La Vache Qui Rit cheese), and a pirate flag. I also give him a little floppy book I made with the stamps about Cal the Monkey and Vern the Cow and their adventure getting kidnapped by pirates. We spend the evening happily stamping things and drinking beer in the street with Hanoiers. Kegs are an oddly integral part of street life here—you can find them at corner stores where you sit on tiny plastic chairs and watch the mopeds parade by, or outside jewelry shops with old men who don't even blink when you sit down with them. At one point, Steven tries to buy two of these ancient guys a round, just because, and they give us a good, long blank stare.

Making friends everywhere!

We sign up for a two-night tour of Halong Bay, which is an hour or so away. It would seem that we still have not learned our lesson about staying far away from group tours. But I promise, we have! There is simply no other way to enjoy an overnight boat trip in the turquoise waters of the bay. It's way too regulated.

Early in the morning, we cram into a tiny bus with a bunch of other English speakers, which is kind of terrifying because we can't do our usual sit-back-and-understand-only-every-tenth-word routine. Now we have to make conversation (gasp!) and it's proving infinitely harder to ignore the guide's microphone monologues now that they're in our native tongue.

Overall, though, the Vietnamese have really got this group tour thing down! Rather than letting their waters run amok with heinous cruise boats, there is a highly organized system of wooden junks, all with bright orange sails—a perfect complement to the turquoise waters. The whole show runs smoothly, and there is not a synthesizer in sight.

Still, our group tour has the feel of, well, a group tour.

Which is why our best day on the water is the second

one when we arrange to break off with the guide for a full-day kayak trip. Paddling around the dramatic karsts together, he tells us about life as a guide—how he doesn't have his own place because he sleeps on the boats so often, how some groups are boring, and others too adventurous for their own good.

We paddle through more turquoise waters, have lunch on the empty beach of a small island, swim and dry off in the sun. In the afternoon, we pass karsts that have bolts drilled into them for rock climbing and for some reason it rubs me the wrong way, even though I like to climb. Steven and I argue about it briefly, mostly about whether it's insensitive to come to a place only for its physical beauty but not its culture.

"Not to generalize, but the climbing community is pretty low-impact," Steven says, "And—oh man, look at that one!" He points to a monstrously striking karst. I stop paddling in awe.

"You know what. Outer beauty wins today."

MEET LAOS

Casey: Welcome to the show, Laos. It's great to meet you.

Laos: Thanks for having me. It's about time. All my neighbors are always hogging the spotlight on these kinds of shows.

C: I suppose it is rather difficult to be tucked in between so many countries, like Thailand and China, Vietnam, Cambodia—

L: And Myanmar or Burma—whatever they call themselves nowadays. What a news hog.

C: Well, okay, let's not talk about them then. Let's talk about you! First off, how on earth do you pronounce your name?

L: Laowwww. No **s**. The French added the **s** when they stormed through back in the day and we just can't seem to shake it, which is so *dumb* because an **s** at the end of French words is silent anyway. Get with it people. Laaaaooooowwww.

C: Duly noted. No **s**.

L: I'd like to talk about being repeatedly featured in the *New York Times* travel section. Now *that's* a paper. They love my little cities and my rivers and my elephants. And they love my cozy and chic hotels that—

C: What about the more rowdy backpacker trail?

L: That's only a small part of my tourism.

BREAKING NEWS

MEET LAOS

Correct pronunciation still elusive, scientists repo

C: Really? Word on the street is that it's taking over the feel of some your smaller towns and dominating the economy.

L: Well . . . truth be told? It's easy money.

C: Like your opium production in days of the past?

L: My agent specifically asked that there be no mention of—

C: Oh right, right, sorry Laos.

L: Laowww! It's Laoooow! What is wrong with you people?!

C: Are you experiencing some kind of Communist/civil war hangover right now? What is going on?

L: I'm sorry, it's just—I'm such a lovely country, I am but—I've got an esoteric language and not a lot of infrastructure and I'm coming into my own in the global economy and . . . it's going to take more than just a few days to get to know me.

C: Steven and I only have a week, but we'll do our best to make the most of it.

L: Well, make sure you check out my Mae Kong River parties.

C: Your what?

L: You'll see.

9:34 am   88°

Back in Hanoi, we look into buses to Laos and realize we'll either lose three days traveling on land or spend thirty more bucks each to fly, so we buy airline tickets from a travel agency in town.

On the quick flight to the capital Vientiane (by the way, don't EVER take Air Laos) we learn about Laos from our guidebook. Once here, we figure out a few other things on our own rather quickly:

1. The food is . . . um . . . weirdly not as good as it is in China and Vietnam.

2. Every single tourist under the age of thirty is required to wear a Beerlao T-shirt—or so it seems, since there is no other reasonable explanation for the overwhelming presence of this item.

3. It is *not* a good idea to drink a lot of Beerlao the night before taking the early minibus for four hours from Vientien to Vang Vieng. (Steven looks good in green. Steven does not look good green.)

The next morning, after a rejuvenating night in our $5 bungalow that looks out at the picturesque mountains, we decide to take a peaceful kayak trip down the nearby river.

Peaceful being the key word here.

"It's so peaceful here!

"I know! Absolutely peaceful!"

"Do you feel at peace? Because I do."

"Me too! It's just us and the river and the mountains and—do you hear something?"

A quiet thumping in the distance turns into the blasting music of a mega river party.

We scramble onshore after our kayak is nearly cannonballed and try to rehinge our jaws. Who are these people? Where did they come from? Is it culturally acceptable here to be mostly naked and entirely wasted before noon?

We watch the crowd of foreigners from one of the quieter corners. Then we watch the locals who are watching the crowd. All the while we are listening to the running commentary from the revelers about the rope swingers.

"That was awesome!"

"Totally dude!"

"She is so hot!"

"I am so hyped!"

"This is crazy, yo!"

Somehow, all this triggers the deep man-urge within Steven to join in the fun that might kill him. He gets in line for the rope swing. I stay back, feeling like a parent at a school dance gone wrong. When it is finally Steven's turn I make sure to get out the camera and keep my ears perked for whatever review he might receive.

Right after he shrieks much like a small girl, I hear the judges:

"That guy has hairy armpits."

I want to tell them: "That was awesome dude! I am crazy hyped and he is so hot yo!" But I keep my judgment to myself.

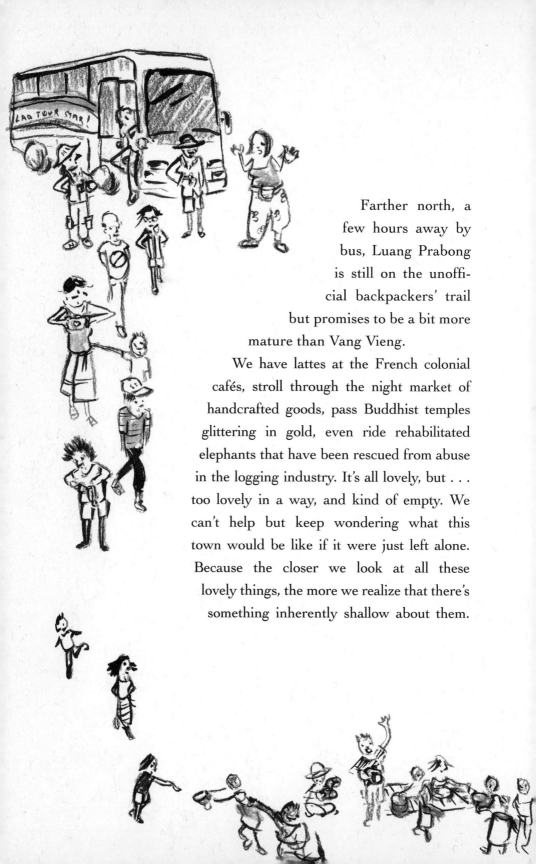

Farther north, a few hours away by bus, Luang Prabong is still on the unofficial backpackers' trail but promises to be a bit more mature than Vang Vieng.

We have lattes at the French colonial cafés, stroll through the night market of handcrafted goods, pass Buddhist temples glittering in gold, even ride rehabilitated elephants that have been rescued from abuse in the logging industry. It's all lovely, but . . . too lovely in a way, and kind of empty. We can't help but keep wondering what this town would be like if it were just left alone. Because the closer we look at all these lovely things, the more we realize that there's something inherently shallow about them.

Laosers certainly don't drink lattes, and I haven't seen a single one wearing any of the flowy pants or multicolored side bags sold at the night market, and I can't imagine that they feel at peace worshiping in their golden temples as sweaty folks set off camera flashes around them. And who says those elephants would prefer to lug around foreigners to logs? What is the real Luang Prabong?

This is, I guess. The old monks who walk the streets every dawn and beg for alms like they've done for many years must be quite used to accepting rice from white girls in tank tops now. And the youngest ones who lead the line have never known it to be any other way.

MEET THAILAND

Casey: Welcome to the show, Thailand! We've *really* been looking forward to catching up with you.

Thailand: Thank you, thank you.

C: Let's cut straight to it: how's your weather?

T: Perfect.

C: Yes! I knew it! And everyone is super friendly, right?

T: Absolutely. We pride ourselves on our hospitality. I hear you are meeting up with two friends who have been living here for a while, Alexandra and Kate, correct? I'm sure they have made many Thai friends who will be eager to welcome you into their homes as well.

C: Oh, we can't wait. It's going to be so nice! And the food is amazing too, right?

T: But of course. Just wait until you taste real pad thai.

C: Excuse me, I think I'm drooling. I'd better get onto some of the hard-hitting questions if that's all right with you.

T: Certainly.

C: Thailand, you are just so agreeable!

T: I know.

C: Okay—talk to me about the 2006 coup.

T: It wasn't such a big deal.

BREAKING NEWS

MEET THAILAND

"He satay-ed my finger!" claims local - Giant lizards

C: But, didn't the military dissolve Parliament? I mean—

T: The heart of the country is with the king, bless his saxophone-playing soul, and he remained unscathed throughout the entire process. My people love him unconditionally. That's why we all wear yellow shirts on Mondays and why I am wearing this yellow "Long Live the King" bracelet.

C: Oh, I thought maybe there was some kind of Lance Armstrong movement going on here. Next: let's talk about tourism here post-tsunami. How's that going?

T: Wonderfully. We received an extraordinary amount of international aid and everything is running smoothly again.

C: Was there at any point thoughts of revamping tourism here as you were rebuilding it? You know—with the sex trade and the druggy full moon parties and all?

T: Have I mentioned our deep respect for religion in this country? We are about 95 percent Buddhist here, and it is quite common for young men to spend a few years in the monastery before entering the rest of professional society.

C: Oh, that's not really what—but it looks like we've run out of time anyway. We are really looking forward to getting to know you in this month we have together.

T: The pleasure will be all mine.

4:45pm   81°

Exclusive interview with Casey Scieszka

nd in Bangkok park · A/C draws customers to 7-11 in d

We leave Laos ready to get to Thailand and connect with Alexandra and Kate, who have been teaching English there since graduation. We're coming to the point where the novelty of not having to work has worn off, and we don't really want to have that "What countries have you been to?" conversation with English-speaking strangers anymore. We miss knowing where to go for an authentic, cheap meal. Hopefully my friends will be able to lead us through some local life.

Alexandra has spent the past eight months in a small town in the northeast called Nan. We are catching her just before she leaves, therefore potentially overwhelming her with hosting duties as she tries to say good-bye to this place she's grown to love. Like she told me on the phone back in Beijing when we first began planning this trip, this last week will be "sacred" for her. And after four years together at school I know that she's a woman who needs her alone time and ritual, so Steven and I plan to stay for barely twenty-four hours. I'm sad that I can't see more of her, but I know that we'll have more time together one day.

Getting to Nan just might take longer than the time we'll spend there, though. We fly from Laos to the Thai city of Chiang Mai and take an overnight bus that arrives in Nan at four in the morning. Then we hop in a cab that drops us off at the one big hotel in town where we use the phone to call Alexandra. I can hardly hear her over the growling and barking of the stray dog in her yard that's apparently keeping her trapped inside. When she finally arrives, in pajamas with insane bedhead, wielding a broomstick, it's nearing dawn. We hug fiercely the way friends do who haven't seen each other in nearly a year. She squeezes Steven too, who she's only met twice before, then leads the way to her house.

Steven and I pass out in the guest bedroom just as the neighbor's rooster begins to crow. A few hours later, we're up and on bicycles taking what we thought would be a shortcut to Nan's most famous *wat*, but what has turned out to be a full-blown tour of the entire town and surrounding area. I want to see everything she wants to show us, to experience the life she has made for herself here, so even though my kidneys feel like they're about to implode, we go on. There is simply no time to be ill.

Actually, there is no time for anything, or so it feels. Steven just watches and pedals along as Alexandra and I rush to catch up, doing no justice to the depth of things we've learned and felt in these nine months apart. ("Take as much time as you guys need together," he said on the bus over. "I'll try and get out of the way.") Climbing up the five million stairs to our last must-see *wat*, I huff and lag and feel sorry for myself and wonder—as Alexandra fights off the wild dogs with her big stick far ahead—if it'll ever be like it used to be again. Between me and her. Between everyone from college now scattered across the globe. I wish I had more time with her. A pang of loss runs sharply through my chest. I keep climbing.

"Aggrhhuhrrraaahhh . . ."

"Steven, I think she needs to go to the hospital."

"How's your medical vocab?"

After our twenty-hour whirlwind with Alexandra, this is how we arrive at Kate's house just outside of Chiang Mai. I am in *pain*, tears coming out of my eyes even when I'm not crying pain.

As the doctors and nurses try to figure out where all my good bacteria have gone and how to lure them back, Kate and Steven have ample time to get to know each other. Whittling away hours in the waiting room together, they alternate between worrying about my mysterious condition and laughing it up playing the board game Steven and I made about our trip thus far. In between visits with various doctors, I come out and laugh with them. It soothes me to see them together. Look at them getting along so well! ("Kate! Kate! Do your cuddlefish impression for Casey!") Steven and I have existed in this small world of just us for a while now, and to watch the two of them interact reminds me that maybe one day

Steven, Alexandra, Kate, all our other friends might live in the same city in the States, and our different crews will merge and we can all hang out somewhere much more fun than a Thai hospital. Like at a party, with all my good bacteria.

At the end of the day, I'm called into an office for a final consultation. I bring Kate in for moral support and of course, translation. The doctor says essentially it's still a mystery. He wants to run further tests tomorrow. Ugrh. He and Kate go back and forth in Thai about what I can and cannot eat until then and suddenly the doctor goes pink and quiet. Kate is looking at him in a confused way then says something quickly, laughing and turning just as pink. The doctor eventually cracks a smile too and everyone returns to their normal color.

Apparently Kate's been learning Thai from her friends. Her foul-mouthed friends who never taught her the polite way to say "urinate," which is why she basically asked my doctor if her home-dawg was allowed to piss like a racehorse tomorrow morning before the tests.

Oops.

So the mystery of my condition has yet to be solved, which might worry me were my veins not pumping with medications that seem to ease the pain and panic. Maybe I can't carry on the best conversations of my life, but I certainly get a kick out of watching Kate talk to everyone. And really, I mean *everyone*. It's taken us half an hour to travel the two hundred yards from her house to the outdoor basketball court where Steven is going to play with some of her students. Everybody in this small town knows and loves her. We chat with a groundskeeper, some teachers, a group of students, a security guard, another bunch of students . . . Kate could converse with squirrels and she'd come out of it with a lifetime supply of nuts.

Eventually we *do* make it to the courts where Kate teaches some of her students how to play Knock-Out before they launch into their scrimmage with Steven—which he *dominates*. Maybe because everyone is too scared of the white giant's bony elbows to guard him. Either way.

Now that we've all worked up a big appetite (hey, cheerleading is hard and you know it), we head over to an open-air restaurant where a woman and her daughter rush over to greet Kate. They carry on in

Thai while Steven and I just smile and nod and feel proud to be associated with the town celebrity. Then the next thing we know we're in the kitchen pounding hot peppers and tiny dried shrimp with a mortar and pestle, going through all the steps of creating a delicious papaya salad.

And it's not just the papaya people who welcome us in. It's the fruit stand folks who also run the shaved ice stand where we get to make our own snow cones; it's her coworkers who coo about her. We are getting the deluxe insider's tour, and we're soaking up every second because in just a few days we'll be on our own again, lost with the rest of the sunburned tourists.

Our last night with Kate, we go out to dinner with one of her Thai friends who calls himself Max. From the way she describes him and panics over the best way to invite him along, even Steven can tell she's got a major crush. Which is why when dinner is over and Max offers to give us all a ride back to Kate's house on his moped, Steven and I say thanks but we'd like to walk off that big meal.

"You sure?" Kate asks, climbing on. I give her a knowing nod.

Steven all but winks.

Kate and Max buzz away and Steven and I meander along the main road, stopping to say hi to the fruit stand family, the papaya salad mom-and-daughter duo, the students who were playing basketball . . . Half an hour later we reunite with a smiling Kate. "What took you guys so long?" she asks.

"We just had to stop and say hello to a few people along the way. You know how it is here."

After a tearful good-bye with Kate, we take a night train from Chiang Mai to Bangkok and arrive early in the morning. Following a friend's advice and figuring it would be nice to avoid the famous backpacker row, we wind up finding a hotel somewhere much worse: the "business traveler" neighborhood, aka sex tourist neighborhood. Oops.

Bangkok's one redeeming factor for us at this point is the giant international hospital. The doctors in Chiang Mai told me to have a follow-up appointment here. So I bring my X-rays and sonograms and prescriptions, hoping to get an answer as to why I feel like my bladder is trying to eat me from the inside out — only to get this:

"The doctors in the north have no idea what they're talking about," says the doctor from the Big City.

"So you know what it is then?"

"Yes. It's nothing."

Oh really? Thanks. You're right! This terrible pain has *totally* been a figment of my imagination! I leave annoyed but relieved that this hospital can't find anything strikingly wrong with me either. I've been feeling better every day since my last round of

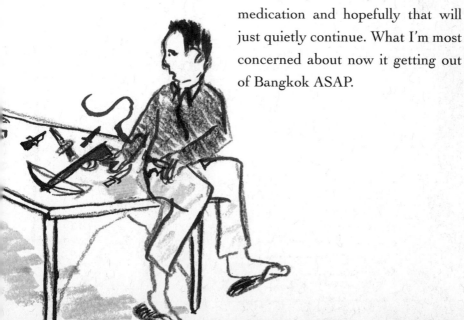

medication and hopefully that will just quietly continue. What I'm most concerned about now it getting out of Bangkok ASAP.

Getting out of Bangkok as quickly as we can, we hop on a plane to the island of Ko Samui and funnel in with all the other tourists trying to reach the eastern islands. It's highly organized and streamlined, which is both refreshing and disheartening; it's looking less and less likely that we're going to be able to quietly enjoy an empty beach. We follow our guidebook to what we think will be the most peaceful spot in Kho Pang Ahn, only to find that the low-key, affordable bungalow joint has recently been renovated into a swanky, full amenities mini-resort overflowing with Swedish families.

"Ughr!" Steven growls and yanks up his sweaty hair.

"All I want to do is throw down all of our shit and stay in one place for more than three days!"

"I know! We're going to wear ourselves out before we even get to Mali."

I drop my backpack in the sand and take off my shoes. "I just need to touch the water before we try and find another place," I say and start walking to the turquoise ocean.

And that's when Steven spots the little shacks lined up at the far end of the beach.

"I can't believe we needed a vacation from our vacation," Steven says.

"I can't believe we got that bungalow for *five dollars*," I say and float closer to him.

"We have arrived!"

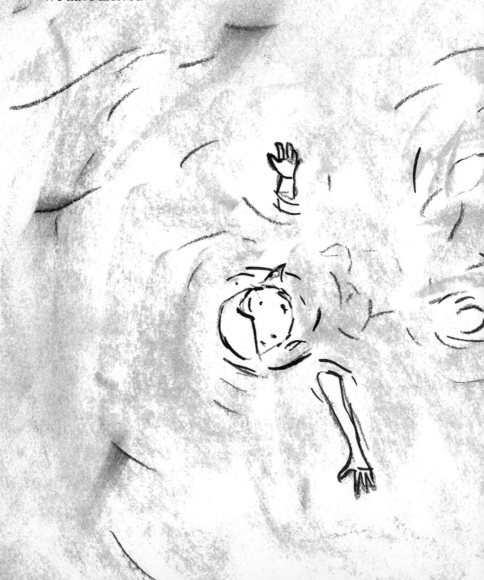

"I also can't believe that you can't float."
"Hey! I can flo—grphbbbrrr . . ."

For ten glorious days we live in our bathing suits, doing nothing but swimming and reading (and reapplying sunscreen). After all those freezing months in Beijing, we've arrived at our beach paradise!

But . . .

There are no markets to buy food, just overpriced restaurants affiliated with hotels, and way too many topless sunbathers. Geologically this is an island paradise, but culturally? What is going on here? Not a whole lot. We were completely spoiled by our insider tours with Alexandra and Kate.

We rent a moped to see what the rest of the island beyond our cove looks like. Much the same. With bigger hotels on some strips, and full-moon party posters stapled to coconut trees. (And half-moon parties, quarter-moon parties, Shiva-moon parties . . . just a lot of parties with a lot of drugs, really.) This place is so physically beautiful, but could be anywhere. There doesn't seem to be much of anything Thai about it.

As we're doing our best to just be here and not worry about the next leg of our travels, I'm thrown a last-minute curveball by the Fulbright folks. Someone in the State Department has suddenly decided that my project's advisor no longer meets the necessary qualifications. I have to find a new one, someone who is affiliated with the University in the capital, and until I do they will be withholding my grant money. As I try to compose an e-mail in which I politely remind them that they accepted my application eight months ago and that I am in Thailand and therefore not in the best position to contact strangers in Mali, my computer freezes and then shuts down. I try three more computers until Steven makes me stop, because whenever I'm stressed or anxious, electronics bear the brunt of it and do things that prompt technical assistants to say things like, "Wow, I've never seen this before." For example, back in Chiang Mai when I was trying to call my parents via the Internet to tell them about my visit to the hospital, Kate and Steven had to send me upstairs until the connection went through.

"Casey," Steven says, putting a hand on mine as I reach for my fifth computer. "Why don't you go check out those sunglasses they sell next door."

"No! I have to write this right now and—" He gives me a look of exasperation. "This is *serious*. They aren't going to give me my grant money if I don't—"

"I know, I know," he says. "It just—it just sucks that this all has to be so stressful right now. We're supposed to be *relaxing*."

"I *know*," I say more firmly than I expect to. "But it's not like I planned for my affiliate to fall through or to get sick, I—" I know I shouldn't go on. "You're right. I'm sorry. I'll write this tomorrow."

So after all this, it's not a huge surprise when Grazia, our Sardinian yoga instructor/fertility expert/astrologist/bungalow neighbor who we've talked to a few times, reads my astrological chart and laughs, "Well . . . you are a witch."

Without any prompting she describes how I probably have troubles with electronics, with the Internet especially, and maybe it started with clocks and streetlights or radios. The fact that she doesn't know me but knows this about me should freak me out but instead it soothes me. I'm not just fucking nuts; I'm an electromagnetic witch! Cool! She says that I could learn to harness this energy one day if I find the right teacher. But for now I should simply try to protect myself. I'm too open to other people's energies and can be hurt because of it. "It's like being very, very empathetic," she warns. "Do not surround yourself with needy people because no one will be helped."

Grazia moves on to my future and talks about how this current phase of traveling and learning new languages is going to continue for a while. But she could say that to anyone on this far-flung beach, right? She goes on about how "settling" in one place will feel suffocating, that it's important that I keep moving. "So I won't really have a home for a long time?" I ask, feeling surprisingly panicked.

"Maybe no," she says. "If yes, then you will take shorter trips because new places and people are necessary for you to feel not dead. But maybe you will have a job with people and they are foreign, or maybe with children because children are very much alive." My heart is beating against my lungs. Why? "What you do is more important than where you are," she says, refolding her legs. "So I don't think you will create a strong attachment to one place for a long time."

I head back to our bungalow with a sense of dread. Why does it bother me so much to think that I will keep traveling? Does it sound bad simply because I'm so sick of it right now? Because I'd hoped to settle somewhere after Mali for a bit where friends and family might be? It's probably because Steven had a reading with her right before mine and his was all about how he needs to find a place and stay there, how he's about to embark on a formative six-month period in his work as it relates to his personal life.

Back in bed, I tell Steven most of what Grazia said, but instead of dwelling on the whole never-have-a-home thing I highlight the end of our talk when she explained how sex is very important to me in a relationship. Another you-could-tell-that-to-anyone insight, I know, but I figure Steven will be happy to hear it. Instead we have a moment to mourn the death of our sex life caused by my mysterious illness. I hear him inhale in that way you do only when you're about to say something serious.

"This is going to sound mean," he says, "but I'm really sick of you being sick."

"Like I'm not sick of it too?" I shoot back and sit up in bed. He pushes himself up as well.

"That's not what I mean," he says angrily. "I knew I shouldn't have said it like that, but it's just—honestly? You haven't been your regular self. You haven't been as fun as you—"

"My regular self? Of *course* I'm not! You're relaxing and reading your book in the sand and all I can think about is how no one can tell me what the fuck is wrong with me. I may or may not feel better and then *you* want to have sex and I have to be the one that says no all the time and I don't—"

We go on like this for a while and reach a point where nothing productive is being said, and we're just angrily repeating ourselves and pushing each other more than we have ever pushed before. I make the penultimate move by imitating him, which makes him say, with such hatred and acid, what neither of us was ever allowed to say in our families, what we've never ever said to each other before:

"Shut up."

I launch myself out of the bed and fumble frantically through my tears for my journal and a pen and rush outside. I spend the rest of the night on the porch, furiously scribbling and sobbing.

He stays inside.

As my breath returns to a regular rhythm and the moon moves higher in the sky, I can eventually distill my many fears to one immediate question: How will we be able to love and live in Mali if we can hardly get it together in paradise?

The sun rises.

"I'm sorry."

"I'm sorry too."

"I just want to be in Mali already."

"Me too."

The most direct flight we can get from Bangkok to Paris includes a layover in Dubai (which is a lot better than stopping in Islamabad, Munich, Cairo, and London—which was our other option). We're wowed by how fancy and clean the airport is. Not so wowed by the seemingly unnecessary second security check that everyone who has a connecting flight must go through. As most passengers start to form a line, Steven and I, without even thinking about it, head straight to the front. And guess who's there with us? Some Asians who don't believe in lines. And who else? Some guys who look and sound like they're from West Africa. They're holding up this line they just cut, going through the metal detector again and again, each round slowly taking off another ring, a studded belt, a necklace, and people behind them are starting to get pissed.

"Fouking hell!" spits a Scottish woman behind us.

"It's like noo one here has ever seeen a line," says the man with her.

"If yooou're gonna skip ahead in froont of all of us cud ya hurry up at least?" she yells.

"Well, now we know at least one thing in Mali that will feel familiar," whispers Steven. "Shall we cut ahead of them too?"

"*Bienvenu, mon cheri, à Paris!*" I say as we step out of the Metro directly in front of Notre Dame.

"*Ooh la la!*" exclaims Steven.

Our bags and jaws drop simultaneously as we enter the apartment my family has rented for the week. It's so clean! And so beautifully French. And really, *so clean!*

After showering (it turns out we aren't half as tan as we thought we were), we head out in search of cheese. The Asian aversion to this delectable dairy

has driven us mad with desire for creamy brie and crumbly goat and knife-sharp cheddar . . . My parents and cousin Eric will be arriving tomorrow (delayed because of snowstorms) so we might as well stock up for them too, right? And while we're at it we should probably get some sausage and wine and bread and…

Several hours and kilos of cheese later we lay nearly comatose on the couches. "Steven?" I ask and he lifts a finger so I know he's awake. "I thought I was a beach person, l but I think I'm really a *Paris* person."

My family arrives the next day and it's a happy reunion, filled with *more* wine and *more* cheese and *more* sausage and—it's no mystery where I got my appreciation for food and drink. Having my cousin Eric in the mix is great fun since he's a varsity-level everything-edible lover himself. After two glorious days of gorging and catching up, Eric heads back home and Steven's parents, Kathie and David, arrive.

We'd been a little anxious about the parents meeting for the first time, but figured with my dad being a children's book author, Steven's mom being a librarian, and us all being in Paris it would all go rather smoothly. And go smoothly it does. It's almost as if the four of them had been hanging out long before Steven and I ever got this hair-brained idea to start dating.

When they're not all gabbing together, they're asking us about Mali. What will we be doing there? Where will we live? What will we eat? What's the weather like? We have just about zero answers for them because really, we have no fucking clue what we're getting into. I mean, we know I'm going to research the role of Islam in the education system there (whatever that turns out to mean), and we've been put in touch with a lady who runs a school that might want us to teach some English and art—but that's about all we got at this point. We don't even know where we'll be staying after we land in Bamako.

But we're not going to worry about that right now. Instead we will simply savor the brie, the Monets, the drinkable tap water and, of course, this time with our parents who continue to be more supportive than we ever could have dared ask for.

Our parents send us off with hugs and kisses and plenty of Pepto-Bismol and sunscreen. Just three hours later, we land in Morocco and have seven hours until our connecting flight to Mali. So we hop on a train and book it from Casablanca to Rabat where we can reconnect with the place where we first met and get one more dose of the familiar before we head off to the *new* place we're going to call home.

Walking down the carless streets of the old medina, we seamlessly enter the flow of the crowd. We know this place. We love this place. The smells of baking bread and roasting lamb and all

those delicious spices are so familiar, and the echo of the call to prayer sends us back to when that was the rhythm marker of our days. We stock up on sticky dates and luscious olives and their signature harsh loofas to scrub off the dirt that will surely accumulate on us in Mali.

Bearing cookies, we head to our host families' houses. Steven's family isn't around, so we head to mine, back to the doorway where we used to make out in the dark and wonder where the hell we were ever going with any of this. When I ring the bell, Amina, my host mother, sticks her head out the second-floor window and shrieks with delight before throwing down the keys.

We are just in time for afternoon coffee—over which we babble excitedly, trying to explain where we've been and where we're going, what's gone on here since two summers ago. Linguistically we're *totally* confused. Chinese is overtaking the little Arabic we can summon. "You don't speak Arabic anymore!" she says to me, laughing and pushing me lightly. But it's okay if I can't express myself in words right now, because my shit-eating grin probably says it all.

When it's time to go, we hug Amina good-bye and promise to get fatter (we are looking a little skin and bones since Southeast Asia), and to be safe in Mali and to remember more Arabic and come back and live here again one day.

"I hope we have Aminas in Mali," I sniffle on our way out.

"We will."

SAHARA DESERT

MALI

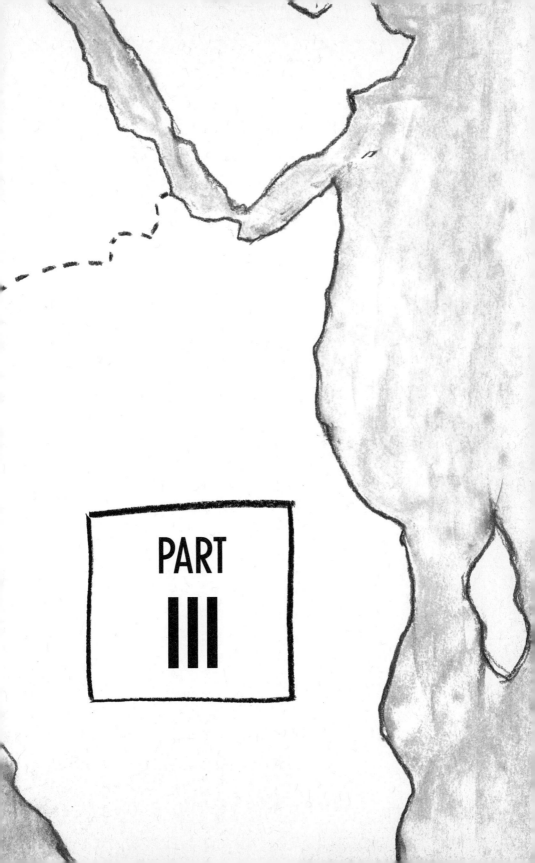

PART

III

It's two thirty in the morning in Mali and it's got to be one hundred degrees. The flies and mosquitoes are swarming and so are the young men who are trying to convince us to hire them as guides. Steven and I are firm but polite for as long as we can be—that is until they start insulting each other in crude English to somehow win us over, at which point Steven cracks and bellows, "Just go away!" Plenty of them scatter, but only to other parts of the benches.

The major upside of it
all is that my good bacteria
seem to have mysteriously returned
so at least I am not feeling ill as we spend the
next few hours fitfully sleeping in turns, waiting for
the sun to rise. There is no way we are getting in a taxi in the
middle of the night to try and find a hotel in a country where we've
never been. I keep stealing glances at Steven as he swats at the flies
that won't let him sleep. What have I signed us up for?

We're grateful for the sunrise despite the heavy heat increasing even more. A place, no matter how potentially hellish, is always easier to face in the light of day.

Strapping on our backpacks again, we head out to where the taxis wait and are absolutely ambushed, like celebrities at a court hearing. In English, in French, in whatever European language they can muster, the taxi drivers ask all at once where we're going. Really, we have no idea. All we have is the name of a small hotel run by two French sisters and a few directions like "Take a left at the hippo." We can only hope it means there are large animal sculptures at the intersections here.

We go with the older man who bothered us the least of the crowd and follow him to his taxi. He tells us some outrageous price, but luckily we read in a guidebook that we should find the sign of regulated prices posted in French.

So far, so good—we've got a ride, and at a fair price. Now if only we could shake this last persistent guide who keeps quoting Bob Marley like it's going to make us change our minds. He goes so far as to get in the cab with us. That's when our driver explodes and gives Steven his first Malian French lesson. After being berated, the guide sucks his teeth, puts up a hand, and gets out.

"I'm not sure I want to know what either of them said," Steven says.

We're quiet for most of the ride, trying to take in as much as we can from our windows. The ground everywhere is red and dusty. There are shacks made from corrugated steel and cinderblocks lining the road. A few women are out sweeping with handleless brooms and babies tied to their backs, or they're walking with buckets on their heads. Men zoom past us on loud mopeds. Our ancient yellow Mercedes audibly chugs along, shaking when it slows down or speeds up. Eventually we get to a bridge where the traffic is a little thicker. There are couples on mopeds now, the women holding on to the men with one hand and their giant head wraps with the other. We cross the Niger River and look at the Bamako skyline. There's not much besides one giant building, which we read in our guidebook is the Bank of Africa.

"I can't believe this is the capital," I whisper.

"I know," Steven whispers back.

It turns out there *are* giant animal statues at each large inter-section, so we take a left at the hippo, but we can't seem to find our next marker: a "big blue building." Finally, after a handful of U-turns, Steven spots a hand-painted sign for the hotel. We pay with the West African francs we picked up at the Malian Embassy in Paris, unload our bags, and ring the bell.

"Holy shit, it's hot."

"Yeah. And it's only seven in the morning."

We wipe the sweat from our eyes and wait.

MEET MALI

Casey: Welcome to the, uh . . . show, Mali.

Mali: *I nee chay!*

C: What? Oh, that's "thank you" in Bamanankan, right? Sorry, I'm just—just a little out of it, that's all. It's so *hot* here!

M: Oh, I know. It's the height of the hot season right now. You are so crazy to be here!

C: Really? I thought the hot season would be summertime.

M: No, that's the rainy season. Of course it's pretty hot then too! Ha ha ha!

C: Oh. Well. Let's see. I uh, think I've got some questions here for you . . . um . . . Let's start with your official language.

M: It's French. But I have hundreds of local languages as well like Bamanankan and Peul and Songhai. Most people around the capital will speak Bamanankan. And I should probably tell you that most Malians don't speak much French unless they've spent many years in school. And not that many people have spent many years in school here.

C: Oh. Well—the research I'm going to be doing is about schools, so I can learn all about that soon enough and, uh . . .

M: Are you okay? You look *really* pink.

BREAKING NEWS

MEET MALI

Mangoes are snack of the season! -Toubab Krewe are

C: I'll be fine. I hope. Um, religion? Mostly Muslim, right? I—damn it is *really* hard to think when it's this hot. What is it, like a hundred degrees?

M: No no no! Don't be crazy! It's fifty.

C: You mean fifty degrees Celsius though, right? That must mean it's like, what? A hundred and twenty something?

M: Why don't I take your little note cards and I can answer the questions by myself and you just sit there. Okay . . . food! Ah yes! Good news about food!

C: Really? That's great.

M: It's rice.

C: What do you mean by, "It's rice?"

M: I mean, it's rice. There's sauce on top most of the time. With tomato paste, or onions. Peanut sauce is also really big here.

C: Like peanut butter?

M: Maybe. But with fish bits.

C: Oh.

M: Excuse me, but I think the cameraman with the funny hair just fell out of his chair. Are you two going to be okay?

11:04 am   122°

d Toubabs by local children - "Is that a donkey or my

After napping oh so briefly in our hotel room (we want to get on this time zone quickly and besides, it's too damn hot to sleep—we're soaking the foam mattress), we head out with our guidebook in search of the American Embassy where we will register. Not something we've been doing in each country, but we figure we should since we'll be here for a while.

Walking around we're a bit stunned and overstimulated. Everywhere is dust and bright fabrics and mopeds and people upon people. We keep expecting to turn a corner and find a downtown with sidewalks and buildings that go higher than two floors, but the tightly packed hustle and bustle continues. The one word we can repeatedly pick out in all the noise is *toubabou*. Roughly it means

"whitey" in Bamanankan, though once upon a time it came from a word for doctor.

Hours later (literally), absolutely drenched and dehydrated, we arrive where the embassy should be according to our guidebook.

Of course it has moved to the other side of town.

We take a cab back and cower in our room until the sun settles a little lower in the sky. "This is not at all like Asia," I say in between gulps of water.

"Except for all the mopeds?" Steven tries. I make a sound that might pass as a laugh.

Having learned our lesson about walking around, we decide to check out the green minivans we saw buzzing through town. We ask one of the French ladies running our hotel what the deal is. She says they're called *sotrama* and we can just hop on any of them that have room for 125 CFA (about 25 cents) and knock on the roof when we want to get off. Easy enough. Except for the fact that the smallest bill we have is five *thousand* CFA. Ten stores later, we have a new tube of toothpaste and change. We flag down a van but there's no room. Oh wait, there is? No, there's not! There are sixteen other people in there! Everyone watches as we squeeze in, all the way in the back corner.

"They're all looking at us," says Steven, ventriloquist style. We try to stifle the urge to crack up, and just when I think I can't hold it anymore, a woman across the way says something to us.

"Pardon?" I ask politely in French, although I'm pretty sure she was speaking Bamanankan. We continue the rest in French:

"What are your names?" she asks.

"Um, my name is Casey and his name is Steven."

"No, no, no, no, no, no," she laughs.

"Yes, it's true."

"What are your *Malian* names?"

"Oh, uh, we don't have any."

"Ah *voila*. You are Fatimata Kanté and he is Salif Keita." Everyone in the bus laughs together.

"Okay," I say and laugh with the crowd, feeling awfully pink from heat, embarrassment, and my general whiteness. I remember I can thank her with the one Bamanankan phrase we know from our guidebook: *"I nee chay!"* I say, and everyone roars again.

"And when did you get here Fatimata and Salif?"

"This morning." That gets the biggest laugh of all.

"Truly? This morning? And already you are on the *sotrama*? Ah, Fatimata and Salif . . ." she chuckles.

It's not until we're back from our afternoon out in the markets and going through our guidebook again that we realize who Steven was named after: Salif Keita, a famous Malian singer who is *albino.*

The next day we make our way to the *new* American Embassy where I meet some people in the Cultural Affairs Department and get my State Department badge that lets me bypass security (Fancy! Thank you Fulbright.). Oddly enough, we have our first Malian meal of rice and sauce at the embassy cafeteria. (It's *okay.*) Everything is shiny and clean and air-conditioned, which makes us acutely aware of just how sweaty and covered in orange dust we are.

The best part of coming here is meeting Aysete, the embassy cashier, who is looking for someone to rent her house. She's just gotten married, and although she loves her place, custom dictates she must move in with her husband. She can even take us to see it right now since she's on her lunch break.

After a very bumpy five-minute drive, we pull up to a gate. Aysete pushes it open and unlocks the front door. Steven and I look at each other like, "Maybe? What do you think?" And then we realize that two other people are in the room. Aysete introduces us and uses our Malian names, which she seems to like so much. (She let out a real guffaw when we told her.)

"So Mohammed here," she says in French, "lives in a room on the roof, but he could leave if you don't think you need a guard. Although he will have to stay for a little while longer because I

can't just make him leave so quickly. And do you want a cook? Because Maimouna here, she cooks for me normally, but maybe you don't want that either."

No guards, no cooks, we just want our own space. A place to live again. So even though there's something a little odd about this place (maybe it's the giant chandeliers in such a low-ceilinged room? Or the heavily upholstered furniture that I could never imagine sitting on in this heat?) we *really* want to move in.

Steven and I confer quietly for a moment—it's two hundred dollars a month, there's enough room for both us to have working space, there's a roof we can hang out on, and she said the neighborhood is friendly and safe. But is this too much for two people, or too little? We don't even know anything about the neighborhoods yet, but what if another arriving Fulbrighter takes it, we should just—

"We'll take it."

"Oh, that's wonderful! When do you want to move in?"

And just like that, we have ourselves a home.

Day three in Mali we head to an Internet café so we can tell our parents we're alive. Baking from the inside out, but alive. And we have a house! Not for another few days, but still. From the Internet café phone booth, we call Maria, the woman who runs that school just outside of the city where we might work. She says she's leaving for a teacher training in another city in two days, so how about we meet up this afternoon, do we have other plans? Needless to say we don't, so after a morning of more wandering, we get into her air-conditioned SUV. Heaven of heavens. Even better than the air-conditioning is the fact that Maria speaks English fluently and has the kind of laugh that can make even the most dehydrated *toubab* crack a smile.

"Where do you want to go? To the school? I also have to go to the grocery store," she says. There's nothing Steven and I would rather do than follow around a mother figure on errands right now. In an air-conditioned vehicle that leads to food no less. (Our Moroccan date and olive supply is running low.)

Weaving through murderous traffic, she tells us more about the school and the nonprofit it's attached to. L'Institut Pour L'Education Populaire is a nonprofit that runs teacher trainings and works on local language curriculum development. IEP (as they usually call it) also runs an alternative school for kids up to ninth grade. Some of the students were kicked out of the public system for different reasons, or just weren't doing so well. "We give them more chances," Maria explains. We talk a bit about what we could do with them—maybe teach English to the older kids, paint some murals around the school, have an art class. . . . Steven and I keep smiling at each other with excitement.

At one point, Maria's cell phone rings. She has Steven see who it is. "Oh no—don't get it," she says. "It's someone looking for a report I said I could write by today and I do not have it! And besides, they are very *French*." She lets out a cackle and we join in, feeling that much closer to her already.

The supermarket looks *just* like a small one in the States. "Oooh, Raisin Bran," says Steven. For seven dollars. Damn it. Looks like things might not be as cheap as they were in China.

Maria picks up some cheese, some hamburger meat, and a bottle of wine. "Do you drink wine?" she asks. I say "sometimes" because I'm still unsure about the social etiquette of drinking in this country.

"Okay, tonight counts for sometimes then," she says and smiles.

We drive up and over the mountain that hovers above Bamako. Twenty minutes later, we're in Kati, the even dustier town where Maria lives. Everything is much more spread out and calm than in Bamako. We like it already.

We stop by her house first since her husband has locked himself out and has been waiting for her to return this whole time. She throws him the keys and laughs (he doesn't look so pleased), then takes us on a tour of the school grounds.

After we check out the classrooms and offices the sun starts to set, the call to prayer reaches around the evening, and Maria invites us to stay for dinner. We gladly accept, excited to eat some home-cooked food. Or anything that doesn't have pits. After splitting the bottle of Chemin du Pope ("If it's the path of the pope it's good enough for me! Now don't be shy!" Maria declares) we are presented with a carbohydrate feast: spaghetti, rice, potatoes, bread, fried plantains. . . . The peanut sauce, *tikka degena*, that goes on the rice is delicious and drippy. We stuff ourselves silly as we learn more about Maria's various travels all over the States, how she and her American friend Debbie met in graduate school and decided to do something with the education system in Mali.

Meanwhile, all around the courtyard, different groups of people are eating from communal bowls — four young men around one, five young women around another, and the children with their own. We're not sure who these people are exactly.

Family? Neighbors? Some of the women have been doing all the cooking. Are they maids? Everyone was introduced to us right when we walked in, and their names, which at this point are totally incomprehensible to us, flew right out the back of our heads as soon as we heard them. We like this place enough to hope that one day we'll know them all.

Eventually, Maria says that Nanu, one of the young men—maybe he's her son?—will drive us back down to Bamako. We tell her we can find a taxi but she insists and Nanu says he's happy to do it. Maria promises that when she and Debbie get back from their teacher training we'll all work out some kind of schedule. "Don't worry," she laughs. "There's plenty of work to do around here. Now you can find your way back to your hotel, right?"

"We're pretty sure," says Steven.

"Oh no!" she laughs. "It's going to be like *The Stupids Go To Town*!"

Maria referencing one of my favorite children's book families ever? This place is going to be amazing.

THE AMERICAN CLUB

The cultural affairs officer at the embassy invited us to a barbeque at the American Club. After sipping Sam Adams and chatting with our country folk, we eventually compute that there seem to be roughly seven types of Americans around:

The diplomat. Easily identifiable as they are the only people wearing full suits in this weather. I guess American officewear doesn't allow for the Malian-style short-sleeved suit. A real shame, because those are fabulous.

Embassy spouse. They're the ones who know about the fancy grocery stores that sell cheese and talk about how driving here is different in Namibia/Saudi Arabia/Ireland/Turkey. Lots of them mix a mean cocktail.

Marine. You know the drill.

Peace Corps Volunteer. Look for the people dressed half-American half-Malian. They might have braids, they might look they've been washing their clothes in a bucket for two years. (Because they have.) Local language champions.

NGO employee. Here to bring better health care/schools/roads etc. . . . Potentially a bit more integrated into Malian culture than most ex-pats since their bosses don't discourage them from doing so (compared to embassy employees who *are*). They tend to stay longer than everyone else.

Tourist. Usually the most sunburned of the bunch. Look for the typical clues: guidebook, bottled water, candy for begging children bulging from their zip-off, quick-dry pants.

Mali-lovers. Whoever showed up on the back of a Malian's moped, decked out in local gear. So far, the only other two Fulbrighters we've met fall into this category. They've spent lots of time in this country before and applied for the grant so they could come back to this place they know and love.

So where do we fit in? So far, nowhere. We're most intrigued by the Mali-lovers, of course, kind of hoping maybe we can be a bit like that one day. That is, until one of them says she loves Bamako so much she plans to be buried here. Not so sure we could ever go *that* local.

THE PLAN

After about a week, we've got a rough plan:

Steven and I are going to stay here in Bamako, until the end of June or so. We will split our time between the house we're renting in a neighborhood called Djikoroni Para and Maria's house in the town of Kati, half an hour away. When we're in Djikoroni Para, Steven will paint and draw and I will do my research, which will most likely consist of hanging out around local schools, doing observations, and interviewing teachers. When we're in Kati (Wednesdays through Fridays—we'll get room and board there in exchange for our work) we will teach English to the older students, try to work some art into those classes as well, *and* paint a series of educational murals around the school grounds. (Not exactly sure what those will be yet, but that's for Steven to spearhead.)

In addition to all that, we'll spend time studying languages. French for Steven and Bamanankan for me since I studied French from third to twelfth grade.

When we're not doing all that, we'll be hanging out with our new friends. Whoever they'll wind up being.

What happens after the end of June? The future gets blurrier the further away it is. We're thinking a month or two of traveling around the country, some time in the cities of Djenne or Segou, and obviously, Timbuktu. We're just going to take it day by hot-as-hell day for now.

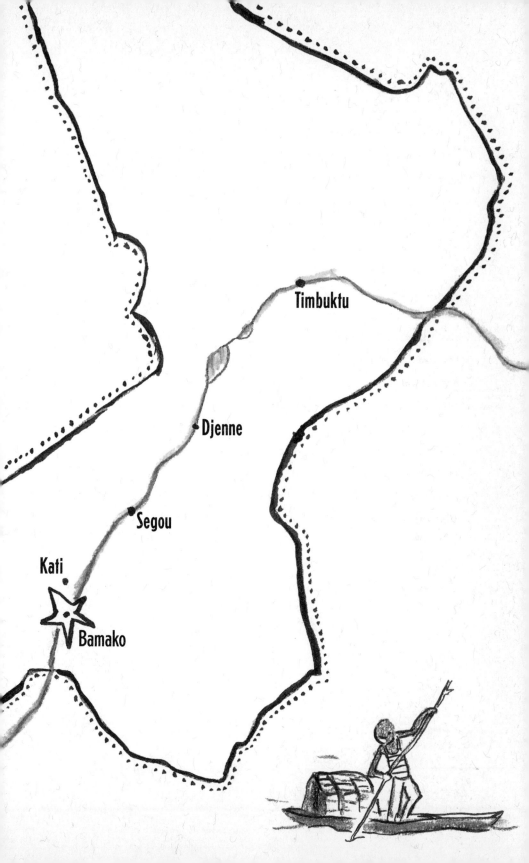

Timbuktu

Djenne

Segou

Kati

Bamako

There are *no* restaurants in this town, which is a big problem now that our olive and date supply has run out. Okay, there are *some* restaurants but they are either air-conditioned and tableclothed ones where a small pizza costs $20 or roadside stalls where you can get beans slapped into a barely washed bowl for 20 cents.

"God I miss our restaurant in Beijing!" says Steven.

"I know. What I would do for some eggplant right now. . . ."

"With a cold beer . . ."

We take another look at our guidebook, fingers crossed and— aha! There it is! It's called Beijing II.

Still getting our Bamako bearings, it takes us a good hour of wandering around side roads until we finally spot the sign. We all but run.

Fluorescent lights? Check. White walls? Check. Mirrored liquor shelf with bottles of *bi jiou*? Check.

We have arrived.

Through mouthfuls of eggplant and shredded pork and tofu and rice, we are transported back to Beijing. We have a big beer each (no Tsingtao, the local Castel instead—but hey, cheap beer is cheap

beer) and gush about how familiar it all is, how we almost feel the panic of not having lesson planned enough setting in. We remind ourselves that we're in Africa, totally free to do whatever we want—this is absurd! We are absurd!

We just might be a little drunk, too, since our water supply didn't exactly last for that long walk. Either way, we're back in Beijing and we feel so at ease.

"*Mai dan*," says Steven, asking for the check. The waitress doesn't even blink and brings it over. I love it!

"Do you think we'll ever go to a Malian restaurant in some other country and feel like this?" I ask.

"Having seen the bean stalls, I'm going to venture to say no. I don't think food will be what we remember most from this experience."

We're moving in today. Good-bye hotel, hello home!

After setting our backpacks down, we take another tour of the place. There's the living room with those velourlike couches, the master bedroom with just a bed, the master bathroom with a Western toilet (yay!). There's the kitchen with lots of cockroaches and no appliances and the other bedroom with all the junk they didn't want to move stuffed inside of it (not so "yay"). There's a little side yard with all the *other* junk they didn't want to move. (Oh boy.) "Is that a wig?" Steven asks pointing to a clump of something brown.

"A weave, I guess. Is that—"

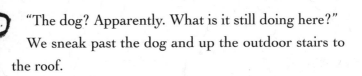

"The dog? Apparently. What is it still doing here?"

We sneak past the dog and up the outdoor stairs to the roof.

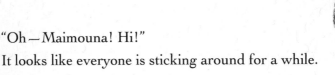

"Mohammed! Oh, uh—hello!"

We come back downstairs.

"Oh—Maimouna! Hi!"

It looks like everyone is sticking around for a while.

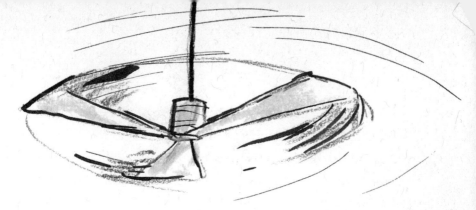

We spend the afternoon outside of the house, walking around the neighborhood trying to get our bearings. Past the cows and groups of children playing soccer in jellies and underwear, past buildings made of mud and corrugated iron, through the potholed dirt roads, by tailor shops with sewing machines click-clicking, and women selling tomatoes or fried dough balls stacked in pyramids. The children follow us chanting, "*Tou-ba-bou! Tou-ba-bou!*" Some of them touch our arms and squeal in horror and/or delight. Even the adults call out to us. "*Eh—toubab,*" they say. "*I nee chay,*" we reply, which is all we know how to say at this point.

Dinner is fried millet balls with some mystery hot sauce we buy from a lady around the corner, washed down with bottles of water. One of the other Fulbrighters who's been here before told us at the barbeque that we could drink the tap water here after a while. That it would just take our stomachs a little time to get used to it. "It's overchlorinated, that's all. You'll have diarrhea for a bit, but you'll probably have diarrhea anyway." Excellent.

After dinner, we lay out a sheet on the floor of the living room since the ceiling fan in there seems to work best. We close our eyes. "This is so crazy," Steven says.

"I know. Really fucking crazy. I'm sure we'll settle into things though," I tell him and kiss him on his sweaty cheek.

And then the fan dies.

"Did I mention that our guidebook says blackouts are rather common here?"

Feeding ourselves is continuing to be rather difficult since we don't have any kitchen appliances (we're planning to get a mini-fridge from that fancy supermarket we went to with Maria and a camping stove since we've seen those sold on the street) and the stores around here seem to sell only tea, powdered milk, and cigarettes. On top of it all, at one hundred and fifteen degrees it's hard to sustain enough of an appetite to motivate you to find food.

Today, though, we've decided to give the trusty tuna fish sandwich a try. We bought a few cans of it from a store down the road, but no bread. Steven says he's seen *boulangerie* stalls around, and maybe because he knows I'll burn to a crisp out there in the noontime sun he offers to be the one to venture out and get some.

I sweat and wait and sweat and wait, and eventually start worrying. Forty-five minutes later I'm about to form a search party with my new neighbors and all their crying babies I've been listening to when finally he returns.

"Where have you *been*?" I ask.

"With Fatimata."

"Who?"

It went something like this: Steven walked himself in circles looking for the bread stands, getting sweatier and pinker and more dehydrated by the second, until finally a woman with three children waved him over to her mango stand under a tree. Speaking no French, and obviously no Bamanankan, turned out to be no obstacle at all in making friends. It's easy to point at people and learn their names. She's Fatimata (like me!) and her three young daughters are Saran, La Vielle, and Nana. Steven, of course, is Salif Keita, which got a huge laugh and might be what inspired Fatimata to invite him to eat lunch with them. Unsure if it would be impolite

to say no, and damn hungry after his long walk, Salif rinsed his
hands with a kettle full of water then dug into the big bowl of rice
with drippy green sauce.

"I was never any good eating with my hands even in Morocco,"
he says. "I don't think as much made it into my mouth as all over
the rest of my face. The kids thought it was hilarious, though." I
laugh and pick a leftover grain off his stubble.

"You didn't happen to find any bread, did you?"

"Oh, sorry. No. But I'm pretty sure they invited us over for lunch
again tomorrow!"

"Tomorrow? Well, I'm not that hungry anyway." And really, I'm
not. I'm just glad he's back. I take a gulp from one of our many
bottles of water. "Tell me more about our new friends."

Steven and I have promised each other to hit the ground running, so on our second morning waking up in our new house we get straight to it. Steven starts painting and I start my research. For Steven that means setting up at the table with his supplies, for me that means putting on a long skirt and my button-down and heading out to find a school. I kiss Steven good-bye and he barely looks up, already absorbed in catching up on some cartoon-a-day entries from our first week here.

I figure I'll start with what's closest to me. In school I was trained to suck up my fear of awkward encounters with strangers and just go for it—ask to do unobtrusive observations, ask to do interviews—ask and you just might receive. It's best to try and enter a site with some kind of gate-keeper, like maybe a friend who knows someone there—but obviously I don't know anyone here, so there goes that. So, with all that considered, I figure I'll just walk until I find a school. I'm hardly fifty feet from my door when I spot one. I'm nervous, and I'm already sweating profusely from the heat, but I'm ready to get to work.

And it's closed. Foiled already! There's a young woman with a baby sweeping the dirt floors. She doesn't seem to understand French, but gestures that I follow her down the block to what turns out to be the director's house. I'm a little mortified to be bothering him on what must be his day off, but he insists he doesn't mind and leads me back to the school so we can have a quick interview. I tell him in French that my project is on the role of Islam in the education system and he tells me what I'm afraid I'm going to hear five hundred more times: "We don't teach religion here. That's in the Koranic schools." (Koranic schools being loosely the Muslim equivalent of Christian Sunday schools.) I try to explain how I mean it in a more nuanced way—like how is the spread of Islam addressed in history class, and is religious dress adhered to more in schools than, say, in the street, etc. But French is sticking to the roof of my mouth, my research questions are so vague and huge right now, and I'm still learning the very basics of the system.

An hour later though, I've got five pages of notes, an armful of textbooks, and a pal. Smiling, he says, "Fatimata, you are welcome to come to my school anytime." So I take his word for it and show up the next the day at 7:45 in the morning to begin my observations.

After four hours of sitting in classrooms, I am transported back to that hazy place called tenth grade geometry. That is to say, I am fighting off sleep tooth and nail. *Barely* successfully, I might add. There's something about the drone of a class reading aloud together, of the call and response of rote memorization, of one-hundred-and-whatever-degree heat that just makes me *tired*.

A bell is struck at noon (a literal bell) and all the students scramble to get their bags and rush out of the classrooms. As I stand up and fully come to, I am filled with empathy. It's no wonder most Malian kids only stay in school for four years. Or have to repeat grades multiple times. (Did I mention that some of the fifth-graders here are well into their teens?) I decide then and there to spend more time conducting interviews than doing classroom observations. Then I join the herd of children and rush home too.

Steven and I find language teachers thanks to the organization through which we studied abroad in Morocco. They've got a small program here and happen to have two excellent language teachers who have some spare time to tutor us. Ousmane will teach Steven French, and Lamine will teach me Bamanankan.

Ousmane is in his fifties and would most likely be deemed legally blind in America. This doesn't stop him from teaching English at the University as well as French to study-abroad students. He and Steven sit down for lessons in his spartan office at the University downtown, share liters of sweet hibiscus juice and bags of peanuts that get stuck to their facial hair, and talk about Malian history, politics, cultural jokes—in short, everything about Mali except for French. Well, they *do* get some basic verb conjugations in there, as well as key vocabulary necessary for Steven to explain to people what he's doing in the country (like "painter," "teacher," "grant," "wife." (We're pretending to be married to avoid potentially offending people). Ousmane slowly reveals himself to be an old-school pan-African socialist, talking about the good old days with the former prime minister and lamenting the weakness of the current democracy. He likes America, and appreciates how hard American students work—much harder than Malian ones, he

claims. He even did a Fulbright himself in Ohio. But most of all, he loves American Nalgene bottles. Why? "I don't know, he just does," Steven explains.

My tutor Lamine is much younger, somewhere around thirty, and talks about Malian culture with equal enthusiasm, but maintains a tight grip on the language lesson at hand. He's the only person I've met who can explain to me the way Bamanankan works—how to conjugate verbs, when exactly to use the different greetings, what the hell is going on with their number system. He loves to point out connections between the language and the culture. Like when saying hello in the morning, you ask, "You and the morning?" as if to ask who is winning in the daily struggle, you or the morning. Men reply, "My mom" (*n ba*) and women reply "My power" (*n ɟe*) because there is some residue of matriarchy left here despite the Muslim/French colonial patriarchy, which has mostly taken over.

Lamine and I have our lessons at the French Cultural Center's café downtown and wind up befriending one of the waiters, Ibrahim, who takes it upon himself to be my second teacher. After my first lesson, I'm not allowed to order my grapefruit soda in French anymore. It's Bamanankan only from here on out.

271

The best part of my lessons, though, just might be taking the packed *sotrama* home and stopping at Fatimata's to try out my new vocabulary on her and her kids and her husband, Mohammed. Steven and I wound up going back for lunch the day after he first met them, and now we see them just about every day since their place is right on the main road and they're always hanging out in their yard, calling people over for tea, for lunch, for shooting the shit.

On my way home from each

Bamanankan lesson, I sit down under their tree with them and they laugh when I use a proverb, or nod along as I explain more about who Steven and I are and where we come from, slowly accumulating the words to express what we're doing here. And we're learning about them too—that Fatimata sells mangoes in the hot season and peanuts during the rains, that Mohammed went to religious school and wound up in construction. With the help of my limited Bamanankan, we are becoming friends. Although I must say Steven is doing a damn fine job winning their hearts as well with an even smaller set of Bamanankan vocabulary. They seem to love his wreckless attitude toward linguistics as much as I do. "Salif, *fui*!" they tell him laughing, meaning he speaks "nothing."

"Salif *bililiba*," he says, which means simply, "Salif is really big." He picks up the middle daughter like King Kong and she screams with delight.

BAMANANKAN

Maria says that Bamanankan (also called Bambara) is the oldest language in the world and is therefore human communication in its most natural form. We are tempted to believe her because it's remarkably easy to just jump into.

For starters, as English speakers, we don't have to stretch our range of sounds too far beyond those of our native language. (A *huge* relief after studying Chinese and Arabic).

Conjugation is relatively simple as well, especially when compared to English and Romance languages.

And many words are logical compounds. For example, knowing the word for "children" (*dewn*) allows you to say all kinds of things. You can turn the word for "tree" (*jiri*) into "fruit" by saying "tree children" (*jiri dewn*). Or express "Malian people" by saying "Mali children" (*Mali dewn*).

It's also easy to cheat your way through certain vocabulary by taking the French word and adding the sound *ee* to the end. This works because when Bamanankan came about, there were no words for things like corner store (*boutique-ee*), or pen (*bic-ee*), or cell phone (*mobile-ee*).

One thing you'll never be able to cheat your way through, though, is greeting people. But that's okay, because this is something you will practice *five hundred million times a day*. In Mali it is extremely important to stop and greet people you know as you pass them. (Which is why we add twenty minutes to our commute time to go anywhere.) You ask them if they are healthy, if their family is healthy, if their children are healthy, if their husband or wife is healthy, if their parents are healthy, if . . . You can go on and on—and get a pretty good laugh if you toss an inanimate object in there along the way like Steven does. ("Is your family healthy? Is your wife healthy? Is your chair healthy? Ha ha ha!") And on top of all that, it is totally appropriate to start greeting *all over again* once you've already had a conversation. ("Yes, that game was really good last night." Pause. "So are you healthy? Your family is healthy? Your—")

The most difficult thing about Bamanankan is perhaps that it has only recently become a written language. This means handy travel phrasebooks are nonexistent as far we've seen, very few people are able to tell you how to spell something when you want to write it down so you can remember it later, and an equally small number of folks are able to explain the rules of conjugation or syntax, etc.

Finally, if you are an English speaker, and in moments of vague agreement wind up saying, "Uh-huh" or in disagreement saying, "Uh-uh," you are *in*. In fact, you might be mistaken for fluent since that's exactly what Bamanankan speakers say, too. So just keep nodding and "uh-huh"-ing until you can start the greeting process all over again. It might take hours until you are discovered.

There's a store on our corner that sells cold water, tea, sugar, cooking oil, sometimes bread. But it's more than a store, it's a *grin*. As Ousmane, Steven's French tutor, explained to him, before independence in 1960, there was an underground newspaper called *Le Grin* and groups of men would meet to have tea and talk about the revolutionary articles. The name of the newspaper has since taken on a new meaning: any group of men who hang around and have tea together.

Steven met our corner's *grin* a few days ago when he was on yet another quest for bread. He has since hung out there a few times, drinking their tea and winning their hearts by translating Akon lyrics. (Akon is a singer from Senegal who moved to America to croon about falling in love with strippers.) I am initially uncertain about joining the testosterone party, but being Salif's lady seems to get me some VIP treatment.

Slowly but surely, we're figuring out who is who, and what they do when they're not brewing tea.

The three guys we know best are Moussa, Djabati, and Borema. Moussa is a law student who likes to sleep late. We think he has a daughter but he's definitely not married. Djabati was born in Cote d'Ivoire (and is thus the best French speaker of the bunch and Steven's unofficial tutor), but his parents were originally from Mali. They've returned here to run a construction business for which Djabati is the driver. And Borema owns the store. He has two daughters, controls the music, and generally speaking, runs this show.

There's also a rotation of older men who come and sleep in the shade and a constant stream of mostly naked children sent to the store to buy things for their families. Other men come for a card game or a cup of tea and then leave. We're still figuring it all out.

It's our first day teaching in Kati. Will our classes with Malian students be that different from our classes in China?

Our first thought is yes. Things are a little more, uh . . . free-wheeling here. We ask, When does class start? Around eight. When does it end? About nine or so. And what do we teach? Anything English related.

We have seventh grade first. "I've got first day of school jitters," I tell Steven as we walk from Maria's house to the classrooms.

"You've already passed seventh grade. I think you'll be okay," Steven says. I laugh.

"I'm happy we're teaching together."

"Me too. I'm going to make you do all the singing."

The students follow us into the classroom without us having to ask, curious to see who we are. We get straight to it.

"My Malian name is Fatimata, but my English name is Casey."

"My Malian name is Salif and my English name is Steven."

"What are your names?" we ask them in unison and suddenly we are bombarded by cries of:

"I'm Akon!"

"I'm Usher!

"I'm Cinqante Cent!"

"You mean Fifty Cent?"

We never learn their Malian names. Just the English ones they have given themselves. Things are starting to feel a lot like China.

The classroom is full of happy chaos and after maybe ten minutes we've got a list of everyone on the board. It looks like this:

Shakira	J.Lo	Usher	
Sean Paul	50 Cent	Jay-Z	
Beyoncé	Nelly	Madonna	
R. Kelly	Akon	Snoop	Lucy

I guess Lucy just doesn't feel she's all that musical.

The rest of the class lives up to their names when we end with a song. It's the most enthusiastic version of "I'm a Little Teapot" I've ever heard. Our musical choice has accidentally tapped into an important part of culture here—tea. And on top of it all, the pots they use are, in fact, always really little.

We learn the Bamanankan word for teapot and doom ourselves to hardly going a day without hearing it chanted as soon as we walk in the classroom.

Barada! Barada! Barada! Barada!

Who knew "I'm a Little Teapot" could be such a hit with the likes of Beyoncé?

Living at Maria's house three days a week is kind of tiring, but fun. Tiring because we're constantly interacting with loads of people, fun because we're constantly interacting with loads of people.

Most of our downtime is spent with ten-year-old girls. There's Djenneba, whose English name is Alice—she's Maria's youngest, who was born just about when Debbie moved in. It was decided that she would be bilingual, and so she speaks nearly flawless English and often serves as our translator with the other girls. There's

Maria's niece Little Debbie, and Mamy, who may or may not be a blood relative but definitely lives here. We play hand games and Connect Four. They wrestle with Steven and he pretends to be a dinosaur trying to eat them. They braid my hair. We make lots of bad jokes and laugh at them really hard. There's something easy about hanging out with kids compared to adults. Awkward silences aren't awkward, and we can ask them questions we probably wouldn't ask grown-ups for fear of offending—like "Who does that little girl in the green dress belong to?" and "When are we ever going to eat lunch?"

Sometimes I look at Steven, crushed under a pile of them all laughing and squealing, and remember back in China when I'd have to convince him that kids wouldn't blow up into a million pieces if you interacted with them. Now look at him. The life of the ten-year-old party.

DRESS UP

Fabric in Mali is an explosion of color and pattern. Initially I think, "Who on earth thought to put pink and green and brown and red and teal and orange *and* purple all together?"

After only a few weeks, though, once I've acquired my own Malian outfits, I start thinking, "Why on earth don't *more* people put pink and green and brown and red and teal and orange and purple all together?"

Jeri is more than alarmed when I call home and make such suggestions.

But in Mali, the more color, the merrier. And as for patterns, choose anything you like! Chickens? Cell phones? Chickens on cell phones? You're bound to find it somewhere. I've seen multiple people with a bathroom pattern. Who puts a toilet on their behind? Plenty of folks, that's who. The only thing better than a toilet on the bum, though, is the president.

We happen to have arrived during a presidential campaign. During elections, in addition to TV/radio ads and posters, candidates campaign by giving away fabric bearing their face and slogan. In a country where not many people have a vehicle on which to put a bumper sticker, wearing your vote head to toe gets the job done. That said, we meet plenty of Malians who plan to vote for someone other than the face they are sporting—which just goes to show that people all around the world love free stuff.

What you wear *with* your fabric can be just as important. Women typically accessorize with a baby tied on their back, a bucket or tray of something on their head (mangoes if they are in season, maybe watermelons or peanuts), a bucket full of surprises on their arm—and if they're feeling really good, high heels and an impossibly metallic purse.

Men, on the other hand, go for a cap (mostly on Fridays to be worn to the mosque), a small charcoal stove on which to make their intensely brewed tea in intensely small teapots to drink from intensely small glasses. A straw hand fan to keep the fire going or the flies at bay is also a popular male accessory.

Dressing locally has been one of the easiest ways to make friends, get better deals on things, and generally amuse ourselves. I'm not entirely convinced these outfits are going to make it back to America so we're getting all the mileage out of them we can now.

Settling into our house is going okay. We bought a mini-fridge from that fancy supermarket, so now we can have cold water. (A SERIOUS necessity here.) And we got that gas stove and even found a wok in one of the cabinets. We hung up a few pictures, and moved some stuff around. All of Aysete's crap, however, is still in the side yard, and that other room is still packed and therefore unusable, and although Maimouna the cook left, Mohammed seems to be taking his sweet time finding a new place to live. We don't want to be too pushy since we feel for the guy—he must be sweating his life away in that hot box up on the roof. But it's been two weeks. And I don't think he's out apartment hunting with those ladies I've seen riding on the back of his moped.

And did I mention the dog is still prowling around too?

"I know this is going to sound spoiled, but I just really want to have some privacy here at home, especially since we spend the rest of the day having none at all," I say, thinking back on the three hundred times someone yelled *"Toubab!"* at me in the streets today.

"I know, I know," says Steven. "I'll go talk to him."

"No! You can't!" I grab his shoulder as he turns to leave. "Your French is too abrupt still."

"Maybe that will work to our advantage?"

Maybe it does. A week after Steven tells him something along the lines of, "You can find a new house now, yes?" Mohammed moves out. The dog, however, cannot take a hint.

The days are going faster now simply because we're being productive. Steven has a slew of sketches and watercolors; I've got over a hundred pages of field notes from observations and interviews at several schools already. And we're getting into the groove of teaching up in Kati.

Being at the front of the classroom again is, actually, surprisingly easy. We know what we're up to now (unlike showing up for our

first classes in Beijing), and best of all we have each other. It is so much easier to run a two-hour class when you've got someone with whom to share the burden. I mean joy.

What's endlessly tricky, however, is teaching English in French to students who speak Bamanankan as their first language. Especially when your coworker's French is a work in progress.

Beyond the issues of language, there are issues of discipline. In Mali, violence often is used in schools as punishment. This school (thank GOD) has an absolute nonviolence policy. But that hole hasn't been entirely filled by an alternative form of discipline, so plenty of the students can get a bit rowdy.

Early on, we figure out that the whole Good Cop/ Bad Cop act we usually save for bargaining actually does wonders in the classroom as well. But eventually we need more than that, and so we bring in the Baseball Rules. Three strikes, you're out. You get a verbal warning, then your English name goes on the board, then you're out.

Maybe baseball wasn't the best pick considering we saw how Mr. Sport, the gym teacher, taught them to play by starting with bases loaded and keeping an inning going until everyone's batted and scored.

Initially no one believes that we'll actually kick them out. By the end of our first day teaching with Baseball Rules, we have a very small class. Our second day at bat goes much better for everyone.

We're at the point where we can say we have friends now. We have the folks who we can just show up and hang out with—like Fatimata and Mohammed (who we've taken to calling Fati-Mo) and their kids, or the guys at the *grin*. Steven's been getting into a pattern of breaking up his painting time with tea breaks there. It's the kind of place where you can always count on running into at least some of your friends, which until we came here we thought only existed on TV.

The *grin* is a triple threat for Steven: buddies, French, and caffeine. Today he's getting a dose of all three as he has tea with Djabati over an informal French lesson, while the others play cards.

"Salif Keita! Where were you today?"

"I am at house to make painters."

"Salif, the artist. The grand artist! thefshrunperungrefrrshish?"

"Pardon?"

"Lesproduconewa draw me?"

"Oh! Yes, yes. I draw you. Tomorrow. Okay?"

"Eh Borema—thendxkdpoejgnlslzmxneigv gqeioymlpk kjahas! Rspeithekch sing."

"Uh—I sing?"

"Yes! Salif Keita, the famous singer. Sing, for skbrodkwiqa!"

"Oh! Yes, yes. Tomorrow also. Tomorrow I draw. Tomorrow I sing."

"Hahaha! Salif, you are strong!"

"Djabati you are strong!"

"Dqoeakdsk pjkoiu Fatimata?"

"Fatimata? She goes to school today. To school over there."

"No, no, no—Fatimata, werxcoietrboko cook food?"

"Oh, uh—no. Not now. Today I cook lunch."

"Eh!! Salif Keita! You cook lunch? Skljljkdfs jklfsdkjl woman!"

"Fatimata works and I work. We cook. Together are better."

"Ha, ha! Salif—you zxmieop psnoef dskcncit sfjhois! Hahaha-hah!"

"Haha?"

CRACKING JOKES WITH COUSINAGE

Cousinage is a nice term for endlessly making fun of people for what their names stereotypically represent. It's a HUGE part of Malian conversation, especially when you're first getting to know someone. That's partially why it's so important to have local names, even if you're just passing through. You can create instant bonds with your fellow whoevers, and join in on the national your-name-eats-beans-and-therefore-farts jokes. That's the number one joke here, I swear. Say, *"Ee bay show doon"* ("you eat beans") to anyone after learning their name and you're guaranteed to get a laugh.

Steven is a Keita, and Keitas supposedly love peanuts, and so he gets lots of peanut jokes. Keitas were also once royalty around the region, so sometimes he can pretend to make other people do things for him. And aside from the famous singer, there is a famous

soccer player named Salif Keita. All in all, Keita suits Steven awfully well since he does in fact love peanuts, and does in fact have an aristocratic profile perfect for a coin. Perhaps he will become more interested in soccer soon.

My name has a little less room for improvisation. Being named Fatimata Kanté is kind of like being named Mary Smith. Fatimata is one of, if not the most, popular girl's name in the region, derived from the name of the Muslim prophet Mohammed's favorite daughter. And Kanté just means I'm a blacksmith.

At least I get to joke that I'm doing all the hard work when Salif just sits around—which gets a surprisingly big laugh in a place where women work their butts off and plenty of men spend most of their days sitting around brewing tea. Hmm.

Teaching, as tiring as it can be, almost always leaves me with a sense of satisfaction. At the very least there's a clear beginning and end to the school day. With researching, though, I'm having a harder time defining what is satisfactory, what is enough, because I could always do *more*.

"I just don't know what the Fulbright expects," I tell Steven over evening mangoes on our roof. "I mean, I know they don't actually expect anything specific in my report but—I just can't tell what a realistic amount of research to get done is."

"That's okay," Steven says, mango juice running down his chin and onto the ground after a big bite. "It means you get to decide."

"I know that. It's just—I feel so *guilty* all the time. Like I'm not doing enough. Like I should be going to more schools, or different kinds of schools. Or I should be catching up on transcribing all my field notes. Or that I should be learning more Bamanankan so I don't have to use so much French in my interviews. But—"

"You can't worry so—"

"But I do. Because then, like—let's say I stay in to type my field notes and then you go out and hang out at the *grin*. I feel bad about not interacting with people more."

"Then you should come hang out when you feel like that."

"But I should also be maintaining really good notes so I can write some great report or something. But I don't even know what I'm working toward, you know? I don't want to do all this research and then just write some ten-page report that three people in the embassy will look at and have that be that." I throw some mango skin to the far corner of our roof.

"That's the thing about being self-employed," Steven says, scooting closer to me. "It's up to you how much you want to do. I ask myself the same questions when I'm painting up here and it's getting hotter and I'm thinking about going inside and I'm like, no, I can't go inside, it's too early, I should work more—and then I start asking myself well what am I even working toward and—"

"That's what I'm saying. We've been here a month already and I'm still not sure what the hell I'm doing this for."

"It'll come."

"It'd better." I sigh and wipe the sweat from my face, then look at Steven. I'm so glad he's here. "Have I told you today that I love you?"

"You can tell me again if you'd like."

Walking home from an afternoon of eating mangoes and bumbling through Bamanankan jokes at Fati-Mo's, we hear: "Are you guys American?" We stop dead and look around. We're used to being called out to, but not in English, and with a perfect accent, no less. Who said that?

"Over here," someone says.

Still stunned, we introduce ourselves to the young woman sitting in the chair outside of the fanciest house in our neighborhood. We've always wondered who lived behind the high walls, the gates, and the guards. "Where did you learn to speak English so well?" I ask her, noting her not-so-local-looking tank top.

"Oh, I grew up in Florida. Well, kind of. I mean, I've lived all over the world but I always went to American schools. But now I'm back here for a little while. You guys are really American? That is so exciting! This just makes me so happy, you have no idea. You have *no* idea. No one around here speaks English! Well, my

parents do a little, and when I talk to my husband on the phone back in Florida he speaks English, you know, but other than that, no. I miss it. Oh, I miss America! Mostly McDonald's. *God*, I miss McDonald's. What I would do for a Big Mac, I swear to God, I *swear* to God, I have to get drugs from the doctor when I see a commercial for it on TV! You might think I'm joking but I'm not. That's how much I miss it. But oh this is so exciting! My parents are going to be so happy to meet you, you should come in. You should meet them! Do you want to come in? It's okay if you don't have time right now, we can do it another time. As long as you're staying awhile. How long are you staying? Why don't you just come in right now. It will only take a second and they'll be so happy."

Meet Fanta.

We can't squeeze a word in to protest, so we follow her past the locked gate and high walls into her house. It's a *palace*, a mansion, a castle! By Malian standards, at least. It's absolutely crammed with stuff—replicas of the Mona Lisa, golden swords, TVs, picture frames upon pictures frames, at least four couches. . . . *And* there's a white horse in the yard, for Pete's sake! It's hard to believe that right next door to all this is Moussa's house with no plumbing and a dirt courtyard.

Fanta's parents aren't home, but we learn that they lived in Saudi Arabia for the past nineteen years, where her father was working at a bank, and they have just come back to Mali to retire. Fanta is elusive about why she's moved back here with them while her American husband is still in Florida. "I'll tell you more as we become better friends," she says as she walks us out.

"Whoa," says Steven as the gate closes behind us.

"Whoa, indeed," I agree.

ELECTIONS

We happen to be here during Mali's presidential election. With the help of Ousmane, his French tutor, Steven fills me in on Mali's political history since Indpendence.

Modibo Keita, a Pan-African socialist at heart, leads the country after independence from the French in 1960. A teacher, an intellectual, he holds on until 1968 when a military coup d'état removes him.

Moussa Traoré, an army general, leads the coup then creates a controlling police state for the next twenty-three years. His grip tightens until strangled citizens, led by students, take to the streets in 1991. Just as he is planning to bomb his own capital, he's ousted in a coup d'état.

Amadou Toumani Troaré (ATT), the commander of the parachute commandos, leads the coup and holds Moussa Traoré in a military camp (right up the block from our house!). ATT is an interim leader until free elections are held in 1992.

Alpha Oumar Konaré is president for the next ten years and (to many people's surprise given the power-hungry history of the region), in accordance with the constitution's two-term limit, holds elections in 2002 for the next president and steps down.

At this point, ATT comes back on the scene, and wins the presidency as an independent with no party. Some people think it shows his ability to transcend petty politics; others think he winds up creating greater divisions.

So right now, in 2007, ATT is up for reelection and he's facing a slew of other candidates, including, most notably:

Ibrahim Boubacar Keita (IBK), his most powerful rival, who is running on a family-values platform and *Sidibé Aminata Diallo*, the first female presidential candidate.

Election buzz is everywhere. We talk about it with the *grin* a lot and hold practice elections at school in Kati; people throw block parties in the name of their preferred candidates; the air seems full of hope to us. Look! Democracy *can* function for the good of the people even in the face of extreme poverty and illiteracy.

Or can it? We talk to Maria and Debbie about it and our understanding of this democratic government becomes more nuanced. Is it really doing much of anything to dig Mali out of this poverty? To promote education? Is ATT such a hero? Isn't it kind of strange that so many of his Ministry leaders are his high school buddies?

Everywhere we go, we see his face and his slogan: *Pour un Mali qui gagne.* For a Mali that wins. When Election Day comes and goes, ATT wins. We'll have to wait and see how the rest of Mali fares.

Steven and I try to share the burdens of living in a house like this, which often means whoever is screaming less steps up and finishes the job.

For example, Steven is the official Cockroach Killer. When they explode from secret places and scatter everywhere, Steven gets the murderous spray and goes on a much-appreciated rampage.

I'm usually the clean-behind-the-toilet and sweep-the-relentless-dust-every-day girl, but today I win double points for removing the mystery turd we find in our bathtub.

Yes, a turd. Whose? No idea.

"It's that stupid dog!" Steven gags as I pick it up out of the tub.

"But all of the doors and windows are locked. There's no way it could get in."

"Oh my GOD."

"What?! What now?"

"It's Mohammed?"

"*What?*"

"He was so pissed he had to move that he kept a key and came back for revenge."

"That is sick and absurd."

"Okay, I don't really believe that, but wouldn't that be kind of funny?"

Only two days later, we find a tiny kitten in that extra room we keep locked and conclude that we must have some kind of magical animal portal in our house. I hope we find a polar bear next so we can follow it back out of the portal into the Arctic because we are so damn sick of this heat.

"One day we'll live in a normal place," Steven says as we lay in bed sweating with our limbs spread out like we're starfish.

"Where mystery turds never appear in the bathtub?"

"And kittens never appear in locked rooms with no open windows." He kisses me on my slick forehead and puts a hand on my belly.

"I love you but I am too hot to be touched right now."

"I know," he says, and flops his arm back down on the bed. "I miss touching you, though."

"I miss it too," I say. "How do Malians make so many babies?"

"Maybe that's the upside of the rainy season?"

We laugh. Then go back to staring at the ceiling fan, willing the electricity to come back on.

Teaching in Kati is coming along nicely, but our mural projects are moving at glacial speed. In between classes and meals up here we create plans and gather painting supplies, but it's tough to execute for a handful of reasons: we can't paint until the sun has set at least a little or else we'll bake to death; Maria and Debbie are often too busy with other things to give us much direction/approval; Nanu, who was going to help us since he is the family painter, keeps disappearing; and the neighborhood kids who don't go to school love to have rock fights around us as we sketch things out.

All this seems to frustrate Steven even more than me, because I at least have my research to fall back on when I wonder what I'm doing here, sweating and shooing children. But his time in Mali lacks a stamp of official purpose other than teaching and painting in Kati three days a week, so when that doesn't go well . . .

"*Ka ta!*" Steven bellows, and the kids scatter.

"Good use of the command form," I tell him, forcing a smile.

"They'll be back in like fifteen seconds," he says. "Can you please ask Lamine how to say something like 'I will use these pencils to poke out your eyes if you don't get the hell out of here'?"

A house always feels more like a home once you host people there. So tonight we're having a little ex-pat party back in Bamako. We cook Chinese eggplant on our camping stove while we sweat and mingle. Just like any old party back home, right?

There are two other Fulbrighters, Alexandra and Chris. (There's five of us in all this year—the other two we met back at the American Club barbeque but we haven't seen much of them since then.) Alexandra's been photo-documenting Islamic scholarship out in the oh so remote town of Timbuktu. Chris's been mostly in Bamako looking at the economics of HIV/AIDS and is just about done. He's also from New York, so we bond over our mutual long-distance love of bagels.

Then there's Jenny, a Berkeley student studying abroad who's been doing her final project up at the school in Kati. And Quentin, the lone Frenchman who's been working at the school as well, doing all kinds of crazy science projects with the kids.

It would be a stretch to find us all in the same room in, say, America, but anything remotely shared goes a long way when you're this far from home.

It's nearly impossible to leave Fati-Mo's without being given giant mangoes. Even with so little—no running water, no electricity, one single room for their family of five—they are so generous. Initially, we can't decide what to give them in return. Eventually, we land upon one of our favorite things—food. For example:

Chinese eggplant (fast becoming our signature dish).

A potato sampler because we Americans have so many ways of preparing this potentially dull item.

Mango ice cream we make thanks to our freezer.

It's great to watch the bowl get passed around the yard to who-ever happens to be hanging about. Most everyone looks skeptical whenever they first taste something, then usually they all slowly come around. Mango ice cream, though, is an instant hit—until everyone experiences brain-freeze for the first time. Now that's a hard one to explain in Bamanankan to people who don't own a freezer.

This week I've decided to pull back from my in-depth interviews and take an informal survey of my neighbors about where they send their children to school and why. I ask Fanta to come along and help me, in part because Steven and I have been trying to find her translation gigs and this will be good practice, in part because she is otherwise kind of a prisoner in her house. The more we hang out with her, the more she reveals about how odd her situation is—some legal trouble, an American husband she left behind. A sudden move to Mali to live with her parents. A father who won't allow her to work and a mother who's equally housebound. It's an obviously complex situation, and Steven and I have been doing our best to be supportive while not getting too involved. Always a tricky balance.

So having Fanta help out with translations of informal interviews around the neighborhood is the best solution we've come up with so far. She won't accept payment, but at least it gets her out of the house, uses her skills, and hopefully adds a little purpose to her days that she otherwise describes as "so boring I could die."

With notebooks in hand, we head out.

Fanta: "Hahahaha!! She says of course you're researching because that's what white people love to do!"

Me: "Did she just say she sends her kids to white school? Does she mean non-religious school?"

Fanta: "Yes. She also says your husband promised to bring her a chicken back from Kati and she's still waiting."

Me: "Fanta and I are both married, thank you very much, Mr. Sidibe. Best of luck in your search for a wife."

Fanta: "She says I need to hurry up and teach you Bamanankan so you two can be regular friends."

Me: "Oh, I know . . . But, hey! I understood that!"

By the end of the day, I've learned that just about everyone would send their kids to private school if they could afford it, that most of the neighborhood already knew my and Salif's names, and that people are just as curious as Steven and I were about Fanta's life behind those high walls.

At the *grin* one day, Steven and I suggest that we all go to the neighborhood dance club this weekend and maybe hang out at our place beforehand since clubs here don't really get going until midnight at the earliest. Everyone excitedly agrees. Djabati busts a move right then and there and challenges Steven to a dance-off.

When we tell Fanta about the plan she laughs and says, "Ooooooh! Do you know what you've gotten yourselves into?" Clearly, no. "You're going to have to pay for everything!"

For the rest of the week up in Kati, we have brief bursts of panic over how many people are going to show up, if it's going to be offensive to the neighborhood to serve alcohol even if we know these men drink occasionally, if people will gawk at how big our house is, how much it will cost to get into the club, etc.

It's such a shame to waste energy worrying that can be spent dancing.

Dragging ourselves home many hours later, the boys are still joking about how Borema fell asleep on the couch before we even made it to the club and who won the dance-off as the morning call to prayer stretches across the sky.

I fall a pace behind and look at everyone in the early-morning light, laughing, and I think, *These are our friends. This is our life now.*

Part of my research includes looking at Muslim private schools called *medersa*. They have the same curriculum as secular schools except everything is taught in Modern Standard Arabic, the language in which the Koran was written, therefore the language of Islam.

So today I'm going to my first *medersa*. I'm nervous—as I always am when entering a new site—but even more so than usual. I've heard so many things about *medersa* already from the embassy people, from Maria, and from the public school teachers. Things like: *medersa* graduates are unemployable since they've learned everything in Arabic; Mali is slipping into extremist hands by sending its children to schools sponsored by the likes of Libya; and how they'll never talk to me openly since I'm a non-Muslim white woman. You know—real pep talks. So I come armed with some freshly reviewed Arabic, a mind as wide as I can open it, and my most respectful (i.e., washed and baggy) clothes.

The hum of children reading in unison resonates in the air as I enter the school grounds. I head straight to the director's office and greet the men sitting about in long robes and religious caps. "*Asalam aleykum.*" They smile. So far so good.

I spend the rest of the morning talking in a mix of Arabic, French, and Bamanankan with the secretary, who has been there for twenty years, as we wait for the director to appear and give the yay or nay for my interviews/observations. It is so refreshing to tell someone about my research and not have them say, "We don't teach Islam here." Instead it's Allah everywhere, though I notice that everyone is very defensive in pointing out that this school is not only for prayers. "Students here learn everything they learn in public school. The only difference is language."

"Of course," I say, even though I'm sure there's more to the situation that just that. I would agree aloud with anything at this point. I'm just so happy to be in a school where someone seems to immediately understand my research.

When I come back for an interview with a history teacher the next week (the director eventually showed up only to look me up and down nod indifferently) we get into more of the details. Many of the concerns I'd heard from people could be somewhat assuaged by our conversation. This school, along with five others they work with in Bamako, is not sponsored by any foreign nations imposing their values; natural science and such subjects are not curtailed in favor of strict religious interpretations, and look—here they are, intellectually engaging with me, the white devil!

On the other hand, I hear some things that *are* upsetting. For example, the assumption that everyone in Mali is Muslim so these schools are not exclusive. Sure, the vast majority are, but certainly not *all*. Most disturbing of all, though, is the language issue. I'm usually all about any kind of multilingual education, but there are several problems with learning in Arabic in Mali, among them:

—Most Malians don't speak it, so it's not a very useful or employable skill within the country (beyond teaching in *medersa*).

—There are few high-school-level *medersa*, so matriculating into the French-speaking high school and university system is difficult (if not impossible) for many of their students.

—Even outside of the working world, how does one apply knowledge learned in Arabic to the rest of life that is lived in local languages and French?

Nonetheless, I leave the interview feeling rather elated (if not daunted by how long it's going to take me type up that transcription). On my way out, I'm stopped by the gathering crowd of kids getting out for the day and the English teacher I met while touring the school. In a loud and clear voice—as if in a language video—he says in English, "Fatimata, it is nice to see you. I am Samba Traoré, do you remember me? Excellent. I wish to invite you for lunch to my home so we can converse in English and you can meet my family." I am slightly embarrassed by the crowd of gawking students we've drawn, so hurriedly I give him my number and duck out. I'm not trying to create any kind of a scene here. As friendly as the secretary and my interviewee were, I have a sneaking feeling it would be easy to overstay my welcome.

A few days later, Samba and I make plans over the phone to meet at the *mederssa* so he can introduce me to his family and practice some English. When I arrive, I greet the women selling mangoes by the door and the children playing in the courtyard, then head over to Samba's classroom. He's excited to see me and introduces me to his students. I tell him I'll just sit on the bench outside where I won't be a distraction until class is finished. A few minutes later, Samba is called downstairs and returns with someone I don't recognize, looking sullen.

"Why did you not go to the director's office when you arrived?" the man demands loudly without any introduction.

"Oh, um—" I'm embarrassed and unsure of what to say. "Please excuse me, I'm so sorry. I didn't—" But I can't get more out than that before he launches into a furious speech, reprimanding me for acting so rudely after they have helped me so much, saying that

they are not required to contribute to my research but so kindly did because I am with the American government and—eventually he starts yelling in circles. I've said I'm truly sorry and excused myself as many times as I can interject, but clearly it's not doing me any good. Initially, I'm not sure if he's mad in the why-didn't-you-greet-us-in-the-proper-Malian way that folks can be here or in that I-run-a-school-and-can't-have-strangers-wandering-around way. Then I get the awful feeling it's more like I-told-the-director-you-would-be-trouble-and-I-was-right way. So now I'm mad. And worried that I'm getting Samba in trouble. But really just mad because I don't think this jerk would be so condescending to me and yell at me like a child if I were a man.

He leaves in a huff, his robe billowing out behind him, and Samba and I are left on the bench in silence. "I am so sorry, Samba. I don't want to get you into any kind of trouble. I—"

"Don't be sorry," he says in English. "They're always sticking their noses into my business. We will leave in just a moment." I tell him I want to go down to the office and apologize to the director too. I do. Not because I'm feeling especially sorry, but because I don't want to make things worse for Samba.

There are about seven of them, sitting around in plastic chairs, including the man I interviewed the other day who now won't make eye contact with me. "I want to excuse myself again for going to Professor Traoré's classroom before coming here. I was not thinking. I'm sorry. And thank you again for helping me so much with my research." The men are either smiling or looking at the ground. I could just spit but I maintain my composure and wish peace upon them in Arabic as I turn and leave.

I soothe my anger at Samba's house drinking tea and cold sodas with his extended family and a few friends. In mostly English, he tells me all about his studies in Ghana and the United Arab Emirates, shows me photo albums from those trips and when he made the pilgrimage to Mecca, and breaks out letters from English pen pals from all around the world. He tells me again not to feel bad about what just happened, that the school has a particular way it wants to be seen—that's why I was only allowed to interview the director's son. (Ah . . .)

I joke with the women about cooking for my peanut-loving Salif Keita and how the babies here are scared to touch me because of my white skin. Slowly, the tension dissipates from my body. It's a shame there are jerks all over the world, and of course I'm going to have to interview some. But at least I can choose who I share an afternoon with in the shade of a mango tree.

PLANNING A TRIP

It's the end of May and we've been here just over two months. Some days we wake up and take comfort in feeling like we have a routine. Some days we wake up and feel like we still have *no* idea what the hell is going on. Often it's related to how satisfied we are with what we're doing. Maybe Steven just did a great watercolor series, maybe I just caught up on typing up all my field notes, or maybe we spent an extra long afternoon with Fati-Mo and the kids—that's a day when we ride the *sotrama* with a smile, knowing exactly where we're going in this crazy city. But maybe both our water and electricity are out and our eighth-graders don't remember any of the vocabulary from the week before and a taxi driver rips us off—that's a day we get into planning our trip.

In the end of June, when school gets out, we're going to take a little summer vacation. Of course, we plan on working along the

way as well—Steven can take his art on the road, I can learn bits about the schools wherever we are. Our goals for that time will be: to see as much of the country as we can, pick two more cities in which to live that will offer new aspects to my research, and *make things* for lack of a better phrase—like drawings and stories and whatever else we are inspired to do.

We mention our plan when hanging out with some other ex-pats at the one cheeseburger joint in town, including Chris, the other New Yorker Fulbrighter. His grant term finishes at the end of June and so he plans to travel then too, and so without much of a chance to think it over, our plans are suddenly merged into one group trip. Trios are often awkward, and we don't know Chris very well, but we're hoping for the best.

The murals in Kati are *finally* coming along! And we're at the point where kids can help us paint now. Most of the time, though, they just want to hang out and talk.

"Casey, are his legs always like this?"

"With all the hair? Yes."

"Ew."

"Actually I shaved today. Just this morning, but it came back already."

"What?!" They laugh hysterically, almost believing him.

Suddenly there's a commotion outside of an empty classroom nearby. A woman is yelling furiously, holding on to a sixth grade girl and the mentally disabled boy that hangs around school a lot. We have no idea what she's saying, but she's having a real go at Nanu, who obviously takes it to heart since he picks up a stick and starts hitting the captive girl and boy. It's terrible to watch. My stomach feels heavy and already I have a lump in my throat—but we're unsure of our place here and we don't even know what happened, and who are we to lecture this community about the ills of corporal punishment? What can we do?

Feeling more sick by the moment, Steven and I keep asking the students around what's happened. All we can get out of them is something about "pornography." Someone finally explains that the girl was taunting the mentally disabled boy and encouraging him to do something inappropriate to another younger girl and somehow this woman got wind of it.

By now Nanu has released the boy who's gone off running and has dragged the sobbing girl off school grounds into the empty street. He's totally lost it. Something has taken over him, something beyond a desire for justice, something absolutely raging and righteous.

"Oh my god, what do we do? We can't just watch this! We have to do something!"

"NANU!" Steven yells louder than I've ever heard him yell before and I am filled with a fierce comfort that I am with him right now.

The kids who Nanu had holding the girl let go and she collapses into the dust, her back already swollen with welts. Nanu is sweating, still clenching the plastic covered wire he was using as a whip.

"That's enough," I say in French, but it comes out in a whisper.

"That's enough," Steven repeats firmly.

"She is a *bad* girl," Nanu pants. "You are disgusting—" he says to her, and then switches to Bamanankan that is too fast and vigorous for us to follow. He shoos the children away and they scatter. The girl picks herself up and hurries off in the opposite direction. Without seeing where Nanu goes, without picking up our painting supplies, we hurry back to Maria's house.

Nanu is only allowed to work in the school office now. We could still use his help with murals, but he's been avoiding us. Understandably so. I don't know what we could all say to one another at this point. At the very least, Maria and Debbie have each said that we did the right thing, that they're glad we told them what happened.

Luckily this frightening incident came at a time when the rest of our teaching experience has been going well. We've recently been told that the ninth-graders will take a national test at the end of the school year that they need to pass in order to go to high school. There's an English section, so hopefully we'll help them secure easy points in that part, which plenty of other kids will automatically fail since they don't have access to English teachers. (Got to love standardized tests, right? Always so egalitarian.)

We give them a test from a few years ago to assess where they are right now. Going over their answers, we realize that these kids have absolutely no testing strategy. And why would they? The only other test like this they've taken was back in fifth grade to qualify for middle school. So along with English vocabulary and grammar, Steven and I do our best to teach the kids how to take a standardized test. We impart tips like, "Never leave a multiple-choice question blank because any answer you pick will have a one in four chance of being right." Neither of us has ever been big fans of standardized testing, and we both believe that the death of learning lies in teaching toward a test, but it feels good knowing that at the very least we're helping the students know more about the enemy that awaits.

At the same time, we're finding better ways to incorporate art and music into our lessons. One of our best centers around Akon's song "Mama Africa," which is all about his love for his birth continent. Going through his verse about the people who left Africa against their will in shackles becomes an opportunity to discuss slavery. It's wild how quickly the students fall into "you" and "we" talk even though clearly none of us are talking about ourselves. Having music in our lesson is a real hit though, and we plan to do it again.

During the cab ride home, Steven and I talk about how happy we are that they got so into singing the song. "I think we need to write Akon a fan letter and tell him how we used his song in a class," I say, only partially joking.

"Dear Akon, My name is Steven Weinberg and my girlfriend's name is Casey Scieszka. We are quite white, as our names might suggest. But we also go by Salif Keita and Fatimata Kanté and you know what? We love Africa too! Just like you!"

We laugh like we've really needed to.

During my security briefing at the embassy when we first arrived, I was told that the best way to deal with the Malian police was not at all. And if for some reason I did find myself in their hands, to mention that I'm with the American Embassy and I'd have a 90 percent chance they'd simply let me go.

Damn that other ten percent.

One Friday night, after a particularly long couple days in Kati (the murals are almost done!), Steven and I go out for some beers to cool down. In the taxi home, sober but tired, we look up and see a truck full of people ahead of us.

"That's got to be a police round-up," I whisper. We look at the sorry faces and feel glad we're heading home. And then the truck slows to a stop right in front of us. A policeman with a rifle gets out and walks toward our taxi. My heart starts thudding.

"*Piece d'Identité*," he says through our rolled-down window. The taxi driver takes out his Malian ID, Steven pulls out his Maryland driver's license, and I . . . realize I have nothing because I wore a dress with no pockets and didn't want to carry a bag. SHIT.

In my politest Bamanankan and French I try to explain that I'm with my husband and he is holding our money so I have no wallet and we are on our way home just up there around the corner and we work here as teachers and researchers and did I say already that I'm with the American Embassy?

The policeman gets into our taxi and tells the driver to head to the nearest precinct. That's when I call the Embassy from my cell phone and get automatically transferred to some kind of help hotline. The guy on the other end can offer us nothing more than, "Just wait it out. I got arrested in Thailand and I spent all night in jail and all the guys wanted was a bribe, so . . . yeah."

I'm still on the phone when we arrive at the station. There are dozens of men in uniform, sitting around, fully loaded, staring us down. We try to tell the driver to stop at the entrance to buy more time. The policeman yells that he must go in. Once in the dismal lot, Steven and I stay in the backseat, holding hands. I'm trying to get something more out of this hotline guy. Can't he transfer us to Post One, the marines who are on twenty-four-hour duty?

As long we don't separate, we should be okay. The men are surrounding the car, yelling at us to get out, getting increasingly louder and angrier until they finally yank us each out of the doors by the arms. I hang up. Things are escalating quickly, they're

separating us and Steven is trying to get to me but they're pushing him back and I feel so alone, so trapped, and so naked—why
didn't I wear Malian clothes tonight?

"We can go work this out inside, miss, just you and us, okay?"
someone says in a voice that causes a surge in my stomach so strong
I think I might throw up. Could this really happen?

"Think of your mothers!" I plead louder than I expected. "Think
of your sisters. Think of them, and let me stay with my husband."

Once inside, I realize I'm literally shaking with rage and fear. There are so many of these men, and they each have guns and fists the size of melons. I don't want to think about what could have happened if they took me in the back alone. But I feel safer with Steven next to me. He whispers that we're doing the right thing staying together, not making too much of a scene.

An officer says he's going to have to take down my full name. He goes through three ballpoint pens before he can finally find one that works, and then once I say it, he is visibly stunned by "Casey Marie Hansen Scieszka." Clearly he's barely literate, and since we've avoided the possible pummeling/rape situation, we've moved on to a bribe, but it's making him look like an ass as we wait it out, letter by painfully slow letter. The dark momentum that had been building up outside is losing strength in this dingy fluorescent office. The men who initially crowded the doorway are slowly losing interest and going back to their chairs under the trees. The few that stay on start getting too curious for the good of their tough façade and soon enough they're laughing when we learn their names and tell them they're no good cow-herding bean-eaters.

The head officer never betrays much emotion as he struggles through all twenty-four letters of my name. By the time he's done, we feel bold enough to ask dryly, "Okay, so how much do you want for all this?"

Six dollars. Six fucking dollars.

Steven demands a receipt.

Fifteen minutes after that, we leave the compound and pass the men who had so kindly greeted us upon our arrival.

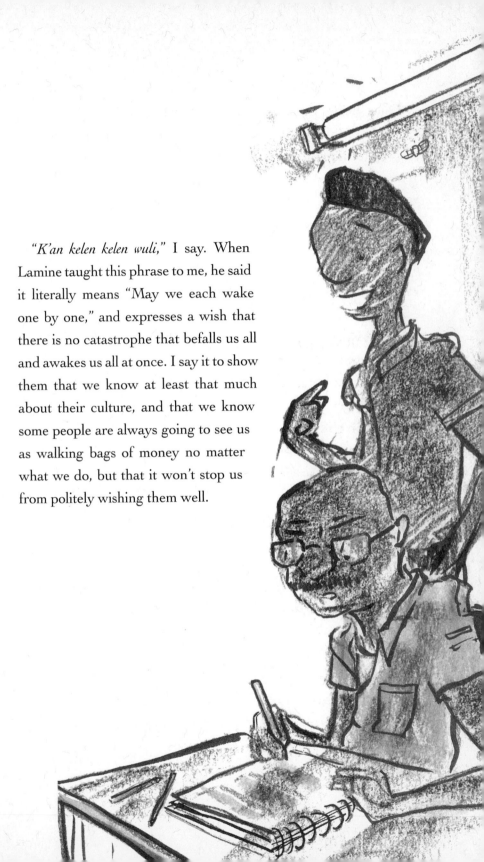

"*K'an kelen kelen wuli*," I say. When Lamine taught this phrase to me, he said it literally means "May we each wake one by one," and expresses a wish that there is no catastrophe that befalls us all and awakes us all at once. I say it to show them that we know at least that much about their culture, and that we know some people are always going to see us as walking bags of money no matter what we do, but that it won't stop us from politely wishing them well.

We come back to Kati the next week, ready to say good-bye. For our final class with the ninth-graders we read Shel Silverstein's *The Giving Tree*. Not because we think we've given so much to them that we've been stripped to sad stumps of ourselves, but because we've been thinking a lot about what it means to give in general—what our friends and neighbors and students and coworkers have been giving us, what it is that we've been giving back. After the story, we wish our students well for their final test and hand out our phone numbers so they can call us anytime to tell us how they did, or simply how they are.

Back at the house, Maria and Debbie host a little soda party for us (and whoever else happens to be hanging around) to say thank you and good-bye. And they give us our very own IEP fabric like all the other teachers wear. ("Finally!" Steven whispers to me. "We are so *in* now.")

Amidst the celebration we learn more about an incident that's been haunting the town—a conflict involving Maria's brother and son and a bunch of military guys who have them locked up now for the offense of "breaking soldiers' knuckles" as they took blows to the head. They've been trying to fight it, but it looks like they're being made an example of for not just handing over a bribe. We tell them about our night with the police and think about how lucky we were to get off for six dollars. How lucky we are that we're in the position to spend the next five weeks on the move.

It's not long before Maria can get a laugh out of everyone again, making fun of how Steven dances like a dinosaur. (He does.) Then we head over to our most recent finalized mural: La Vache Qui Rit and La Vache Qui Pleure. At Debbie's suggestion, we've taken the Laughing Cow cheese logo and reworked it to show students how sad the crying cow is when she eats plastic bags and litter, and how happy the laughing cow is when she eats mango pits and other biodegradable goodies. The kids got to do the vast majority of the painting, and despite the constant threat of paint fights breaking out, it was well worth it. We pose for a final picture in front of it and say good-bye.

And suddenly we're leaving tomorrow.

Fanta said we can store all the extra stuff we don't want to schlep around with us at her house. We, specifically our backs, are very grateful to her. She's also offered that when we return to Bamako for a few days we can stay at her house since we're giving up ours. Standing around in her kitchen (which looks like we could be back in America) we exchange all our important numbers just in case, and talk about the next five weeks. "You guys are going to be off on this crazy adventure and I'm going to be stuck here," she says. "I really might die without you. Honest to God." We've slowly learned to not take everything she says literally, but still—we *are* a bit worried about what she'll do when we're gone. Her parents have her mostly trapped in the house since she's unemployed and they don't trust her to go out alone. Our presence has allowed her a lot more freedom than usual. But she's a grown woman; her life is not our responsibility. We hug and say good-bye.

At the *grin* the guys get excited about all the places we're planning to see and add their own suggestions. Borema, the corner store owner, writes down the name of his hometown and says we have to stop and say hello to his family. Djabati says if it weren't so dangerous right now we'd have the best time of all going down to Cote d'Ivoire, his birthplace. And Moussa just keeps squeezing our hands and saying, "Ah Fatimata! Salif! We will miss you!"

We will miss them too.

Our last neighborhood stop is Fati-Mo's. They brew up some extra sweet tea and we hang around, bumbling with our Bamanankan and dancing with the kids until the sun sets. They think we're absolutely nuts to go all the way out to Timbuktu. They haven't been farther east than just outside the city limits. It's strange to think that we're about to see so much more of the country than the average Malian does.

"When you come back it will be the rainy season," says Fatimata. Mohammed makes rain noises and hand gestures just in case we didn't get it.

"Yes. Rain, come!" Steven beckons to the sky in his utilitarian Bamanankan. "Come to Djikoroni Para!" Their middle daughter La Vielle does a little rain dance and we all laugh.

"She is Salif's girlfriend," says Fatimata. "She's going to cry tomorrow when he doesn't come." She pretends to wail.

"Oh Salif will cry too," I say. "He's a very, very big baby." Even little Nana laughs for that one.

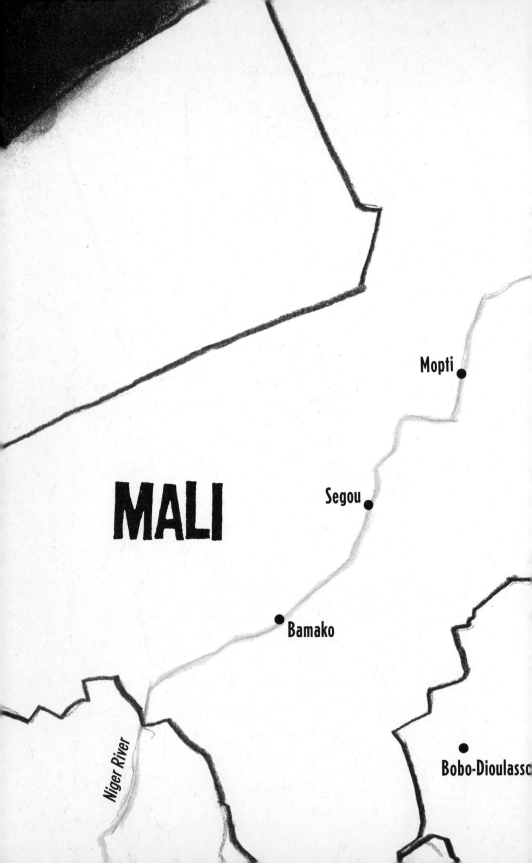

MALI

Mopti

Segou

Bamako

Niger River

Bobo-Dioulasso

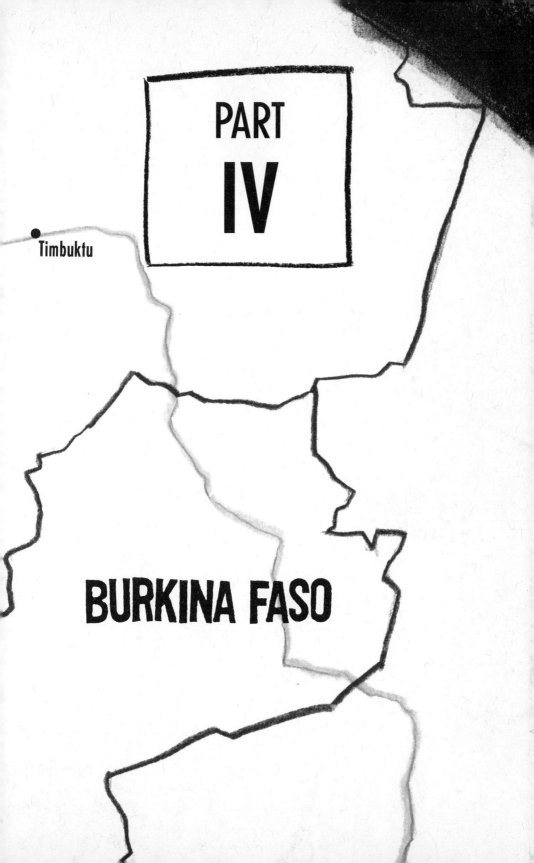

PART
IV

Timbuktu

BURKINA FASO

It's not quite seven a.m. and Steven, Chris, and I are waiting, with backpacks in tow, for the bus to load.

"Do you think the sheep are going to yell like that all the way there?"

It feels good to be on the road again! Well, metaphorically speaking, since literally the roads are a *mess*, mostly lacking pavement and/or regular maintenance. It's as hard on these ancient overloaded buses as it is on the ass. Travel slows down even more when you factor in the hitchers who ensure you never go more than ten minutes without stopping. And things get nice and cozy when they sit in the aisles with their chickens/buckets of mangoes/baby triplets. We pass the time with games of 20 Questions or making up crossword hints to things we see around us. ("Three across, hopefully it's not loaded." "Umm . . . that guy's hunting rifle?")

Once off the bus, the guides are hard to shake, especially since it's off-season and they're so desperate for work. Steven and I have

gotten pretty good at the firm "No thank you," and people will usually back off if we explain nicely in Bamanankan that we live in Bamako so we know how to buy food for ourselves, but thanks. It's rattling the hell out of Chris, though. He nearly came to blows with this one guy who followed us from the bus station as we were looking for a hotel. We were shocked by how quickly he escalated the interaction by yelling and physically threatening the guy. I suppose, as he said, he hasn't had to deal with this very much since he's black and therefore isn't usually spotted as a foreigner so quickly from afar. But he's going to have to get used to being hounded if he's going to travel with us *toubab*.

After a few days in the towns of Segou and Mopti, we find ourselves on the water in a canoelike boat called a *pinasse* heading north (but downriver) to Timbuktu. Compared to the packed buses, six people on a boat the size of, uh, a very small boat, feels quite liberating. There's Steven, Chris, and me, plus Mabo the boat owner and guide; Amadou, his twentysomething nephew; and Alasan, his ten-year-old son. Mabo seems to be a tender guy, with a real affection for his kid. Amadou is the most serious of the bunch

but no less friendly. Alasan is adorable. For whatever reason, we trust these guys immediately.

And now, for the next four days we're going to putter along the high banks of the Niger River, past village after tiny village until we cross Lake Debou and, on Chris's birthday, arrive in Timbuktu.

Mabo warned us that we might run into rain now that the wet season is beginning. He forgot to mention the dust storms.

As one looms ahead, we pull ashore to a five-house village. It's the first we've seen in maybe an hour. The goats are huddling together, the children are being called inside. A mountain range of dust clouds rolls quickly and so quietly toward us. We stand in awe until the wind picks up, at which point we're ushered into a mud house where the two small windows and one door have been barricaded with heavy rugs. We sit in the darkness, listening to the wind and animals howl. There's a young woman in here too and a boy who might be her brother. She turns on a flashlight, so harsh to our eyes already, and shines it on the blanket next to her. We watch as she lifts it to reveal a baby smaller than any I've ever seen. I imagine her giving birth in this very room. How different my entrance to the world was.

The young boy says something and she replies, shining the light in his face. Their skin is lighter than Mabo and his family's, their features sharp and slim. Whatever they're saying it sounds like an Arabic-influenced combination of Portuguese and Finnish. "Do you think that's Peul they're speaking?" I whisper to Steven.

"I have no idea," he whispers back, and then all is silent again.

We are enclosed in the apocalyptic orange clouds.

Then quite suddenly, it's passed. Hesitantly, we crawl out and see the storm moving away on the other side of the river, a silent rolling giant.

Every day we putter ahead.

"That's a *great* tree," I say.

"First thing I'm gonna do when I get home is get a blueberry bagel." Chris laughs. "Hahaha! America here I come!"

Neither Steven nor I can come up with a polite way to ask him to stop talking about what he's going to do when he gets home. The best we can do is nod along or try and redirect the conversation.

"I *really* like that tree," I say again.

Two beautiful days later we are unfortunately being towed upriver by pirates. And really, that's not so bad considering the day's earlier highlights include:

—Getting to Lake Debou only to realize it's too low to use a motor since the rains have barely started.

—Struggling to push ourselves along with hand poles under the baking sun, calculating that will add at least five more days onto our trip, which we don't have since Chris really wants to be in Timbuktu by tomorrow.

—Turning around to go back to find a ride in the last big town.

—Watching our motor fall off the boat and sink down the deepest part of the river.

Such is travel in Mali.

After working out some sort of trade with these men of the black-sailed boat that happened to be passing by, Mabo is apologetic and doing his best to hide his despair over the lost motor as he sits and watches the horizon. Steven is drawing portraits of the crew, hoping to win them over just in case they do turn out to be real pirates. Little Alasan hasn't left his side much since being given some paper and a pencil of his own to play with. I'm going back and forth between helping Amadou in the "kitchen"

(i.e., back end of the boat) and sitting up front with Mabo, putting my legs in the water, so happy to feel a breeze again. Chris is under the boat's canopy with headphones on taking practice GRE tests.

I could spend another week on the river in this boat, easily. Steven too. We've seen things we never could have from the road, like Bozo fishing villages and hippos. But Chris is running a tighter ship, so to speak. And keeping to a set itinerary is proving rather difficult in a country where things unapologetically move at their own pace. So it's been stressful for him and for us in turn. And I think his frustration is reaching a boiling point since this is the end of his time here. He's just so over it all. We are not.

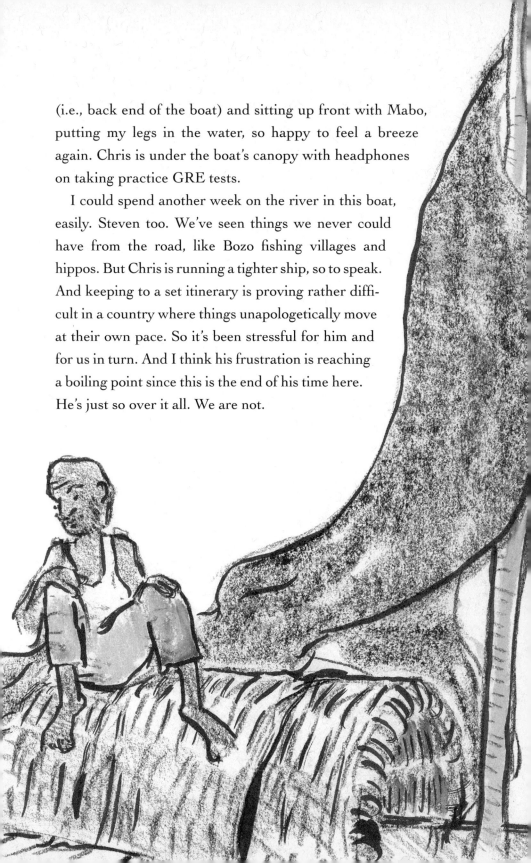

After a few hours, we pull to shore and Mabo points to a town in the distance where we can catch a ride north. He says he and Alasan will walk us there and help us negotiate if we'd like. Amadou will stay and watch the boat. Sounds good. (Well, more like the only thing we can do at this point.) Then, rather sheepishly, he asks if he can have the rest of the money we owe him.

That doesn't sit very well with Chris, who adamantly believes he owes this man nothing since the agreement was to get us to Timbuktu and he hasn't, and that in fact it's Mabo who owes us a full refund. Mabo explains that he's already spent the money we gave him on the fuel (which we used) and the food (which we ate), so he has nothing to give back to us, nothing to pay the guys who towed us, and nothing to get himself and the boys home. As Chris is alternately yelling in English about responsibility and the downfall of Africa and silently shaking his head in a rage, we try to negotiate something with a watery-eyed Mabo. Amadou has disappeared, but Alasan is watching, horrified, and our tow-guys are just outside. Mabo is mortified. Maybe he isn't running the most reliable business in Mali, but nothing is reliable here. And that's the risk you take when traveling in the third poorest country in the world.

Sure our business transaction has in some ways failed,
but our human interaction doesn't have to.

In the end, we give Mabo enough money to pay the
pirates and agree that we'll keep the rest since we're
going to have to use it to get up to Timbuktu. Mabo
tells us to come back to Mopti and find him again, that
he and Alasan will take us on the best day trip ever,
free of charge. "As friends," Mabo says to us. "Okay?"

Chris gets on the bus silently.

"Okay," Steven and I say and wave good-bye.

Someone call the Guiness Book of World Records—we've found the fattest woman alive! And hilarities of hilarities, she lives in a country where most people don't have enough to eat and she's sitting right on top of me! I mean, next to me in this 4x4 packed with no less than thirteen people.

And we thought the boat was small.

But hey, as long is this old thing holds together for the next six hours through the roadless desert, we should be in Timbuktu by tonight. Unfortunately, that won't be in time for Chris's birthday as it was yesterday. There were no more rides leaving until this

morning, so rather than celebrating on camelback with a sleep-over in the Sahara, we stayed in the rather shitty town of Douenza and made a cake (aka, crackers and cheese spread), drank champagne (aka, Seven-Up, and vodka) and had a birthday party (aka, crashed the high school graduation party held at our crappy hotel). After some very necessary drinks and laughs, we got in a few hours of sleep before waking up at the ass crack of dawn to claim our seats in the 4x4.

And what seats they are.

Off the buses, off the boat, out of this 4x4 and . . . onto a camel! Welcome to Timbuktu. These shaggy, disgruntled spit machines are certainly not what you'd call comfortable, but definitely fun. Well, at least for the first twenty minutes. Then you start getting saddle burn in all kinds of places and realize why your guides are walking.

We're here thanks to Alexandra, the fellow Fulbrighter who's been in Timbuktu for many months already. She's arranged this night out in the Sahara and I can't tell you what a relief it is to have someone else in charge of making plans.

We take a break on a dune to play some Frisbee with our guides and their friends who have magically appeared and "happen to" have jewelry for sale on them. When the boys start arm-wrestling, I sit on a dune and think about how different the southern edge of the Sahara is from the northern. Back in Morocco, the dunes of Marzuga are bright orange and as tall as city buildings and there's not a living thing in sight. Here the sand is creamy, the dunes small and partially covered in shrubs. It's beautiful, but oddly, not barren.

Then we're back on the camels as the sky turns to pink then to cool shades of blue that will be black by the time we reach the nomad camp. Chris takes a moment to call his dad from his cell phone just because he can. We all find it rather hilarious, but the guides don't care.

We arrive at a tent and see a carpet and lanterns spread out before it. Gladly, we dismount our camels and dive into a delicious meal of couscous and juicy chicken. At one point we hear a small "meow" and sure enough there's a cat that smelled dinner too. Steven is allergic so he does his best to shoo it but it just won't listen, which is what prompts one of the nomads to pick it up and chuck it like a baseball out into the dunes. (Yikes!)

After, we lounge about, digesting, talking, looking at the stars. At one point, the village leader comes over to talk to us (through a French-speaking guide) about life in the desert: sleeping in tents, getting water from wells, moving with your animals to new places where they can graze. He talks about the government's promise to build more roads to Timbuktu so rice can be brought in cheaper, and how lots of nomads around here send their children to schools in town nowadays. I find myself wondering what it is that makes people hold on to a lifestyle like this. One that is so challenged by governments and nation borders, by global warming and desertification, by the growing city whose lights we can just make out from here.

Maybe the Sahara imparts a certain stubborn toughness on all those who live in it—which could be why the cat is back and snuggling up on Steven again in no time.

TIMBUKTU:
WHAT WERE WE EXPECTING ANYWAY?

For all the hype and mystery that surrounds its name, Timbuktu the town is rather, um . . . quaint? Here's how it measures up for us after a few days:

Things we expected to find in Timbuktu and found:
   —Sand
   —Lots of donkeys
   —Plenty of camels
   —More Tuareg nomads than anywhere else
      in the country
   —Tourist-hungry guides

Things we found in Timbuktu but were not *expecting to find:*

—A reluctance from people to talk about the specifics of the ancient manuscripts that are being restored around here. (Because we're not Muslim? Because we're foreign? Because there wasn't enough time to really get into it?)

—A crazy mix of ethnicities visible in people's faces.

—A desire to come back and set up camp in August for a few months and get into the two points above.

Many bumpy hours southwest of Timbuktu, we find ourselves in Sevaré, a small town just outside of Mopti (where we first took off in the boat). It's home to many NGOs and hotels for people like us who are about to head out to Dogon Country. Dogon Country being the must-see series of cliffside villages around here, so different from the rest of Mali in just about every way.

We give ourselves a day to recover from the epic ride through the desert. Chris takes more practice GRE tests in his hotel room, Steven and I wander around town making preparations for the next three days we'll spend hiking. In the evening we reconvene with the other guests for the family-style dinner the hotel serves. There are two other people staying here who both happen to be from the States as well: a former Peace Corps volunteer now working for an NGO in the region, and a math teacher working in Ghana. It's refreshing to talk with someone other than ourselves, especially with people who have similar interests and travel experiences. We share a few laughs over transportation horror stories then somehow, maybe it's Angelina Jolie's fault, we start talking about

international and interracial adoption and things get ugly with Chris. He's rolling his eyes, tapping his fingers on the table impatiently and interrupting people only to repeat himself. And there's not much you can do once someone erects a wall around themself made of "You don't understand because you're not black." Especially when you've already agreed many times, "That's what I'm saying. I *don't* understand."

As mortified as I am to be associated with him right now, I'm relieved when Chris storms out like a child. All this building aggression wasn't about just me and Steven. For the past few days, as our conversations have shifted toward arguments, we've started to worry that it was all because of us. That we had become one of those couples who are terrible to travel with. But he argued with the guides, with bus-ticket vendors, with Alexandra, and now with these people we only just met.

Regardless of where this rage is coming from, it's not something we need to be around. And so, the next morning we head our separate ways.

This is Dogon Country. Walking, walking, walking, past grand baobab trees, down steep cliffs alongside barefoot women balancing full buckets on their heads, past clustered villages echoing with the sounds of people greeting each other in languages we've never

heard. "*Seyo! Seyo! Seyo!*" they yell, even when they've long passed one another. It's hot, but the air is clean, and it feels so good to be crossing distances with only our two feet.

Actually, we've got ten feet all together: there's me, Steven, our guide we got in touch with thanks to Alexandra, and an Italian couple who may or may not have expected to be doing this tour with other people. After feeling awkward about the possible confusion for the first ten minutes, we warm up to each other easily. I mean, how could we not—they're Italian, just like our astrologist who we met in Thailand *and* they're puppeteers. After hairdressing, puppetry is our favorite travel lie we use to spice things up.

It's a good thing they introduced themselves first.

And beyond their fascinating profession, these people are fun. We can have conversations with them about education and charity and travel and history. They don't berate the guide about anything. They don't pine for home. They're new to Mali and so full of wonder for it.

This region is so different from the rest of Mali. For one, it's the only Animist stronghold in this predominantly Muslim country—most people here believe in spirited plants and animals. The languages sound nothing like the Bamanankan we know from Bamako, or the Tamshek and Songhai and Peul we've heard on our trip so far. And these villages are isolated in a way that none other are, tucked into the shadows of cliffs pocked with small man-made caves and hugged by the desert that is slowly encroaching from the other side.

This is the "other" that people come to see. And guess what's slowly morphing life here into a photocopied version of itself? Us. Tourism. We walk around as quietly as we can, and give the elderly men we pass kola nuts as a gesture of gratitude, but still—the kids follow us, calling out, *"Ca va bidon! Ca va bon bon!"* barely greeting us before demanding water bottles or candy. On our second day of hiking, we hear drums from a village ahead and see the tops of their famous eight-feet-tall masks bobbing over the tips of the graineries—a funeral dance! No—well, yes, but it's not a real funeral. Once we get closer, a young woman on her way to a well tells our guide that a wealthy Frenchman has simply paid for the village to reenact one for him.

It's the tourism paradox—you come to see something different, you bring money that you hope will help with the community, the community uses it and starts to change because of it, but a façade of the old must be maintained in order to keep the money coming. . . .

Still, it's so damn beautiful here, and it seems

tragic that any of it should be lost. But who are we to wish stagnancy upon a place? Or is it called preservation? Does it matter what we call it when the desert creeps a mile closer every year and promises to wipe out all the sustaining life-forces here regardless of how anyone feels?

Really, though. So. Beautiful.

Aghruhhhaooooohghhhffurghaaaah . . . .

When we get back to Mopti from Dogon Country, something hits our systems. Hard. Bad water? Bad food? Bad luck? Just *bad*.

Even though it would probably do us best to just stay in one place with a bathroom very nearby, we're on the road again, heading to a town down south called Sikasso. Dogon was magical and fun and

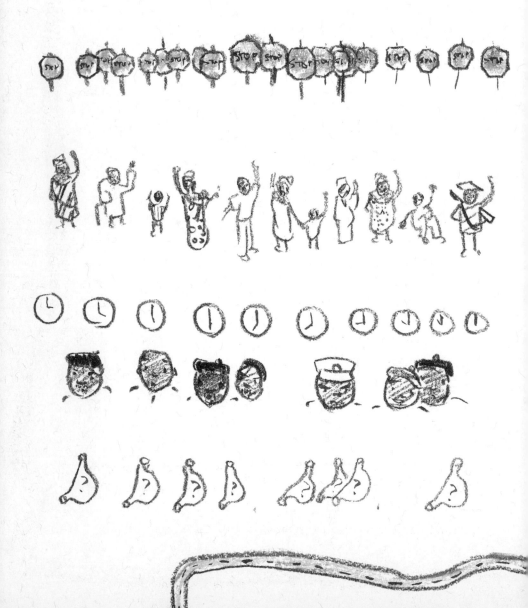

fascinating and so much more relaxed than any of our travel with Chris. But we've got more places we want to see—like southern Mali, and Burkina Faso (because it's right next door, because it has the best name in the world).

To best understand how our bus ride from Mopti to Sikasso goes, I'll give it to you in numbers:

 # of stops made (23)

 # of times we run out of gas (2)

# of hitchers (11)

# of hours on the road (15)

 # of police checkpoints (10)

 # of close calls experienced by our digestive systems (14)

And # of days needed to recover? We'll have to see.

TOP FIVE THINGS WE LOVE ABOUT BURKINA FASO

1. Its name

The only country name in the world that is possibly cooler than Burkina Faso is Burkina Faso's former name: Upper Volta. So basically, Burkina Faso wins twice. (For political history nerds: the United Nations Security Council has permanent seats and rotating seats, and Burkina Faso is on the rotating seats list. That list is alphabetical, so jumping from U to B in 1984 made more than a few countries mad about skipping. And you thought that was only in lunch lines.)

2. Its rotisserie chickens

Farther south = more green land = fatter chickens = streets lined with rotisseries = happy Steven and Casey

3. Its hippos

We only love the hippos since they were so kind as to not flip over our tiny boat, drag us to the bottom of Lake Tengrela, and drown us. Which, according to our guide, was a real possibility. So glad he told us once we were already on the water.

4. Its bicycle and moped rental spots

After that most heinous bajillion-hour bus ride, Steven and I have taken transportation matters into our own hands! I must admit, though, biking is tough, even on flat land, now that we've lost a combined forty or so pounds of muscle mass in the past few months. And riding a motorcycle through narrow, sandy roads full of stubborn and/ or oblivious children and donkeys is awfully dif-ficult as well. We've now got the tire burns to prove it. *However*, all bodily harm is out-weighed by the freedom to move at our own pace.

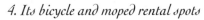

5. Its name

Seriously. It is SO COOL. Burkina, why don't you make more T-shirts with your name all over them?

Due to my fat ankle caused by severe tire burn, our desire to stop unpacking and repacking, and our interest in possibly living here for the last leg of my grant, we decide to set up camp back in the town of Segou for a week—which is EONS in *toubab* tourist time. So, simply by being recognized after a day or two of walking around, we've made some new friends—like the

Lebanese dude who works at our hotel, the guys who run a paper supply store, the man who has the best sandwich place in town, the accountant who might have an empty office we could use if we come back here. . . .

When we're not limping about, we're in our hotel room with the door open to the courtyard and the summer rain, working. Steven's taken over the desk and is making a small and precise watercolor series of a young boy who loses his mom in the color and chaos of a market. He's also finishing two pieces to give to his mom for her birthday.

I'm spread out on the bed with my field notes I've had printed and bound, coding them, trying to identify patterns and themes. I've also got my new notebook from the stationary store that I'm filling with a story.

After a month of never sleeping in the same bed for more than two nights, we are savoring this stability. This stillness. This replenishing rain. Steven goes on little adventures to find things he knows I like, like yogurt and fruit and candy. I go on little adventures to find things that I know he likes, like whiskey and peanuts and mysterious street food.

"I really want to live here after Timbuktu," Steven says, looking up from painting. "I get a good feeling about this place."

"Me too," I say, and go back to writing.

We work in content silence.

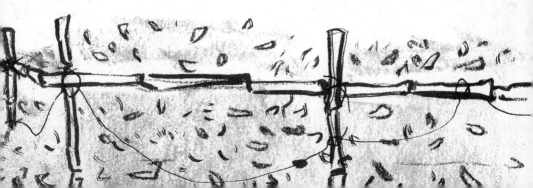

What Segou offers, beyond the possibility of more friends and more tranquility, is a life on the river. Sure our place in Bamako was only a half a mile or so away from the Niger, but it's polluted there and the banks are crowded and interrupted by heavily trafficked bridges. Here it's calm and quiet and the whole town is greener than any other city we've seen in this country. And there's a small riverside restaurant with a double-tiered patio that goes right to the water's shore where you can drink your beers, eat your peanuts, and watch the bats swoop over the wooden boats as the sun sets your day into night.

It also happens to be a fine place to celebrate Maria's phone call of good news: twenty out of our twenty-four ninth-graders passed the national exam and are going to high school next year.

Our week in Segou is done and now it's time to head back to Bamako. On the four-hour bus ride, we call Fanta to let her know what time we're getting in. "Oh, you guys are coming back today? I'm out getting my hair done but, uh, that's okay. Just call me when you're in the neighborhood." We hang up.

"She definitely has not asked her parents if we can stay like she said she did."

"Shit. I know. What do we do?"

We show up with big smiles and a liter of baobab honey and hope for the best. Her mom seems a little surprised, maybe a little dazed, but not mad. Phew. Then we go upstairs to set our bags down and hear stern, muffled voices. When Fanta returns she says something about how her dad is at his other wife's house, so her mom is mad about that. "It has nothing to do with you, I swear."

We take Fanta out to dinner at our favorite Chinese place to stay out of her mom's way. We gorge ourselves while she picks at eggplant sadly. We keep trying to tell her we don't want to cause any trouble, that we can just go to a hotel, but she insists we stay. We head back and settle in, ready to pass out.

Then we hear screaming.

When Fanta finally returns to our room, puffy-eyed, her face streaked with mascara, she says we can stay for the night but we have to leave in the early morning. We evaluate our situation. It's midnight. We have nowhere else to go with all of our shit. And not just the stuff we traveled with — but everything we brought to Mali that Fanta was kind enough to let us store here for a while. There are no hotels in the neighborhood, and Fatimata and Mohammed's place is just one room barely big enough for all of them, how could we impose?

We have no choice but to stay the night and leave before the roosters get going. At six in the morning we haul all of our stuff downstairs and into a cab that one of the family guards has hailed for us. It should be a discreet time to exit, but Borema catches sight of us as he's opening his store. I hardly notice, though, because I overdid the Chinese food last night and I'm thinking my inners might explode all over this cab any second now.

We head back to the first hotel we stayed in. Should we be surprised that it has since closed down? "Just go with it, honey," says Steven, squeezing my hand. "We've been on the run for a while — embrace this part of your Jewish identity."

"I'm only culturally Brooklyn Jewish, if that," I whimper. "And you're only half. Besides. I bet the Jews didn't have an epic case of you-know-what everywhere they went."

"You never know."

We try to check in to a somewhat nice place next to our favorite Chinese restaurant but it's full, so we wind up at an okay hotel just down the road. It doesn't really matter, though. We plan to spend most of these next two weeks before heading back to the states briefly for a wedding and some family time, outside of our hotel room, hanging out in Djikoroni Para.

After showering (and feeding me lots of Pepto and Steven lots of coffee), we head back to our neighborhood. During a happy reunion with the *grin*, Moussa invites us to his place to have some *to*. We've had this slimy millet creation before, most notably in Dogon Country where it looked and felt remarkably like mucus (maybe that's what got us so bad?), but Moussa promises his sister makes the best in the world.

From the little *to* we've tasted, she does. But even better than the *to*, is the time we spend sitting in Moussa's room, talking about how the elections turned out, his school experiences, what Timbuktu is like today compared to how it used to be. Moussa is our age, so in many ways we can relate to him easiest out of everyone. But maybe it has nothing to do with our age, just everything to do with how he understands why we get so tired here, so hot, so worried that some people see us as walking money, and so grateful and giddy that others don't. He's the friend we could bring back to America and everyone would be like, "Yeah, Moussa rocks." Because he absolutely does.

Our reunion with Fati-Mo's family is just as happy. We slip right back into our usual antics—dancing, making funny faces, enjoying peanuts instead of mangoes now that the season has turned. Suddenly an afternoon rainstorm swoops in, and fat raindrops begin to pelt us. "Come! Come!" Fatimata calls as she hurries into their house with the girls.

The rain beats down on the corrugated steel roof and we all huddle, laughing and soaked already, in our shelter. Their house is a room—a room we've never been in before since they spend most of their days near the tree and the well in their 'yard.' The room consists of two beds, two mosquito nets, and a small shelf. Fatimata moves a bucket into the middle of the floor to collect the rain. "It's the rainy season now!" she laughs, and catches some drops to playfully flick at little Nana. I take the captive moment to tell her (in my rusty Bamanankan) about our hippo adventure in Burkina. She and the girls nod along, doing their best to follow as I bumble about, "A boat in a lake. No *brbrbrbrbrbrbrrrroom*. Just [charades for pole]. Watch out! Hippos! Right here! Me and Salif! Fatimata and Salif and ten hippos! Not good."

They laugh and remind us that they'd been saying all along we should just stay in Bamako.

Back at our hotel, I realize that in the madness of our travels I've been better at taking my anti-malaria pills than my birth control. Rather than wait it out on my own, I tell Steven.

"Casey, I have to tell you something," he says in a wary tone that makes me feel instantly nervous. "I don't want you to be pregnant. At least, well—not now."

How have we gotten to this? To "not now"? I tuck myself underneath his arms and we kiss. He smiles at me in the most darling dopey way and my whole body warms.

"Yeah," I say. "For now we've got La Vielle. She should be more than enough for a while."

Steven is going back home a week before I am. The Fulbright only allows me to leave the country for two weeks, and besides, we each have some catching up to do with ourselves.

We check out of our rather dingy hotel and move my stuff into the nicer one down the road now that there is a room available. There's wi-fi and air-conditioning and a pool. In short, it's heaven. And the perfect place for me to write — because that's my main goal for this week alone. To finish that story I started in Segou. To somehow consolidate everything I've learned from my research so far into a fictional form.

After an afternoon with the *grin* and Fati-Mo ("Fatimata is going to cry without Salif!" they all say and laugh), we head to our Chinese restaurant for a last meal together. This time we bring along photos from Beijing to show our waitress friend, which she gets a real kick out of. "Ah! Beijing!" she says, and grins for each picture and choppy explanation. We order a feast to celebrate.

"It's going to be so strange," Steven says in between bites of stir-fried green beans.

"To go home after a year of being away?"

"That, and to see everyone and eat whatever we want, but . . . I was more thinking about how weird it'll be to be apart."

"I know. It's kind of crazy that we've spent at least *some* of every single day together for the entire year.

"And after a year of hardly ever seeing each other."

"Well, it looks like that's worked out now doesn't it?" He smiles.

"It certainly has." I raise my glass of beer. "To our wonderful adventure continuing, to your safe return, and a happy reunion at home."

"To all that and your story."

We cheers.

Things are different already and it's only my first day alone.

I sleep in until eleven. I eat only yogurt and vanilla cookies all day. I don't speak a word of English (until Steven calls to say that he made it home safely). Maybe three hundred more Malian men ask for my hand in marriage than usual. And I spend over five hours straight just *writing*.

After a few days, though, it's ever so clear to me how happy I am to usually have Steven somewhere near. We've developed such a great partnership for so many things, from simple bargaining to the bigger challenge of teaching. But I'm seeing how it's in so many other ways too. We've got this kind of back-and-forth with our friends here that relies upon the combination of our different kinds of humor, our individual language skills, and our general ability to play off of each other. And our different genders grant us access to different parts of life here, but together we get the best of both worlds. For example, the *grin* is a place of all men, and although I am comfortable with each of them, I still feel like I have lost my chaperone somehow. When women I don't recognize walk by I want to call out to them, "I know I'm breaking Malian gender norms here, and it's not my intention to be that white lady who thinks she can do anything. I promise!"

The upside of being a woman without a male partner has been that I've been granted more access to certain family intimacies with Fatimata and her girls. Externally visible things like helping cook lunch (something she would never let Steven do no matter how many times he asked), and less obvious things like the casual comfort of me playing jump rope games with the girls all afternoon when she goes to the market. Fatimata even breaches new topics of conversation with me—like if I plan to breastfeed my own children one day. (I say yes, which for some reason, despite all the breast-feeding that goes on around here, she finds surprising. And by the way, I'm not pregnant. Hooray!)

What benefits the most from being alone is my Bamanankan and my writing. I speak Bamanankan all day, and in just a week it improves as much as it did in my first two months here. (Immersion, immersion, immersion. Nothing better than learning languages the way we did when we were all babies.) Then once the sun sets I go back to my hotel and try to get my bearings back in English, fol-lowing behind my characters who seem to lead the way themselves until I'm too tired to go on.

There are moments when I wonder if I'd come to Mali alone I would have learned more Bamankan (certainly) or done more research (definitely) or written more stories (of course). But none of that would be worth what I have done with Salif Keita.

Having spent at least some of *every single day* together over the past year, Steven and I can't quite go cold turkey for our time apart. We talk on the phone most evenings.

"I'm still turning around to tell you things and scaring strangers," Steven says. I laugh.

"Me, too. I really confused this old lady on the *sotrama* today when I pointed out a guy's fabric that had showers all over it. Oops."

"Oh! The lady from White Lion back in Yangshuo wrote and sent pictures! She wrote all the details of exactly what kind of school stuff she put our donation toward."

"That's so cool!" I say. "Forward it to me so I can look."

"I will. I'll do that when we get off the phone." We pause.

"It's so weird to talk on the phone now," I say.

"I know. It's kind of like college. Speaking of time warps, have I told you enough that I feel like I'm in high school again? I'm sitting in my basement right now watching MTV Jams and eating a burrito."

"Oooooh," I groan. "Mexican food."

"Yeah, sorry to tease you. It's pretty great to have all this familiar food around. And coffee. Mmmmm . . ."

"I'll be there soon enough. Anyway—you were saying that you have been magically transported back to high school?"

"I *have*. And I don't like it. I just"—he thinks for a moment. "I don't know how to explain everything that happened in this past year, and most of the time I just don't want to anyway."

"That happens to everybody, though," I tell him. "Don't worry."

"I'm not really worried, it's more—I just wish—I don't know actually."

"Seriously, don't worry. Have you ever met or heard of someone who spent a year abroad then came home and was like, 'Hmm, everything feels just wonderful. It's like everyone understands what I've been through and how I want those experiences to inform my life back home!'"

"Well . . ."

"I'm only being so firm about this right now because I'm going to need you to tell me the exact same thing when I call you from Brooklyn all weirded out."

"Okay," he laughs. "But could you say it one more time so I can really remember it for you?"

My week alone in Bamako is over, Steven's week of D.C. time is done, and suddenly we're in the dappled green of northern California at my friends' Portia and Griffin's wedding. All five of the women I lived with senior year are here for this small but immensely special occasion, so not only are we celebrating that one of us has found her partner, we're also having fits of giggles and happy tears over the fact that we're all here for it together.

Along with Steven.

What a trouper. He's my date. And Alexandra's, Kate's, Julia's, and Rae's too. Except for the time he spent in Thailand with Alexandra and Kate, he's only hung out with all these girls during his few visits to Pitzer. But he's managing to fit right in. It's like they have all picked up on how comfortable Steven and I have become with each other over this past year and accept it as the group norm. And I love all of them and him for that.

The only difficult part of this is being the only unmarried couple at the wedding (and therefore being asked by every third person when *we're* planning on getting married) and having to condense our wild and formative and confusing and not-yet-finished experiences abroad into a single sound bite.

But really, it doesn't matter what we're feeling right now. Because this day is not about us. It's about our friends who are getting married and everything they are saying to each other at this moment, under these trees, in front of everyone who loves them.

After the wedding we buzz down to San Francisco quickly to see more friends, then fly back across the country to Brooklyn for a handful of days before we have to return to Mali.

Two weeks is a *really* short amount of time when there are so many people to see, so many bagels to eat, and so many amenities to enjoy. But we're cramming it all in there. And more. Today we're walking around Chinatown with my dad in search of hand-pulled noodles (We got him hooked too.).

"Maybe we should live in Chinatown when we get back," Steven says. We've started thinking about Life After Mali, if only because everyone keeps asking us about it. We're considering living in San Francisco. Doing lord knows what, but that's why we're trying not to think about it too much right now.

We can't find hand-pulled noodles anywhere. Manhattan's Chinatown has mostly southern-style restaurants. So we settle on

a place with delicious-looking ducks hanging in the window. It's no Muslim noodle joint, but by the end of the meal we're full and happy that at the very least this place has cold Tsingtao beer.

"I bet I can find a noodle place by the time you guys come back in December," my dad says. "I would happily accept that mission."

With full bellies, we walk around in search of gifts for our friends back in Bamako. Where better to find souvenirs than Chinatown, right? This is the first time Steven or I have been abroad, gone home, then returned to the same place. It's great to have friends we know who we want to find specific things for. Like school supplies for the little girls, music for the *grin*, cookies for Fanta and lots of tea varieties. . . .

It's also great to be able to stock up on things for ourselves. Stuff we've run out of (Pepto, sunscreen, hand sanitizer, water tablets) and stuff we wish we'd thought to bring the first time around (more underwear, protein bars, episodes of *Lost*, oil paints). And there's a certain element of stress that's gone too. Usually when we're getting ready to go somewhere we have only a minimal idea of what we're getting into. But now we know.

For the most part.

We overdid it last night. In every way. We went out too hard with my brother Jake, my cousin Eric, and a bunch of my childhood friends. And we fought when we got home. Drunkenly, confusingly—over what? It's hard to tell. Over everything, maybe? All the talk of marriage, of what we're going to do after Mali, of what we have and have not accomplished in the past year, what the hell we're going to do in Timbuktu, just how quick this visit had to be. And now, after a transatlantic flight, we're still hung over, puffy-eyed, and pissed, and we've got seven *more* hours to kill in the Paris airport before we fly for six *more* hours to Bamako.

"This blows," I say and consider how much trouble I would get into if I ripped off these arm rests so I can actually lay down.

Steven refolds his arms and legs. "Yes, it does."

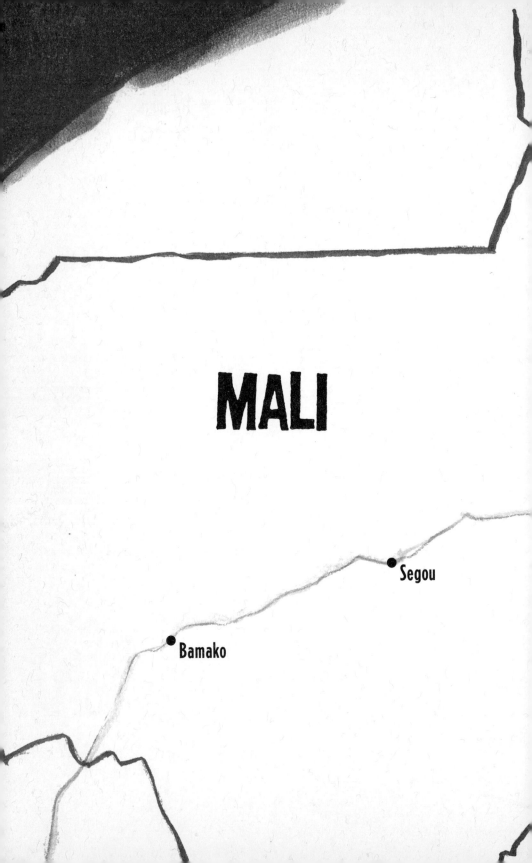

MALI

Segou

Bamako

● **Timbuktu**

PART
V

Niger River

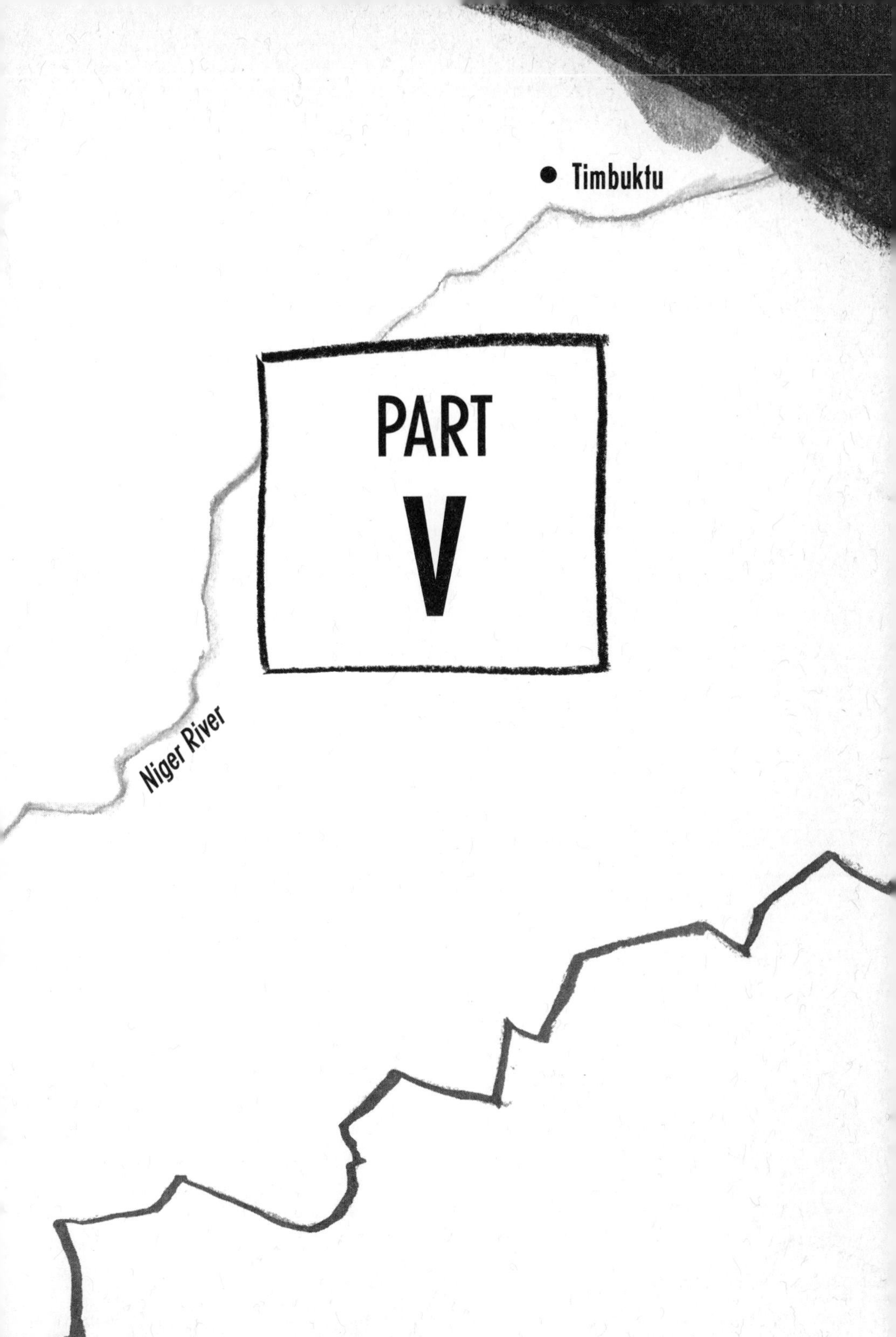

"**F**atimata! Salif!" The neighborhood kids are as happy to see us as we are to see them.

Adding to the joy of our reunions is the Santa sack full of the small goodies we've carefully picked for all our friends. Stuff like De La Soul and Bonnie Raitt cassettes for the *grin* boys to listen to while hanging out together (among many other odd picks— it's really hard to get ahold of cassettes in the U.S. nowadays!); a variety pack of tea for Mohammed so he can try something other than Malian green mint; peanut butter for Fatimata to show her the American version of peanut sauce; school supplies and Twister for their kids. We run into a few awkward encounters where people are like, "Where's my big stereo?," but for the most part everyone seems to understand that these are small gifts that represent our big gratitude.

The person who wins All-Time Best Reaction to a Gift is Nana, Fatimata and Mohammed's youngest daughter. She's already jumping and squealing with joy because we're back (and so am I— I nearly cry when she first spots us and runs halfway up the road into our arms), so I guess it's kind of easy to push her over the edge from excited to ecstatic by giving her a small stuffed hippo and, more important, a photo of herself. She screams with delight and wets herself on the spot.

As tempted as we are to stay in Bamako with the people we already know and love, we've promised ourselves we'd try to live in the ever-mysterious Timbuktu. Steven is excited to draw the city's mix of people, I'm ready to continue my research in a place that was once a thriving hub of Islamic education—we want to keep pushing ourselves to go further into what we don't know.

We decide to cut the six-day journey into one by taking a plane. A nonstop journey to Timbuktu! No buses stopping for hitchers, no boats losing their motors, no 4x4s with the world's fattest ladies. NONSTOP.

Mopti

Hah.

Halfway through the flight we start descending.

"Um, excuse me? Have we arrived in Timbuktu already?" I ask the flight attendant.

"No, no, no," she smiles. "We're stopping in Mopti."

We triple check our ticket stubs. They definitely say nonstop. Hmm. The mystery of Timbuktu begins.

Timbuktu

We haggle a jeep ride from the airport to Fondo Kati, the ancient manuscript library/guest house where we stayed with Alexandra our first time here, because it's where we'll be shacking up for the next few months. We're greeted by Hawa, the co-director of the library, which she runs with her husband Ishmail, and several of her children. We say hi to the women cooking and a young man brings us to our room. He flicks on the fluorescent light and I have a flashback to first entering our Beijing apartment. It's a little bare, but at least the walls are a bright turquoise—and I'm sure it'll feel more cozy once all of our stuff is strewn about.

The best feature of this whole set-up is that we have our very own air-conditioner! Granted it's labeled in Russian and might have been made when the U.S.S.R. was in fact still the U.S.S.R., but hey, it works.

According to our plan to hit the sand running, we set down our bags and head straight out to the streets, ready to talk to anyone. It's much like when we first moved to Djikoroni Para, with people

calling out to us, children following in our wake. Except the streets are made entirely of sand and people don't only want to say hi, they want to sell us jewelry. Which is why we're happy to run into somewhat familiar faces: Moussa and Abu, two of the Tuaregs with whom we played Frisbee in the desert. "You really came back!" Moussa says, visibly surprised. "How long will you be here?"

"Probably two months. We'll see."

"That's plenty of time to see all of Timbuktu and go out to the desert again. I am going to show you so many things!" His enthusiasm is contagious.

On the way back to our new home, we stop off at the patisserie that serves not pastries, but ice-cold beverages. On top of the joy of our easy arrival and chilled beer, our waiter—like almost no one else up here—speaks Bamanankan.

We toast: "To Timbuktu."

Our first morning, we get out of the house early (before the sun rises too high) and set off to the merchant quarter where hopefully Steven will draw a few a portraits and I will get in some informal interviews about where people go to school and why. We wish each other good luck and split off.

This neighborhood seems mostly Arab, and I've heard that the Arab community in Timbuktu is the hardest to crack. Hopefully our limited Arabic will help.

I pick a store at random. A man in an orange robe sits, fanning the charcoal for his teapot amidst the stacks of plastic buckets, heavy blankets, and other things he sells. I greet him in Arabic, which he returns, a little surprised. I tell him my name and before I can go on he asks me if I'm Muslim. I say no, and he says that Fatimata is a Muslim name.

"That's true, but it is only my Malian name."

"So you're not Muslim?"

"No," I say and try to smile.

"If you're not Muslim, that's not good," he says and kind of wags

a finger at me. So I shrug, force a smile, and walk away. At least I'm not planning on doing all my interviews in the street like this.

A few doors down, I manage to engage a handful of people—men and boys, to be precise, since there isn't a woman in sight. They tell me about how they didn't go to "French school" (meaning public school) and don't send their children there—only Koranic school, where children memorize the Koran and the sayings and practices of the Prophet. In a way this is exciting, because these are exactly the sentiments I would love to hear more about, but I'm having a hard time expressing myself in Arabic and French and I'm growing uncomfortable with the crowd that's gathering.

A man interrupts me as I'm talking to two young boys and asks if I'm Christian. When I was asked this in Morocco I answered honestly: I was raised without any religion but I take a great interest in them all, hence my current research. But instinctively, I'm uncomfortable saying that here, so I kind of nod. At that moment I notice that the man in the orange robe from the store has joined the crowd. Hiding behind the others, he starts to lecture me about how I must convert to Islam because it is the only path to salvation, to righteousness. He goes on and on, wagging that finger all the while. I wish I had the guts to tell him that's it's unfair to refuse to interact with me alone, but to then berate me in public.

Some teenagers come to my rescue and start talking to me about wanting to learn English. But I'm still uncomfortable with the way the others are staring at me, like I'm some kind of a show. So I drop the husband bomb and go off to look for my *toubab*.

I duck into the Maison des Artisans, which is essentially a place where Tuaregs sell their jewelry and leatherworks in a retail store setting so tourists will be more comfortable. I collect my bearings, and in the process get a handful more interviews with craftsmen and women, and their friends who hang around. I feel less rattled now that I've engaged in some friendly and informative conversation.

I head back out into the sun and turn down a side street Steven and I walked down yesterday. There he is, with his giant sketchbook out. "Boucoum, this is Fatimata!" he says, jumping up. My heart surges and I realize how relieved I am to see him. I can't believe Alexandra lived out here alone for so long.

Boucoum, a large man in a sweeping powder blue robe, offers

me a stool. I accept and join them in the shade. "Salif says you are doing research about religion and schools here," he says in French, pushing up his glasses that still have the 100+ sticker on the lens.

"Yes, it's true," I say. Steven is smiling in a boyish way. He loves this guy. And after only a minute I know why: it's because this man can talk about Jesus's role in the Koran, Karl Marx, and the conditions in North Korea all in one breath. Now *I* love this guy. Especially because he is holding on to the spotlight and is totally willing to include answers to my research questions in his wandering monologues. This is how I find out that he sends his two sons to Koranic school, because if he even thought about sending them to a secular school his father would roll over and die and then haunt him for the rest of his life. To his dad, attending a school like that is akin to giving Mali back to the French. "This is the African tradition," Boucoum says and laughs. Before I can ask him to clarify, he's talking about how Jimmy Carter once brought his mom to Timbuktu.

All too quickly it's time for lunch, so we make our exit. "Salif and Fatimata, come back anytime," he says and smiles. We will.

After only a week, we've built a routine: Up early, buttered bread and tea in the common room, Steven with his sketchbook in the streets, me with my notebook at the libraries or the markets or schools, back to Fondo Kati for lunch of sauced rice, typing up field notes and napping until the sun goes down a bit, and then back out into the sand streets for more drawings and interviews, a cold beverage at the patisserie, back home for sundown, type up more notes, read or watch Brazilian soap operas with the kids in the courtyard, and then go to bed.

Sometimes we have appointments too—today we have a date to interview and sketch some Tuareg teenagers named Mohammed the Magnificent and Abdul who we met a couple days ago in town. We rendezvous where we first met and they walk us to the northern part of town, the nomad quarter. We enter a courtyard and settle onto some plastic mats and are joined by another (not so magnificent?) Mohammed. They bring out a small charcoal stand and put their tiny teapot atop, fan the embers and say they are at our disposal for all of the questions we have about Tuareg life.

Clearly they're doing it up for the tourists with their turbans wrapped across their faces and their robes, the ceremonious three cups of tea. But we've been clear with them from the beginning that we're not here to buy any jewelry, so we get right into the sketching and the questions. They talk about how they go to Koranic school, how they'd like to go to French school but since they have to work they can't or their parents don't want them to, how they've never gone south to see any of the rest of Mali, how they all have a brother or a father who's done the fifty-two-day trek to Morocco to trade goods. . . .

Between the second and third cups of tea, they take out their jewelry. We explain to them again that we didn't come here to buy anything, and that we were very clear about that from the moment we met. The less magnificent Mohammed gets visibly upset. "But I'm leaving on a caravan on Friday!" he says. Yeah, right.

Suddenly, all pretenses are dropped. They take off their turbans, put away the jewelry and disintegrate into teenaged boys, asking us for cigarettes, and making jokes about how Tuareg men are very "strong" and that is why there are so many children running around. We laugh, mostly because we're relieved to not be living in some weird tourist play anymore.

Nervous that it would be easy to spend all his time at Boucoum's and meet no one else, Steven went on a mission yesterday to find some more *grins*. He met some Arab guys who teach at a *medersa* during the school year. One of them, named Hana, has agreed to give us Arabic lessons, so we're meeting him this afternoon.

At four o'clock exactly ("It is not Malian for you to be on time!" he says in French), we find him at the predesignated corner and head across town to his place. During the twenty-minute walk he tells us about himself.

He was born in Timbuktu but moved to neighboring Mauritania at the age of eight. "The *medersa* here are not strong, so in order to have a complete Arabic education you must go to a more Arab country." He says he's proud that he speaks better Arabic than most Malians, and keeps insisting that what they learn in Koranic

schools and *medersa* here is not nearly as good as what you can learn in an Arab country. A purist I suppose.

So why come back to Mali? His whole family is here and has been for five hundred years. And the civil war, which had been tearing apart the north during the early nineties has since settled down. Now he teaches Islamic history at a middle school level *medersa* and does translation and cataloguing at a manuscript library down the road from us. "But they give me almost no money. There is not enough money anywhere in this country. It's so poor," he says. It makes me wish we were paying him more than $8 an hour for the Arabic lessons, but that's the trap here—you want to help, but you don't want to set the standard that foreigners will pay twice as much as anyone else.

When we arrive at Hana's house, there's an old man with crazy eyes outside, swaying and dancing and mumbling to himself. We quickly duck into Hana's place and close the door just in time. *"El beboon,"* he says, meaning "the door" in the most formal Arabic. And so our lessons have begun.

Hana *is* totally a purist, insisting we start at the beginning with each letter of the alphabet. It's a good review, but at the pace we're going we might never get to anything new. At the very least, I get to take a good look around since I don't have to pay such close attention. His place is dismal. There are two carpets and a small foam mattress. That's it. There doesn't seem to be an excess of anything but sand out here.

After our lesson, we head to the tailor so I can get another absolutely giant outfit made. I can barely conceal my reluctance as I'm explaining the design to the tailor and he laughs and says, "Ah, Fatimata doesn't want to dress like an old woman."

"Exactly! Not in this heat. But I have to for my research, you see?" He does. He promises to make me something even Salif won't take an interest in.

On the way back, we decide to stop at the patisserie (what else are we supposed to do until dinner's ready?) and run into Hana and some of his buddies having tea on the side of the road. In Arabic we tell them that Hana is a great teacher and he smiles. One of the guys speaks a little English and, after asking where we're from, asks me if I thought 9/11 was "nice."

"No," I say. "It wasn't nice. It was hard and horrible for everyone."

I see Hana kind of hit the guy on the arm. The guy says something about how the attacks did a lot for

Bush's job security or something like that—he's trying to qualify what he just said. I'm having a hard time following, though, because his English is choppy and he's kind of laughing, all while I'm trying to catch more of Hana's reaction in my peripheral vision. Instead of creating more of a conflict, I try to switch the focus to all of us agreeing that none of us are big fans of Bush's policies. I finally catch a glimpse of Hana giving his friend the evil eye—not the kind that says "Not around them" but the kind that says "You shouldn't ever be saying that." Then suddenly it's the call to prayer and they all must leave.

"Well," says Steven as we pick a table at the patisserie. "I guess that explains the bin Laden stickers we saw in the market."

"But does it? What the hell? I wonder if people out here even realize what that symbolizes to us. Then again, how many people who wear Mao shirts know anything about what he actually did?"

"So true," says Steven. We shake it off, decide it was a fluke encounter, and drink our beer.

After nearly two weeks of the unbearable heat and sand in the city, we decide to try the unbearable heat and sand in the desert. We've done this before, of course, but that doesn't stop us from looking forward to a cool and peaceful night of connecting with infinity under the stars.

Everyone here seems to have a camel or a cousin who has a camel or a camel that has a cousin, and a really "authentic" nomad camp not too far away that we can go visit for a "very good price." We break a lot of hearts when we choose to go with our new friend Mohammed who I met our second day here at the Maison des Artisans.

After a few hours of riding camels into the sunset, we arrive at the camp, which is nothing more than a tent and a few mats. Once the sun sets and we can't draw or take notes anymore, we have some dinner (rice with an extra sandy kick) and then lay down under the full moon.

And that is when the party begins. The donkey party that is.

Apparently, when donkeys are well fed and find themselves all together under the light of a full moon they like to hee-haw for hours until you think you really can't take it anymore. Then they will hee-haw louder and more desperately so you will start to think maybe something is wrong, like maybe there's going to be an earthquake or a UFO landing—can't animals sense these things before

people can? The light of the moon will
make you feel like you are trying to
sleep in the dentist chair and it will
not cool down. Not until the last
hour of the night, just as the sun
is rising and Mohammed is telling you it's time to have breakfast
and get back on the camels.

You will take the stale bread
and look over at the neighboring camp and see a
man stumble out of
his tent over to a
donkey, which he
promptly *thwacks*
with a big stick. And
although you are gener-
ally against the donkey
abuse you see so often
in this country, this
time you think to
yourself, *He totally
deserved that.*

Back in town, we shower off the sand and, despite getting maybe an hour of sleep last night, I get ready to interview the director of another ancient manuscript library. I put on the special potato sack our tailor made me and do my best to make my boy-short hair look less like a faux-hawk with a tail and more like, um, some kind of traditional female haircut. (Did I mention I chopped it all off before heading to the desert in a fit of heat-induced rage?)

When I get there, I'm greeted by the head librarian, a somewhat elderly man I've interacted with the few other times I've come in here to interview people. His family has origins in the south, so he speaks some Bamanankan and kindly calls me "Bamanan *muso*" (*muso* meaning woman). Eventually, the director is ready to see me.

I'm very excited to interview the top of the food chain here, because every time I try to get someone to go into any depth about the manuscripts, they resist. Initially I thought that resistance was coming from a reluctance to talk to a white woman about something intellectual or religious. But lately I've been getting the feeling it's because they don't actually do much in the way of analysis here.

During the interview, we cover a range of topics:

On Timbuktu's future "We need to return to the time of glory." (As in, re-create life in Timbuktu as it was five hundred years ago.)

On globalization "International influences are mixing with our strong traditions now and women are wearing jeans just like prostitutes!"

On modernization "People are watching immoral shows on television and can use the Internet to look for all kinds of things—like porno!"

On his wife calling twice during the interview "She is jealous I am with a beautiful woman."

To be fair, he touched upon much more mild topics, as well, but these are the sentences that bounce around my head as I walk home, furious that I had to sit there and silently scribble away and just listen.

Or did I? What is my role here anyway? Passive collector of information? Researcher hoping to help? A person who doesn't like the idea that if I stay quiet, these men will believe I agree with them?

After one particularly unsuccessful morning drawing in a new part of town (the kids were too rowdy, the men actually too still from boredom to make an interesting portrait), Steven decides to head home for lunch early. On the way, he comes across a group of men sitting in front of one of the many moped parts shops in town.

"*Wandasubu*," says Steven, greeting them with the one Songhai phrase we've learned from the kids at Fondo Kati.

"Eh!" they say in unison—the high-pitched Malian sound of surprise—and call him over.

"What's your name?"

"Salif Keita."

"Eh!" they laugh again. No one in Timbuktu has been this pleased by either of us having a Malian name. Honestly, we've kind of missed it.

They insist he stay for the next pot of tea, and over the strong brew they talk about what it is he's doing here and what it is they all do (moped repair, teacher, radio D.J.). Eventually, the teacher says he wants Steven to give him a non-Malian name.

"Something great. Like Bill Clinton. Or Albert Einstein. Yes, I want a scientist."

"Okay . . ." says Steven, trying to think. "Your name is Hans Bethe!" To the best of his French abilities, he explains how Bethe, after helping the Manhattan Project create the atom bomb, spent much of his life advocating nuclear arms control around the world.

"Yes! My name is Hans Bethe!" says the teacher.

Steven is pleased with the choice too. "They both have good, solid heads," he says to me later at home.

"Oh, yeah? I hope you told him that. 'Hey new friend, you have a solid head. Really, it's a compliment!' "

We're constantly thinking about the balance of taking and giving here. Is research a form of taking? Is asking people to sit for a portrait a form of taking? Can we make it all a form of giving without involving money? And what about with new friends? What do they expect to get from us when they give?

For example, our pal Moussa. He's been nothing but friendly since we met him during our first trip, and on our first day here, when he was so happy to see us. But for some reason we can't stop feeling suspicious and anxious. He's taking us to a "divorce party" this afternoon, and as intrigued as we are by what that could possibly be, we're afraid of so many things that come with it—will we have to pay him? Will we be interrupting something that is private? Will this be more of a tourist show than a normal, local event anyway?

Even after the party is winding down, we're still not sure. At the very least, we now know what a divorce party is: after separating from her husband, a Tuareg woman wears only simple clothes, no jewelry and no make up for three months. She then has a reentry to society party where a musician called a *griot* sings about her, and she can show off her beauty once again in bright whites, big jewelry, and smoky eyes. After this process, she is considered by many to be even more desirable than a never-married virgin.

As the party dwindles down we've got kids swarming around us and an old lady asking for money and the divorcée seems to have disappeared without us getting a chance to say thank you or goodbye. It's incredibly awkward.

On the walk back to town we think about Dogon, and how these rituals seem somehow sullied by us witnessing them. It's like I tell Steven: "I mean, I wouldn't want a bunch of Malians I didn't know crashing *my* divorce party."

As for Moussa's intentions, we're still not sure. He dropped us off at the party, went somewhere else, then came at the end to pick us up and walk us back to town. But why? There's something about this town that holds us back from fully trusting it.

We walk home slowly, stepping around the green lakes of puddles that have accumulated from the rain, past all the kids who want to shake our hands or get money. As we near the Arab merchant quarter we see a crowd in the streets, watching and laughing at the crazy man we've seen around Hana's place. He's half-dancing and swaying in the middle of the road. We try to cross the street to avoid him but he follows us and almost gets hit by a car. I let out a sound of surprise and he starts kicking sand at us, getting closer as we hurry to pass by. The men all around are laughing and roar even louder once he grabs me by the arm and I have to

yank myself free and run away. Steven ushers me down the rest of the road quickly as the men continue to laugh. My chest is exploding and I feel betrayed and vulnerable and unwelcome.

After having some Sprites at the patisserie to calm down, we are followed home by a group of about fifteen little boys. Although they're no older than ten, they're still menacing, talking aggressively in our direction, demanding money, going so far as to hit me on the butt and try to untie my traditional wrap skirt. We try to shoo them, but it doesn't work, and neither does ignoring them. We pass a group of men watching a soccer game on TV outside and they yell at the small gang, with hands raised to hit them, and they scatter—only to return half a block later. The kids know that while those men would hit them and tell their families, we never will. So they start throwing sand at us and once we are "safe" inside the doors of the Fondo Kati compound they even throw *rocks* at us over the wall. A small one hits me in the head and a big one misses Steven by hardly five inches. We rush outside but by now they are only laughing shadows disappearing down the road.

We are powerless in so many ways. These kids don't know us, we don't know them. And we'll never be able to talk to them about the absurdity of throwing rocks, not just at us, but at a library that is doing its best to restore their town's place in the world. And we don't have enough friends around who can help us. We feel angry, unwelcome, and unsafe. Is it because we're white? Because we're not Muslim? Because we don't give them money?

Back in bed I have to agree when Steven says, "Today was hard."

I've been sleeping in more. Or at least trying to. And we've been having to force ourselves out the door and into the streets. It would be so easy to just hole up in here, away from the sun and the sand and the people who stare at us (and throw rocks). But wouldn't we kick ourselves for wasting our time out here in the magical, mystical Timbuktu?

You have to give yourself a break sometimes, though. If you don't properly recharge and take moments to privately process everything that's going on around you, you'll burn out quickly. In China it was easy to do that—we had a nice place to live, work was done at the end of the school day, people didn't stare at us, and it wasn't one hundred degrees every day. Here it's a little harder to find relief—that's why we have an evening beer at the patisserie, why we carefully ration our consumption of Starbursts and *Lost* episodes.

Better than that, though, is the relief we find in

returning to our favorite pastime we've been neglecting for a while: making silly things together.

Feeling confused and rejected by this absurd town, we create an absurd story about a guy named Idirssa who runs Constructive Construction. It's a construction company that keeps taking on projects from international NGOs that aren't actually related to buildings or bridges or roads—at least not in any kind of literal way. Requests for metaphorical "paths" to employment and "bridges" between traditional and modern education turn Timbuktu into a construction site that in the end might not be so constructive. It's not supposed to be a heavy-handed critique of international aid, but . . . Okay, so maybe we have passed a few judgments, but at this point we're having fun finally being able to turn our observations of the absurd and tragic and complex into something that makes us laugh.

Never before has an afternoon gone by so quickly here.

Our other favorite indoor pastime is eating the children who live here too. I mean pretending to eat them. Although I'm not so sure the littlest ones always remember that it's a joke. Steven does look especially hungry with that hot sauce in hand.

RAMADAN

Ramadan is the month-long Muslim holiday of fasting, which cele-brates the time the Prophet Mohammed received his first rev-elations from Allah. From sunup to sundown, nothing is to cross the threshold of your lips (except if you are ill, prepubescent, elderly, on the road, or menstruating). In some places, like Morocco and Egypt, the harsh day is balanced (some might even say overwhelmed) by a festive night of food, street life, and the best TV programs of the year. Here in Timbuktu, we have yet to find that post-sundown party. Changes we are witnessing/participating in include:

No food No more street snacks. Good-bye delicious fried dough balls.

No water Must hide our water bottles in our bags now and take stealthy sips in empty alleys to avoid sinking into dehydrated aggression like everyone else.

No tea A very boring *grin*. Now these guys really have nothing to do.

More religious dress People appear to float down the streets in large robes.

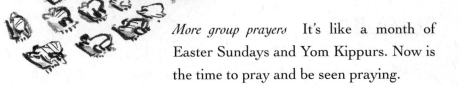

More group prayers It's like a month of Easter Sundays and Yom Kippurs. Now is the time to pray and be seen praying.

Higher racial tension "The blacks aren't real Muslims. Most of them don't even fast," says one of the guys at Hana's *grin*. Uh-oh.

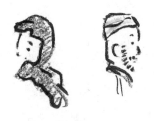

Less male-female interaction All thoughts of sex are forbidden during the day. (As is the act, of course.) Some men avoid the temptation by avoiding interactions with women altogether. Especially non-Muslim women. Not so great for interview-based research.

Fewer willing models In Islam, it's forbidden to visually depict the Prophet Mohammed. Some people take this to the level of forbidding any kind of portraits. Not a great turn for Steven's project.

Different TV programs Prime-time television is no longer dedicated to our beloved Brazilian soap opera. Hours of Koranic chanting and religious sermons will have to do.

I opened a bank account here when we arrived, since there are no ATMs in Timbuktu. I'm starting to wish I'd gone with the old cash-under-the-mattress system, though, because every time I come to get money, I spend half an hour deflecting the director's advances. And what's worse than listening to his clichéd compliments (My eyes are like oceans? *Really?*) is having to hold my tongue. With most men here who overstep my boundaries, I can give a firm no and at the very least throw the word *husband* around. But I'm scared of committing some kind of bank fraud, so I tell the director I'm not married. Which was kind of stupid, for the obvious reason that now he thinks I'm fair game and we told everyone else in town that we *are* married.

Why even lie about being married in the first place? In Mali, unwed couples don't live together. And sure, our friends here don't expect us to change everything about ourselves and become just like they are, but they do expect us to respect certain values, certain norms. And I want to. (Most of the time.) I didn't come here to convert people to my way of life. I came here to experience something new. But I'm seriously worried I might lose my shit on the next dude who thinks it's okay to tell me

about how pretty my goddamn hair is when I'm trying to complete a professional transaction.

So I bring Steven along with me to the bank today. As I'm doing bank business, Steven is sketching and hanging out with the director's underlings. Including Jeune Afrique, a man nicknamed after the French language newsmagazine because he's such an avid radio news listener. There was once an article written about him in *Jeune Afrique*, much to his pleasure. He keeps photocopies of it in his desk and hands them out regularly. Steven is finding him hilarious and entertaining. And Jeune Afrique takes a liking to Steven as well, which is why he keeps introducing him to everyone who comes into the bank.

"Salif, come, come—you two must meet," he says, ushering over a young woman dressed to the nines. "Salif lives at Fondo Kati and, Salif, you know the director Ishmail, right? This is Ishamail's—" He stops himself mid-sentence. After fumbling around for a moment he lands on "sister."

Hmm. On the walk home, Steven tells me about the odd exchange.

"They're hiding something from us," I say.

"Well, definitely," Steven agrees. "You should have seen her face. She was like 'No, no, no, don't say it!' Do you think it's Ishamail's mistress or—"

"Or second wife."

We walk for a few silent paces in the sand.

"Why would they lie to us?" Steven finally asks.

"The same reasons we lie to them," I tell him.

"Well . . . we don't even know who she really is."

"No, we don't," I say. "But—either way I think now we know we can't ask."

"I don't want to draw right now," Steven says and sets down his sketchbook on the table of the common room. We've just finished our usual breakfast of instant coffee and day-old bread with butter.

"Then don't," I say, and pick back up my collection of Virginia Woolf short stories.

"But if I don't go out and draw, then I'm just going to feel all cooped up in here."

It's our usual paradox. Sometimes we want to take a day off, but what does that even mean? What would we do?

"Why don't you finish that Gengis Khan book? I thought you were getting into that."

"Yeah," he says and pulls on his hair so it stands straight up. "But I just can't sit still right now."

"Then you should leave, because that's what you want—"

"But maybe I don't want to draw all day. You know? I thought that would be great but it's kind of boring. Does that mean—"

"No, don't even say it. It doesn't mean it's not what you really want to do. It's just like me with writing. We want to do these things in comfortable places. Or places where we can at least take a break and not fear that we'll bore ourselves to death."

"Yeah maybe, but—that doesn't change this. I can't just stay in here. I feel trapped."

"Then go," I say. I can feel the fingers of guilt grabbing on to my ankles. If he goes out, then I'll feel bad for staying in and not getting any interviews done today and—

"Okay. I'm going to go. Maybe I'll just go get a coffee at one of the hotels in town. Even though

I already had coffee. No—I'll go to the moped shop *grin*. But I don't know. Ever since Ramadan started it's really boring. What's a *grin* without tea?"

"Well, I don't know. Just get a coffee from one of the hotels then."

"Yeah, okay."

"Okay," I say and open my book. "The sunscreen is still in my side bag from yesterday." Then he's gone.

I try to write in the common room. Then in our bedroom with the air conditioner on.

And then I cry. It doesn't really make me feel better, but at least it exhausts me enough to fall asleep.

The next day we go around town sketching and interviewing together. There was no need to make up since there was no fight. But we each feel in need of some extra support lately.

On the way home for lunch, we come upon some children playing in stagnant water who want to shake our hands. I go for the double-handed wave high above my head. Steven says, "*Ca va.* Um, no thank you."

"No thank you?" the older of the two asks.

"Good-bye!" I try with a big smile and pull on Steven to keep walking.

"That is not proper," the younger one says, getting in front of us. "You *must* take my hand."

"We said hello and we are in a hurry to get home. See you next time!" I try again.

"You must take my hand. It is the African way," says the other, now blocking our path too.

"Steven, just shake their hands," I say in English.

"Did you see that muck they were playing in?"

"What are you saying? Are you a racist?" the older one asks, visibly mad. "You will be in trouble when I yell to everyone. Do you want that? That is the military camp." He points to the compound where there are a few men in uniform with guns hanging around. Men we try to avoid.

"Please don't yell," I say. "Listen. Wait one moment and listen to us. Since we are *toubab*, everywhere we go children want to shake our hands, to touch us. Lots and lots and lots of children every day. But it makes us sick. Our bodies are different from yours because we did not grow up here and so, sometimes we are sick from that."

"Yes, it's that," says Steven, nodding along.

"Do you not like Africa?" asks the big one, still riled up.

"No, we like Africa very much," I say in my calmest voice even though I'm starting to feel like yelling too. "That is why we live here. Did you know that? We live at the library down the road and we have many friends in town and when we see them we shake their hands every time."

"Yes, but only our friends," Steven adds firmly.

"So if you two are our friends, we will shake your hands too. So what is your name?"

"My name is Mustapha," smiles the big one.

"My name is Brahim," says the little.

"Hello. My name is Fatimata," I say and extend my hand. We all shake.

"My name is Salif," Steven does the same.

"Look! Now we are friends, and when we see you in the streets we will stop and say hi. Do you understand?"

"Yes, yes, I understand," says Mustapha. "Ha! Fatimata and Salif!" They laugh and go back to playing in the muck.

We trudge the rest of the way back to Fondo Kati.

DRINKING BUDDIES

I spend the day writing a demented story about a manuscript restorer who is haunted by the ghosts of Timbuktu's tragic past, while Steven paints watercolors of ducks pecking away the faces of bored men. Symbolic expressions of how we're feeling recently? Maybe. So what better way to drown it all than with booze, right?

We head out to the only hotel in town we haven't been to yet and find some watery, overpriced whiskey and—who are these other American guys? We do a comparison between Steven and the one closest to us:

fake Ray Bans

faux-hawk

generally "skin and bones" physique

three-day shadow

partial Malian outfit

flimsy flip-flops

speaking French and bits of Arabic, Bamanankan, and Songhai

sporty sunglasses

America-themed tattoos

buzz cut

generally "enormous and ripped" physique

short shorts

desert camouflage T-shirt

speaking English

    All clues point to . . . U.S. Army personnel. But what are they *doing* here? We've heard rumors that the Malian government allows U.S. troops to do desert training for Iraq in these parts. Maybe it's true. Maybe that's why, unlike nearly all the other *toubab* travelers we cross paths with, they haven't talked to us, or even waved. We're in completely different worlds.

    But we're all drinking whiskey.

We've got a date with Mohammed's camels this afternoon. Steven's going to draw them (he's tired of asking people to sit still), and I'm going to tag along (I'm tired of asking people to talk to me).

Since we're early, we wind up at an empty hotel at the desert's edge, talking to a staff member named Malik. "The Libyans bought this hotel," he tells us. "They're going to knock it down soon and make it twice the size. It will even have a swimming pool. They're buying everything in Mali. But they're so racist, like all the Arabs here, you know? That makes it very difficult to work with them, but we do, because a job is a job and there aren't very many here in Mali. Truly, though, they are very racist. They think they are the only real Muslims in the world. But like I said, very good at business." He interrupts his surprisingly frank monologue to ask us if we are looking for a room, what we're doing out here. We tell him about our camel date. "Ah, the Tuaregs and their camels. They spend all their time walking around town looking for tourists, hassling them, and never thinking about what it feels like to be followed like that. All for jewelry!"

"Well, at least this guy doesn't sell jewelry," I say.

"What's his name?" asks Malik.

"Mohammed."

"Of course!" he says, and we all laugh. We make plans to return another day before heading off for our camel date. I feel refreshed in a way that I haven't since . . . since I don't know when. It's been a long time since someone has spoken with such openness and sympathy. I've been feeling so misunderstood and isolated lately. Which, I believe, is why I unexpectedly burst into tears this morning. Again.

We head off to the edge of the desert to wait.

I float on the feeling of being understood for as long as I can. And then, sitting behind a bush to avoid the setting sun as we wait with Mohammed for his brother and the camels to arrive, I float a little further until I arrive at Timbuktu blankness. It's kind of like the really bored, sad, and unmotivated cousin of Buddhist meditation; there are no thoughts, just emptiness, but instead of that feeling of pristine connection to the oneness of everything, it feels like, well, nothing.

I look at Steven, following the nearby goats around to draw them until his camel models come. Watching his subjects more than his paper—just like we're taught to do in art class. He looks content. Happy even.

When Mohammed's brother finally arrives with the camels, he explains that they

did not have their legs tied together last night and had therefore wandered farther than usual. Steven gets straight to drawing them and I go back to staring at the bush. Eventually Mohammed breaks the silence by asking me to buy him four goats. "Two of my wives have died, Fatimata, and I am scared I will die too and my children will have nothing. But with goats they will at least have milk and something to eat or sell. Buy me two goats. Or four."

I've already filled today's crying quota, so instead of getting sad about being treated like a human ATM, I tell him I'll talk with my husband about it and try to force a smile. Then go back to feeling nothing.

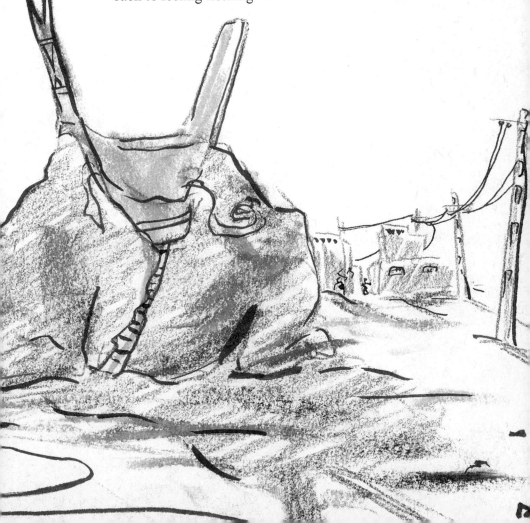

I head out to the cyber café this morning to connect with the world outside of Timbuktu. After the usual trek in the sand, I arrive soaked through with sweat. I feel better after reading a few e-mails, but annoyed by how slow the connection is, how my flash drive isn't working. My electromagnetic field kicks into overdrive and my computer fizzes out and crashes. Just then Steven arrives. "I'm heading back to hide in a book until lunch," I say and squeeze him on the shoulder. I want to hug him but I can't here.

When he returns to our cool cave an hour later he says he has some news. In the *New York Times* there was an article about rebels shooting at a U.S. Army plane that was doing food drops in the desert just east of here.

It's time to leave.

Or is it? I can't tell if either of us has accomplished much of anything in the month we've been here, if leaving would be copping

out, if staying would be unnecessarily dangerous. After another lunch of rice with tomato sauce we lay about the common room and talk. Steven is reluctant to go. I can tell he worries that leaving early would be taking the easy way out of a challenge. "But it would be selfish of me to say we have to stay because of my portrait project," he says.

"As selfish as it is for me to say we have to leave because I'm sad." We sit silently as the air conditioner hums. "But it would be stupid to stay, right? If we were having the time of our lives and getting all kinds of crazy work done, then maybe it would be worth the risk but I just . . . I just don't think it's worth it. The people at the embassy would probably flip their shit if they even knew we were still here and . . . Do you think you would actually collect that much more material in the next month? Or would it be kind of more of the same?"

"It's hard to say," Steven begins. "Even if I was going to get more portraits done I wouldn't be happy doing it if you were miserable the whole time."

"I don't want all this to be put on me."

"No, no—I didn't mean it like that. I think . . . I think we should probably go. Like you said, it's probably just not worth the risk. I mean, we've seen all those military guys around. Who knows if something is going on that we don't even know about and—"

"That's what I'm saying. Let's just—let's just go."

We wait for the afternoon to come. I feel better. Not free yet. But better. I watch Steven digesting our decision. I don't want to disappoint him.

But I have to go. We have to go.

Once the sun has lowered in the sky we head over to a hotel to find out about getting out of town. The idea is to simply fast forward our plan and move to Segou as soon as possible, as opposed to a month from now. And instead of taking a plane back to Bamako, or the nightmarish combo of 4x4s and buses, we'll take one of the big river boats. I imagine the calm of being back on the Niger.

From the hotel, we're directed to the official government-sponsored Tourist Bureau where we meet Baba. He's very formal, very friendly, but not exactly full of helpful information. He says one of the two passenger boats just passed Timbuktu and is on its way to the town of Gao right now but should be back in a few days.

We head back to the hotel where we first asked about boat schedules and have a soda on the terrace. Steven has a tonic, I have a Fanta Fiesta—things we never order. It's a silly example, but we're already feeling different, not trapped by the routines we have formed around ourselves. We talk to the waiter for a bit and he shows us some books about Mali. "I will look at anything to distract myself during Ramadan," he laughs. Then we quietly watch the streets from above. Life looks normal. Even once the

sun sets and the call to prayer is ringing out, people are still sitting in the wire chairs by their mopeds, walking in the street. It's not at all like the rush and hustle then swift silence that we experienced during this holiday in Morocco. Eventually some men form rows to pray together and a line of begging children grows in front of a man giving out food, but it's all at the classic Malian speed. Not speedy at all.

"I think we're going to surprise ourselves with how much we've done once we leave this town," Steven says on the walk home. "I really do."

We're meeting up with Moussa today—our friend who took us to the divorce party. He takes us to his house—two rooms with plastic mats and a small courtyard with a nomad tent in it. We sit down in one of the rooms and he turns on a standing fan then starts to make tea with a small charcoal stove like everyone has. As the tea brews, we talk. About how he gets hives from fasting and therefore doesn't, about his brother who sells jewelry in Segou, about the American military guys in town who request knives not jewelry, about how many people speak Spanish in America, about the cost of health care. I feel more and more like I'm talking to a friend, like I can tell him what I really think about things. I can tell Steven does, too.

The only thing looming over our time together is this "question" Moussa has for us that he's been referring to for a few days but hasn't come out and asked yet. Finally he brings it up. I breathe deeply. Please don't have this be about money; please don't have this be about goats. "Fatimata, Salif, I want to make sure you want to come to the desert with me," he says.

He's talking about a five-day trip to his cousin's town we've had in the works for a week now. Immediately I say yes, because we would *love* to get out of this city with him, to see an actual nomad village, to wake up and go to sleep in the Sahara for five days straight. But of course we can't now. It would be outrageously stupid of us to do with everything that's going on. But we can't tell him that we have to leave yet—we haven't even told anyone at Fondo Kati—so we can't say anything. I really don't want him to waste his time, though, so I am very firm about telling him to not make any specific arrangements yet since we are still unsure of the dates. I promise myself that when the time comes I will give him a full explanation.

At one point, two of his friends stop by. Of course, they want to sell us jewelry. Steven and I keep insisting we're not interested right now while Moussa quietly tends to the tea. We're kind of annoyed, but not as much as they are. They all but stomp out.

We stick around for a little longer, talking about what it means to be fat in different cultures, what we studied in college, and how weird professional sports are. When it's time for lunch, he walks us back to the main part of town. When we get to the Arab merchant quarter he cuts through a herd of goats toward a side road. As I'm thinking about what an idiot I feel like for ever doubting his intentions he says, "I don't like that street. Bad business happens there, trust me." I tell him about the crazy guy who grabbed me and how everyone laughed. "That's not right," he says, shaking his head. After a moment of silence he continues, "I'm sorry for my friends who came. I told them they could come to talk if they wanted, but only to talk. I was very clear about you two not wanting to look at jewelry. But, you know."

We know. And we're so damn happy he knows too.

It's time to tell everyone at Fondo Kati we're leaving. "We have some sad news," I say to Hawa in the courtyard. I'm nervous.

"You are leaving," says Hawa.

"Yes, it's true. With everything going on in the desert right now—"

"I understand. Truly I do. Right now things are peaceful, but at any moment something could happen. It wasn't always like this, you know," she says with a sigh. I nod along. Steven starts playing with Abawe, her little daughter, who just can't get enough of him. "Since 1991, everything has been okay. A few incidents here or there, but we could live peacefully. Now, for the past year—the air is changing. We do our best to live a normal life, all of us, all of us who have nothing to do with the conflict. But we live in fear, always wondering if tomorrow there will be fire and bombs in the streets. It can drive you insane."

"I know, I know. It's such a shame. Such a terrible thing. You have been so kind to us, really. Thank you for everything."

"Oh, it's no problem, truly. The children love you. Just look." Steven is holding Abawe upside down. "She is crazy for him."

"Look—he is crazy for her, too!"

We go inside and pack our things, then head back out and say a million good-byes all around town and tell people that if the situation settles down before the end of November we will come back. (Something we only half believe ourselves.) And if not in November, one day in the future, even if it's many years from now. People's overall reactions mirror the way they act when you've been sitting around for three hours with them and finally you have to go. "What? *Already?*" they say, and you want to ask, "What do you mean 'already'?"

During the good-byes around town, we decide to have a soda break with Malik, the employee out at the Libyan hotel on the edge of the desert. The other day we had an interview/drawing date with him and again and he opened up so instantly.

His reaction now is much like Hawa's, "Yes, you should go. You know we used to be able to sleep outside. But now you never know what will happen. You never know what people are capable of."

He swats at a large bug. "Those things will kill you, by the way, if they land in your food or your drink."

"Oh my god, we never knew," I say, scooting away.

"They *kill* you?" Steven asks as it lands between our glasses.

"I know," Malik says and shakes his head. "Here, there is danger every-where."

The next morning we're officially on the road again, standing in front of the boat upon which we will spend the next five days. Engines are growling, animals are groaning, people are yelling. The floodlights from the boat illuminate a teeming chaos of things loading and unloading, bottlenecking at the single narrow ramp. It's a fucking mess.

We are happy to have two escorts: Baba from the Tourist Bureau who has brought us our tickets, and Amadou, our Bamanankan-speaking waiter-friend from the patisserie who happens to also be taking the boat tonight. We're going to bunk up with him in a four-bed cabin and hope no one else takes the last bed so we can leave our stuff in the room without worrying about it.

The two men push on board with us and we step over crying children and frantic goats and elderly folk sleeping, until we reach an empty room. We turn on the lights and a swarm of moths and bugs start hovering around the low lamp on the ceiling. I catch a quick glimpse of two bunk beds and note that there are no openable windows before we flick the light off again.

"Oh boy," I laugh and wipe sweat from my eyes with my forearm.

"I call top bunk?" Steven says wearily. "Or bottom? Maybe just a new bed altogether?"

There is no escape.

It's only our second morning and already I have cabin fever. The days are hot, the nights are worse. This is *nothing* like the peace and tranquility of our other boat ride. As the sun gets higher in the sky, the slivers of shade get smaller and the people and the animals more restless. Wannabe guides are trolling the decks and can't seem to take a hint.

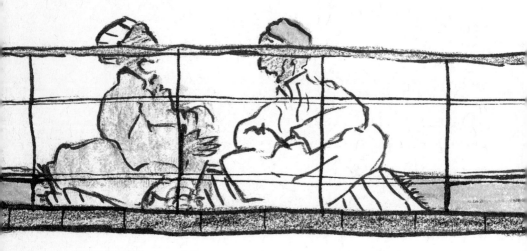

This whole setup leaves a lot of time for brooding. And no amount of journal writing can exorcise the feeling that I'm wasting time. On this boat, in Timbuktu—in Mali really.

As I've been telling Steven, I think what I really miss is variety. It's like everything is the same here. That was the sense of doom that was taking over me in Timbuktu. I didn't want to get up for a new day because I felt certain it would be just like the last. Is that the same melancholy that has taken over that whole city? Is that what Steven was capturing in everyone's faces?

The worst part is I'm totally doing this to myself. *I* applied to come here, *I* decided what my project would be. No one is forcing me to do anything. Then again that whole process began two whole years ago.

When I'm pouting, Steven is drawing. He's pretty burnt out from sketching in the streets, but drawing is his only escape. Not that people are leaving him alone. He keeps attracting a crowd.

And when he asks people to not hover over him or to give him a little space, everyone just comes closer. It's suffocating, even to watch.

Soon enough we'll have some space of our own. Just a few more days now. In the meantime, we'll do our best to entertain ourselves drawing up our own silly tarot cards, elaborating on our Constructive Construction story. We try to laugh. Or at least not lose our minds.

Our third day on board, we're called over to the kitchen. Something about our tickets. Amadou, our bunk buddy, comes with us. The man behind the counter doesn't even return our greetings. "Are these your tickets?" he demands.

"Yes."

"Is your name Maimouna Kanté?"

"My Malian name is Fatimata Kanté, but I have a different English name."

"So you are not Maimouna Kanté?"

"Well, I am—does it say that on the ticket? I think my friend forgot my Malian name. He was confused." I hadn't even noticed we had names on our tickets.

"Is that Salif Keita?" He points to Steven now. I explain that, like me, he has an English name and a Malian name then ask him as politely as I can muster what the problem is.

"The problem?! The problem is you are not who you say you are!" He waves his finger in my face. "You have someone else's tickets. This is fraud! Do you act like this back in Europe? Do you lie about who you are?"

"Sir, I'm not trying to lie. We bought these tickets from someone at the government's tourism office back in Timbuktu and—"

"Listen to me. You cannot come here and lie like this. This is fraud! This is illegal and I know you know it. You know how to read, don't you?"

"*Yes*, I can read." I feel like smacking his sweaty face. I look at Steven and I can tell this French conversation is moving too fast for him but he's pissed too nonetheless.

"Then you knew that you had someone else's ticket but you didn't care."

"No—those *are* our tickets, we paid for them—like I said we got them from the government tourism office. A man who—"

"You are lying!"

"No, I'm not! Please, sir, just listen for a moment—"

"No, *you* listen!"

"She's sorry," Amadou butts in. "You are right, she understands." He gives me a pleading look.

"I understand what you are saying, but it's not true," I say as calmly as I can manage. "Do you understand what *I* am saying? What else were we supposed to do? We went to the *official* office. These are tickets from your *government* and—"

"You have to pay for your own tickets or you get off the boat."

"These *are* our tickets. That's what I'm saying. And we are not going to pay twice just because we are *toubab*!"

"You would not behave like this in Europe," he says, wagging that finger again. I could tell him that in Europe, where I am *not* from, they have this craaaazy system where people's tickets are checked *before* they board a boat to the middle of nowhere. But instead I ask to see the captain. Amadou tries to apologize on my behalf again, driving me to be even more firm about not acting sorry at all.

"The captain will tell you the same thing. You must pay or we'll leave you in the next village." An option we just might have to take him up on.

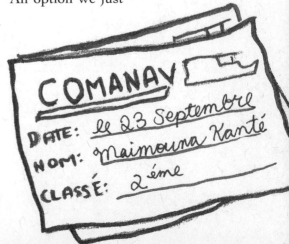

COMANAV

DATE: le 23 Septembre

NOM: Maimouna Kanté

CLASSÉ: 2ème

Lucky for us the captain has more sense than his first mate, and after talking to Baba on the phone, he decides that we can stay without paying more. "Next time be more careful," he says.

Next time. Right.

The next day, we're still on the boat. Still moving at the speed of a mostly dead reptile. Still stopping in every tiny town.

"This is going to take hours."

"Whose cows are those anyway?"

"I don't know. But do you think they had to buy tickets for them?"

"Hah. Right—I'd like one for Daisy and another for Old Bessie and—"

"Oh my god!"

"Holy shit! It just fell right in!"

"We are never going to make it to Segou."

Day five. We start slugging from our secret whiskey stash and talk about how hot it is, about how dirty we are, about what the population explosion will do to Mali. . . .

"You're such a sad drinker now," Steven says. "I don't like it."

"Hey—I don't like it either," I say, and feel even sadder. And kind of mad, too. It's like back in Thailand when he didn't like me being sick. "It's not like I'm doing this to torture you," I say, holding back the tears. "I just want to go home and get the fuck out of here."

"Look, I think Segou's going to be really great. We can get a place to live, and hopefully we can rent that studio space from the accountant in town and—"

"I know, I know, but I'm just so *sick* of talking to people about Islam and pretending I believe in God, and it's just so damn *sad* to sit in schools and do observations and look at all those kids and know that most of them won't be able to get a job even if they try. I just—"

"It's hard, I know. Your project is really hard," he sighs and rubs my hand with his. "But you've done so much already. You have hundreds of pages of field notes!"

"Right, but for what?"

"It's okay if you don't know exactly what right now. You'll figure something out. That's what this time in Segou is going to be for. Hey Virginia Woolf, you'll have a room of your own!" I don't even smile. He runs a hand over his head. "I don't like it when you talk like this. We are our own bosses. We can do whatever we want."

"But I *can't*! I can't go home. If this was just any regular job I would quit in a second."

"I don't know what to tell you. I'm not so happy either right now."

"I just want to get off this fucking boat already. I feel so trapped. Am I just a sad person now? What's happened to me? I never felt like this China."

"Because things were never this shitty in China."

"It's true. It was all 'la la la! We finally get to live together! La la la! Let's eat some more delicious food for a penny!' "

"Look, we have just *one* more day of this, and then we'll be in Segou. We won't even have to leave our hotel room for a week if we don't want to."

My chest tightens. "But then I'll just feel *guilty* for not—"

"I—" he starts, but can't seem to come up with anything else. I try to wipe a tear discreetly and look at the black water.

We should arrive in Segou tomorrow. Lots of the people and the crying babies and the bah-ing goats got off in Mopti (where during a brief walk on shore we ran into Amadou from our first Niger River ride!) so the boat is a little quieter now. Still hot as all hell, but quieter.

There's a rainstorm somewhere in the distance, so the lavender clouds are lighting up in brief flashes. I'm watching the riverbank roll by slowly. It's mostly arid land dotted with five-house villages every once in a while.

Then we pass the tree.

It's the same tree that we saw from our tiny boat with

Mabo—that ride, that whole trip, it was another transition. This is an omen! And a good one, too; the tree is filled with birds happily chatting and fluffing their feathers. It's a host to so much life in an otherwise empty place.

I watch it until I can no longer make it out in the darkened sky.

"Did you see the tree?" I ask Steven later on. Maybe he missed it. Maybe he didn't remember it.

"I did," he says and grins. "It seems like a good omen, doesn't it?"

"That's just what I was thinking," I say and put my head on his shoulder.

PART
VI

This is me writing, this is Steven painting. We've been living in the town of Segou for two months now, absurdly enough, at a radio station.

That office above the stationery store was already taken when we arrived, and we couldn't find any places to live that weren't empty concrete villas twenty minutes out of town. That's how we wound up renting two offices here at the radio station. One for working, one for living.

In a way, it's kind of dreamy—the impossibly short commute, private studios of our own where we can just write and paint. And in a way it's kind of a nightmare—there's no kitchen, our bathroom is the public bathroom, there's no privacy, the hundred-degree heat gets trapped in the concrete, the bus station is right below us. . . .

The plan has been to use this time to process Timbuktu, to process all eight months we've spent in Mali, and make

something of it. "Make" being a purposefully vague term here. Steven is making paintings from the sketches he drew in Timbuktu; he's making stencils of donkeys; he's making illustrations for a children's book about China that he was hired to do. I'm "making" more research and a final report for the American Embassy/USAID/Fulbright/Malian Ministry of Education/whoever else I can convince to read it. I'm making more fictional stories, and sometimes I'm just making bags for my friends out of all the crazy fabrics from here. Together we've been making our Constructive Construction story and other book proposals we hope will come to life once we're back in the States.

On good days, this all feels like enough. On tough days, we have a hard time answering when we ask ourselves, "What are we still doing here?"

The *biggest* question we face every day, though, is actually, "What the hell does Mali's future look like?" The longer we live here, the more we worry about it. The population explosion, unrest in the north, desertification, dependence on unsustainable foreign aid, education woes up the wazoo, a giant unemployment problem . . .

We don't want to leave Mali after nine months and feel like all we did was take, take, take. Then again, how pompous is it to think that we can "help"? Or tragic and shortsighted to think that we can't?

The more you think about it, the more confusing and paralyzing it is. Take this example: Mali used to have a *very* high infant mortality rate partially due to babies dying from malaria. The solution to that seemed obvious enough—distribute free (internationally provided) mosquito nets to mothers with young children. That was done and *voila*, thousands more babies live past their fifth birthday. A great success! Except . . . women are still giving birth to about seven babies each even though most of them are surviving thanks to the nets (along with other advances, of course). This means that there's been a *giant* population explosion, which is now straining the country's resources and leaving too many people unemployed. So does that mean you *don't* give out mosquito nets? That you don't

want those babies to survive? No way! But . . . what do you do? Promote birth control? How? By handing out condoms like mosquito nets? What happens when people refuse them because they say that Allah says "be fruitful and multiply"?

What Steven and I return to again and again when we talk about all this is that it seems as if some of the aid work in Mali lacks long-term sustainability, institutional memory, and local input. I say, "some" NOT "all," because there are *plenty* of people doing awe-inspiring work that's changing lives for the better for the long haul. People like the folks of this Segou-based NGO that we just found out about called Mali-Enjeu, which trains Koranic students in employable skills alongside their traditional religious education. Or Maria and Debbie with their school and teacher training/curriculum development. These operations are homegrown solutions with long-term vision and great institutional memory/accountability.

Which is exactly why we jump on board with both of them and ask, "How can our skill set help your operation accomplish its goals?"

We spend many an hour talking about this. Usually at hotel patio cafés, surrounded by begging Koranic students.

With Mali Enjeu, identifying our useful skills is simple enough. We speak English and can relate to the mind of a tourist, so we design a poster that asks visitors not to give money to begging Koranic students (which might be taken from them by their *marabout* and teaches them that begging is sustainable) but *rather*, to donate to Mali-Enjeu. Much like the signs for White Lion that caught our eye back in Yangshuo, China, we specify exactly what the money can go toward. Five dollars' worth of soap, ten dollars' worth of books, a hundred dollars for a water filtration system . . . Like this, we can help other people help other people.

With Maria and Debbie's Institute for Popular Education, we've already used our English skills by teaching and our visual art skills by making the murals. But

we keep wondering if there is something else we can do with them that's even more long-term.

One afternoon, as I start moaning about how my short stories are never going to serve any purpose, Steven is hit by a bolt of genius: my stories can be used in schools. We can hire Lamine (my language tutor) to translate the one that's set in Bamako and Kati into Bamanankan and it can be used by Maria and Debbie's Institute as local language material. *Voila*. The research that I funneled into a fictional form can become an educational tool.

During all my classroom observations, it pained me to watch kids memorize verb charts in French or Arabic and then whisper and giggle to each other in whatever other languages they *really* speak. I kept asking myself, what would it mean to learn in one language and live in another?

I'm obviously not the first one to think about all this, as there are even laws about how many hours in the classroom must be taught in the local languages. BUT: hardly anyone is enforcing it, the vast majority of new teachers aren't being trained for it, *and* there simply aren't enough materials written in these languages to be used.

That's where IEP comes in—training teachers in local language curriculum along with developing and distributing local language books. Steven's and my part will be the creation of a new text (with illustrations, of course!) as well as the funding for printing. Between our friends and family, we can certainly raise enough money to print a thousand books. This could even be the start of a more long-term partnership.

We leave the café downright giddy with hope.

Part of what has spurred all this thinking about what our role here will amount to, beyond the fact that our time in Mali is wrapping up, is that tourist season has begun. (There's a direct correlation between the increase in visitors and decrease in temperature. And, by the way, never before has eighty degrees felt so chilly.) It's great, because now the guides have other people to harass; it's not so great because now prices for everything have gone up. (Coffee is twice as much? Come ON.) It throws us back into our ever-returning identity dilemma—are we long-term tourists? Temporary residents? Honorary locals?

Overall, our unusual role in this town allows us to pop in and out of lots of different social circles. We can hang with the radio *grin*, we can befriend the Lebanese who run a hotel and supermarket, we can party with the Peace Corps Volunteers, we can be peers with local artists, we can share tips with tourists. . . . It's great to have such a variety of pals to bounce back and forth between. But honestly, sometimes it feels like having a big group of friends but no *best* friend we can really confide in. Usually we try not to dwell about who we miss back home, but today we allow ourselves to be sentimental because it's Thanksgiving.

For our feast, we're having a spread of everything from the States that we could find at the Lebanese supermarket. It's *just* like we do it at home! With the exception of the turkey, the stuffing, the cranberry sauce, the pumpkin pie, the extended family . . .

Nearing the end of our feast, Moussa from Djikoroni Para calls. "I'm coming to Segou tomorrow to visit you!" he says. In the spirit of thanks and giving, I tell him he is more than welcome to stay with us as long as he wants. Steven and I toast another round to him. Then another to Mali. And another to Beijing. And another to Brooklyn. And another to Bethesda. And . . . wake up really dry-mouthed and hung over with our mosquito netting on top of us like a blanket. My phone rings again. It's Moussa.

"Fatimata! I'm here!"

So I'm not going to lie—Steven and I were a little nervous about what we would do with Moussa all day for however many days he planned on staying. (The Koran says that as a Muslim you are required to host even a stranger for three days—does the line blur for Muslim friends of non-Muslims?) Apparently we forgot that the average Malian dude is quite content to spend much of the day simply hanging out with a pot of tea and some friends.

Moussa's never been to Segou before. Most locals don't travel the country much at all; we've seen more of Mali than nearly all of our friends who were born and raised here. So it's great to be walking around with him and hear him say, "Oh Fatimata, Salif—this is the spot!" again and again. He likes this town, he likes our quiet life here.

It's also refreshing to show someone what we've each been working on. It can get a little like airplane air with me and Steven—we make things and show them to each other then make more things and show them to each other, again and again.

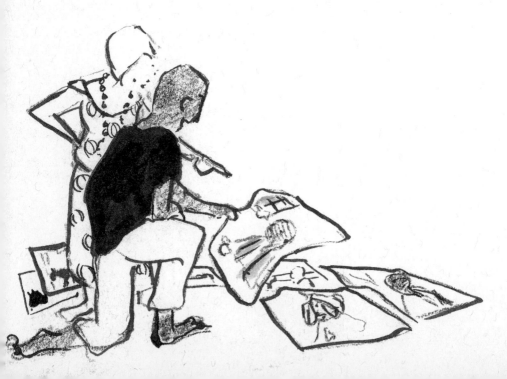

"Salif, these are very strong," Moussa says, looking at all of Steven's paintings spread out on the floor. He takes a swig of orange soda. "Look at you—*le grand artiste*!"

Our conversation turns toward the future—what will Steven do with these paintings? What are we going to do once we're back in the States? We tell him that really, we don't know. We ask about what he plans to get into after he finishes law school.

"I don't know what kind of law I want to practice. I still have another year, so I don't have to decide. But I can either go into private or public, and I think I want to do public."

"What does that mean? Can you serve more people like that?"

"Yes, I think so," he says. "I can work on international issues, with the poor, or work with the government. Maybe there's not as much money for me but—" He laughs and shrugs. "I don't know yet."

"That's great!" says Steven, enthusiastically popping peanuts. "The world needs more people like you, Moussa! Mali needs you!"

"Salif Keita!" laughs Moussa and puts his hand out for a shake. "You are too kind. Really. Both of you."

And for the first time in a while I want to cry because I'm so happy.

Moussa the good Muslim is leaving this afternoon after three days here. Steven promised a fellow painter he met in town, a French guy named Adrien, that he would check out his studio, so Moussa and I have the morning together. I take him down to the river again since he liked it so much and it also happens to be my favorite place in Segou to simply sit. Maybe it's the water. In a landlocked place like Mali, a river feels like the right place to be.

"Ah Fatimata, this is the good life," he says, closing his eyes and breathing in dramatically.

"It is, it is," I say. "It smells much better than Bamako, no?" We laugh. I don't want to leave it at this, though. It wouldn't be entirely true. This is not *always* the good life for me. "Sometimes it's hard here," I say. "Even though Salif and I are doing what we love, and have all these friends, we still miss America."

"Yes, America. Your families must miss you very much."

"Yeah. It's been a long time now. We left back in August 2006."

He sings the classic sound of Malian surprise: "Eh!"

"I know!" I say. "And it sounds kind of stupid, but it's difficult to be a *toubab* here because so many people look at us and talk to us and—"

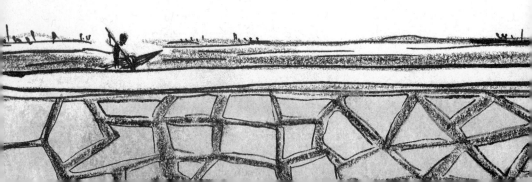

"Ask for money—"

"Yes! Exactly! Sometimes I feel like I'm a human bank, you know? But—"

"That's not right," he says, shaking his head. "That's not fair."

"Yeah, but I understand why some people think that. The children especially. And with my research, learning about the Koranic students—I don't know how to tell them 'I don't want to give you money because I don't think that helps the big picture for you.' It sounds mean but—" I look at his face and he is nodding along intently. I feel understood, and that's all I want. I don't want to dwell on it; I don't even want to say another word about any of it anymore. I just needed that look from someone other than Steven. From a Malian friend. "There are lots of people I miss in America and parts of my life there, but Salif and I are going to miss our friends in Mali, too, you know."

"That's why you will come back," he replies with absolute certainty.

Three weeks later, we're on our way back to Bamako.

The only advantage of living next to the bus station this whole time is that it's sinfully easy to move out and catch a ride.

After just three hours, we're at the final checkpoint before the capital. All the buses are idling, and the ladies selling food are yelling, and everyone's talking loudly and listening to ring tones on their phones—but it doesn't bother us. The weather has finally cooled down and we can appreciate anything and everything. We are leaving Mali in just six days.

We head up to Kati for a day, as planned, to finish the final details of our murals and figure out what else we need to do for this new book project. It's great to see everyone again, to have them laugh at us for having gone all the way out to Timbuktu. ("We *told* you there's even less out there than here!") We wind up disappointing some of the kids, though, because when they spot us at school they think it means we're back to teach for the rest of the year. (It kind of feels good to see them so sad about it. Is that wrong?)

What's especially exciting, though, is hearing about Maria's plans to use my story. I was so nervous to hand it over to her and Lamine. These people were the real test. I'd taken quite a leap, writing from the point of view of a Malian mother of three. And even though I had packed it with things I had heard from the mouths of Malians themselves, there was the giant possibility that what I created was essentially not realistic. That's why I nearly faint from flattery when I see Lamine and he asks me, "How did you do it? How did you know how a Malian thinks?"

"I guess I've spent a lot of time listening to people for the past nine months," I say.

Hanging out in the courtyard before dinner we tell Maria we're so happy we've found a way to contribute to her inspiring efforts.

"Do you want to keep giving?" she asks and laughs. "After Salif Keita makes the cover and draws me ten more books, you two can just stay here and teach English forever, how's that? I am too busy now that Debbie is back in America until Christmas. We're always so busy here. As soon as we're finished with one thing there are ten other things waiting right behind it." She sighs heavily. We can only imagine what it feels like to face this country's problems every day and know that you will face them for the rest of your life. But if anyone can do it with a sense of humor, it's Maria.

With no language lessons or research to do, we have all the time in the world to just hang out with our former neighbors in the streets of Djikoroni until sunset every day.

We've planned some specific activities, as well, like a field trip. Today we are taking Fati-Mo's kids (Saran and La Vielle only, Nana's still too little) to the National Museum. We've asked Moussa to come, too, because we think he'd like it as well and will be a great help with translation. We also really want this family and the *grin* to become even better friends. (If only because it's fun when all your friends are friends, right?)

When we show up in the morning as planned, Moussa, Saran, and La Vielle are all dressed up—along with three of the neighbor kids Kao, Maimouna, and Iba who we hadn't quite invited. Uh-oh. I guess we'll just cram them all into one cab. It's not like we haven't seen eight people stuffed in one before.

Part of the reason we want to go to the museum with all these kids now is that aside from the fact that they probably will never have the opportunity to go with school or their parents (it's seen as too expensive, possibly irrelevant), the current show is photographs taken by Africans of Africa. What better way to be introduced to modern museum culture than to have it celebrating your home through the eyes of your people?

The whole thing turns out to be a hit. They are totally intrigued by all the photographs ("This is Africa, too? Really?") and definitely get a kick out of the small-scale replicas of Mali's famous monuments in the garden outside. We have an impromptu dance party near a miniature mosque of Djenné and end with some sodas at the museum café.

Deciding where we can best catch a cab to head back, Moussa says maybe the zoo. "The zoo?!" squeals La Vielle.

And that's how our field trip turns into the ultimate field trip. For the kids at any rate. As they are loving the monkeys tied to trees and the tiger with hardly enough room to turn around in his cage, Steven and I are cringing at the sign outside the lonely ape's cage that says, "Don't feed Samba cigarettes." The one part Steven and I do find amusing is the fact that every fourth enclosure or so is labeled something exotic like "zebra" or "crocodile" but is actually home to a donkey. When we point this out to Moussa he explains, entirely straight-faced, "This is very good grazing land."

It's our last day in Mali. Already? Finally?

Djabati (Mr. Dance-Off from the *grin*) has offered to drive us around the city for all our last-minute errands in the car that's usually reserved for his dad's construction company. Moussa comes along for the ride, and together we take on the crowded markets in search of last-minute gifts and whatnot. The Muslim holiday Eid, or *Tabaski* as the Malians call it, is coming up, so it's kind of like going to Macy's a few days before Christmas—that is to say,

insanely crowded. And instead of Christmas trees for sale all around, there are packs of sheep that will be slaughtered for the festivities.

We briefly consider buying one and sharing it with the neighborhood, but then think better of it. So our party plan now is to bring back watermelons. They're gigantic here, in season, easy to share with lots of people — and don't require any slaughtering or roasting.

We pick up our bags from the hotel, check out, and head back to Djikoroni where we will hang out until midnight, at which point Djabati will drive us to the airport for our 2 a.m. flight to Morocco. (We are taking a weeklong layover and meeting Steven's family there before heading home.) We go back and forth between making tea at the *grin* and having dance parties at Fati-Mo's. Steven is finally, fully initiated into the *grin* by making an entire pot of tea on his own. We sit in the low wire chairs, listening to the tapes we brought them from America, and make promises to write and call. "Don't forget about Bamako," they tell us over and over. "Don't forget about us!"

How could we?

They ask what we'll do when we get back to the States. We don't know. Hang out at our childhood homes for a while? Eat crazy quantities of all the food we've missed? Move to San Francisco? We ask them about what they're going to do. "The same thing we do every day!" says Borema and gestures to all of us sitting around

outside his store. And it's probably true. When we came back after our trip around the country, or even coming back now after our time in Timbuktu and Segou—nothing had changed. And when we ask them what happened while we were gone, we can never get anything out of anyone. What if we come back in a year? In five? In ten? It's not like China where you blink and all of a sudden there's a luxury hotel where there was once an empty lot. Will Mali have changed? And more important—for the better? For the worse? How will all of our friends fare?

Fatimata and Mohamed's girls fall asleep before we leave. Which is probably for the best since I'm literally sobbing when it's time to say good-bye.

Fatimata tells us, "They will cry tomorrow, too, when they see there is no Fatimata and no Salif."

"We'll come back," I say.

"We'll come back," Steven echoes.

"*K'an kelen kelen wuli*," she says. May we each wake one by one.

And now it's time to go. We cram into Djabati's car with as much of the *grin* as we can fit.

"Ai! Salif! You are too big!"

"No—it's you Moussa. You are just as tall!"

"Borema, can't you move over?"

"Eh! I'm already out the window! Papy you're taking up so much room!"

"You boys—quiet down back there."

"Oooh! We're in trouble with Fatimata!"

"In America, parents tell their children who are fighting in the car, 'I will turn this thing around if you don't stop.'"

"I will turn this thing around if you don't stop!"

"But then we'll miss our flight!"

"And then you can stay. Perfect!"

Just a few hours later, we're back in Morocco. Back in Rabat, back in the old medina—on our way to see Steven's host family. We ran into one of his host brothers on the street who said we should come by for afternoon tea. "I think I was just too nervous around them when I was living there," Steven says as we make our way over. "I never really knew what to do, and they didn't seem to like me very much."

"Maybe now that you're an especially well-traveled young man with a respectable lady friend you'll wow 'em and set it all straight," I say and smile.

We walk the familiar streets to his house, with teatime cookies in tow, and marvel at how much has changed since we first came here more than four years ago. Skate-board punks outside Parliament? Women in jeans in the medina? Maybe it's because we're coming from a country that's so desperate for change but has a hard time making it happen that we find this kind of fluidity here to be a good thing.

"I like the new Morocco," I say.

"Me, too," says Steven. "Here—take my hand." And I do, my breath shortening to display this kind of affection in public.

We ring the bell. We wait. No one is home.

"It looks like we'll just have to come back to Morocco again," I say. "In the mean-time—straight to Amina's?"

"Shkoon? Ahh! Casey! Steeeven!"

I love surprising her like this.

"She remembered me!" Steven grins as I open the door with the keys Amina has thrown down.

"I know! Isn't she the best? We have to come back and live in Rabat again." I've got the same silly smile he does.

"We definitely do."

I pull open the heavy door. "Hey, do you think we'll ever go back to Djikoroni and surprise everyone there?"

"It wouldn't be such a long trip if we were already in Morocco . . . ," Steven says with a conspiratorial smile.

"Quite true," I say. And maybe out of habit—a habit I hope never to break—we pause and kiss before going upstairs.

"Caaaaaaaaseeeeeeey?" Amina calls down. "Steeeeeeeeeeeven?"

ACKNOWLEDGMENTS

Thank you to our agent Steven Malk for guiding this book through all its stages, to our editor Nancy Mercado for taking such a project on, to Kimi Weart for helping us couple our words and art, and to all the generous people we met throughout our travels.